For Mic
with love
from Darren

Concepts of Justice

CONCEPTS OF JUSTICE

D. D. Raphael

CLARENDON PRESS · OXFORD

OXFORD
UNIVERSITY PRESS

Great Clarendon Street, Oxford OX2 6DP

Oxford University Press is a department of the University of Oxford.
It furthers the University's objective of excellence in research, scholarship,
and education by publishing worldwide in

Oxford New York

Athens Auckland Bangkok Bogotá Buenos Aires Cape Town
Chennai Dar es Salaam Delhi Florence Hong Kong Istanbul Karachi
Kolkata Kuala Lumpur Madrid Melbourne Mexico City Mumbai Nairobi
Paris São Paulo Shanghai Singapore Taipei Tokyo Toronto Warsaw
with associated companies in Berlin Ibadan

Oxford is a registered trade mark of Oxford University Press
in the UK and in certain other countries

Published in the United States
by Oxford University Press Inc., New York

© D. D. Raphael 2001

The moral rights of the author have been asserted
Database right Oxford University Press (maker)

First published 2001

All rights reserved. No part of this publication may be reproduced,
stored in a retrieval system, or transmitted, in any form or by any means,
without the prior permission in writing of Oxford University Press,
or as expressly permitted by law, or under terms agreed with the appropriate
reprographics rights organization. Enquiries concerning reproduction
outside the scope of the above should be sent to the Rights Department,
Oxford University Press, at the address above

You must not circulate this book in any other binding or cover
and you must impose this same condition on any acquirer

British Library Cataloguing in Publication Data
Data available

Library of Congress Cataloging in Publication Data
Raphael, D.D. (David Daiches), 1916–
Concepts of justice/D.D. Raphael.
p. cm.
1. Justice—History. 2. Political science—History. I. Title.
JC578.R358 2001   172'.2'0922,dc21   2001032874
ISBN 0-19-924571-1

1 3 5 7 9 10 8 6 4 2

Typeset by Cambrian Typesetters, Frimley, Surrey
Printed in Great Britain
on acid-free paper by
T.J. International Ltd.,
Padstow, Cornwall

IN MEMORIAM
UXORIS DILECTAE
SYLVIA DAICHES RAPHAEL
TAM SAPIENTIA QUAM VIRTUTE PRAESTANTIS

Acknowledgements

Chapter 7 is a revised and slightly extended version of an article that was published in *Perspectives on Thomas Hobbes*, edited by G. A. J. Rogers and Alan Ryan (Oxford: Clarendon Press, 1988). Chapter 16 is a revised and slightly extended version of an article that was published in *Revue internationale de philosophie*, 127–8 (1979).

Contents

1. What is Justice? — 1

Part I Ancient Roots

2. Justice in the Bible — 11
3. Aeschylus' *Oresteia*: The Development of Justice — 19
4. Plato's *Republic* — 30
5. Aristotle — 43
6. Jurists and Theologians — 56

Part II Modern Shoots

7. Thomas Hobbes — 65
8. G. W. Leibniz — 80
9. David Hume — 87
10. Hume's Critics: Kames and Reid — 104
11. Adam Smith — 113
12. J. S. Mill — 126
13. Henry Sidgwick — 139
14. Hastings Rashdall — 150
15. Peter Kropotkin — 160
16. Chaïm Perelman — 168
17. David Miller — 183
18. John Rawls — 196
19. Robert Nozick — 214
20. Brian Barry — 220

Part III Historical Fruits

21. Fairness — 233
22. The Developing Role of Justice — 242

Index — 251

Chapter 1

WHAT IS JUSTICE?

What is justice? It cannot be captured in a simple formula like 'the rendering to each person of what is his'. That traditional definition from Roman law gives the principle of justice for settling disputes in civil law, but it does not cover the justice of criminal law or claims made in the name of justice outside the sphere of law. The idea of justice has complex ramifications. Yet it would not be true to say that it lacks a unity binding its different elements together. The meaning of justice is pretty well captured in a more familiar term, 'fairness', which is not at all obscure and is readily grasped even by young children. 'Justice' and 'fairness' are not in fact synonyms, and in Chapter 21 I examine the differences between them; nevertheless they are very close to each other, so that it is usually possible to substitute one for the other without serious change of meaning.

Although the idea is familiar and readily understood, it is not easy to pin down. Justice is a complex concept that pervades social thought to an unrivalled extent. It is basic to law, ethics, and politics alike. Its nearest rival is liberty, which is equally basic for politics, and a beacon for law and ethics, at least in democratic thought. Even non-democratic societies give overriding importance to a concept of justice. The notion of justice is more complex than that of liberty and one aspect of the complexity is to link together the structures of thought that constitute law, ethics, and politics.

In the law, the idea of justice is virtually all-embracing. Although we may distinguish the letter of the law from the spirit of justice that underlies it, the language of justice is used of the system of law as a whole. We speak of courts of justice, and judges are often given the title of 'Justice' (Mr Justice, Lord Justice, Chief Justice).

In social and political ethics, the idea of justice does not cover the whole field. Justice is one virtue or ideal among several. It can claim to be the foundation of social ethics but not the apex. So far as society is concerned, justice is the most fundamental virtue and so may be called the most important. But when judging the actions of individuals, social thought does not rate justice as the highest, the most admirable, virtue. Justice is expected as a matter of course, while courage, self-sacrifice, and devotion to the poor and helpless are more highly esteemed. In political thought, as I have said, justice shares with liberty the honour of being the basic ideal.

As between its use in social ethics and in political ethics, the concept of justice does not differ in character. It remains the same ethical idea. This ethical notion of justice is not quite the same as the legal notion of justice, but the two are connected. The idea of justice always has an ethical tinge to it, and that can be seen in legal usage. When lawyers appeal to principles of 'natural justice' or temper established law with principles of 'equity', they acknowledge that their system of law is meant to serve an ethical purpose and to follow ethically acceptable methods.

Justice, like Janus, has two faces, one conservative, the other reformative. These two faces are apparent both in the law and in the thought of social and political ethics.

The conservative aspect of the law needs no emphasis. The primary function of law is to preserve the order and the smooth running of society as it now exists. A system of law that has got beyond the primitive stage usually distinguishes between criminal and civil law. Criminal law prohibits behaviour that is harmful to individuals and to society as a whole. The punishment prescribed for crime is not meant to satisfy the victim for the harm done to him, but to defend society from the harm done to it. It is intended to repair the breach to the social structure that is caused by breaking society's rules. If the criminal is also made to compensate his victim, this remedial action, distinct from punishment, is intended to make good the damage done to the individual, again a matter of conserving the status quo. Compensation for the victim is in fact more akin to civil law, where damage done to an individual or a group is treated as a breach of a right that must be made good. In general, disputes in civil law concern people's rights, and the decisions of the courts are intended to preserve or restore an existing system of rights, 'to render to each person what is his (right)'. In both criminal and civil procedures the function of legal justice is to conserve an established order.

But that is not the whole of the legal process. Laws are made as well as applied. They are made by legislatures and in some degree by judges. Sometimes a new statute (an Act of the legislature), or a judgement of a court that has the effect of making a new law, is simply the correction of an anomaly in the existing system. But more often new laws change the existing system and represent the reformative aspect of legal justice.

Statutes make changes in the law to give effect to current ideas of what would be fair and proper. Examples of such changes in the twentieth century that come readily to mind are laws intended to remove inequality between the sexes or people of different colour; laws affecting the family, changing the rules about marriage, divorce, inheritance, and the protection of children; laws about social security, making the whole community responsible for the basic needs of those who cannot help themselves; laws about protection at work, both for health and safety and to prevent unfair dismissal.

The progressive aspect of legal justice shows itself much more often in statutes, Acts of the legislature, than in case law, judgements of the higher courts. That is to be expected, as a consequence of the different functions of the legislature and the judiciary. Politicians are elected to the legislature in order to express the will of the people, and one of their main tasks is to enact laws serving that purpose. Judges are appointed to apply the law, fairly and efficiently, not to change it. But from time to time there are good reasons for judges to change the law. The legislature is too preoccupied with the multifarious business of politics to make all the changes that are needed to iron out injustices (unfairness) in the law as it has developed in decisions over the years. When judges take on this task, they are sometimes a bit like legislators in reflecting general opinion of the day – but on broad moral principles, not on any and every contentious issue.

The Supreme Court of the USA has been especially ready to amend the law in the spirit of natural justice, which for practical purposes means the moral outlook of reflective people. Take as an example the celebrated case of *Brown v. Board of Education* in 1954, when the Supreme Court ruled that segregated schools for children of different colour denied 'equal protection of the laws', in breach of the Fourteenth Amendment of the Constitution. Formally the judgement was interpreting a nineteenth-century document, but in real terms it was reflecting twentieth-century ideas. No one supposes that the people who adopted the Fourteenth Amendment in 1868 thought they were outlawing segregated schools, and indeed the judgement of 1954 virtually overturned an earlier ruling of the Supreme Court in 1896 that equal protection of the laws was not breached by segregation if facilities were 'separate but equal'. Less striking but equally valid examples can be found in the case law of England and Scotland. Lord Denning, when Master of the Rolls (head of the English Court of Appeal for civil cases), said in a judgement of 1979 that, while the law of the nineteenth century had attached great importance to rights of property, there had more recently been a change of course: 'Social justice requires that personal rights should, in a proper case, be given priority over rights of property.'[1] In 1989 Lord Emslie, the Lord Justice-General of Scotland, changed the criminal law of that country by ruling that a husband could be guilty of rape against his wife. His examples prompted a Member of Parliament to propose that a similar

---

[1] *Davis v. Johnson*, [1979] AC 264, at 274.

change be made to English law by statute; it was in fact made in 1991 by the Court of Appeal in a judgement delivered by Lord Lane, the Lord Chief Justice, and was then confirmed by the House of Lords in its judicial capacity.

In social ethics, as in law, the concept of justice has both a conservative and a reformative role. The conservative role is to maintain the established order of things, taken to be entitlements. A person is entitled to the things that he has acquired, provided that the method of acquisition was not itself wrong. He is entitled to keep, use, consume, or dispose of them, as he may choose. People are often thought to be entitled to their place in an established order of differentiation, without the need to consider whether that order is independently justifiable. Many people, including most trade unionists in Britain, think it is unjust to erode existing differentials in pay for different jobs; if one group of workers has overtaken another, the second group thinks this is unfair and that the balance ought to be restored as a matter of simple justice.

But justice is also given the reformative role of changing the existing pattern of entitlements by taking account of merit and of need. Alongside the conservative tendency to retain established differentials, there is a reformative tendency to ask whether the differentials fit the relevant facts. We do not think it just for an individual to continue to remain always on the same level of pay; if he becomes more valuable through training, experience, or greater maturity, it is fair and proper for him to be promoted. The existing position of groups is no more sacrosanct. Ambulance workers ask whether their job is really worth less than the job of firemen. Is it less skilled, less dangerous, less useful to the community? Should ambulance workers be regarded as essentially members of the health service or of the emergency services? So should the arrangements for settling their pay be similar to those for nurses or to those for firemen and the police? Then what about the claims of need? If the pay for workers at the bottom of the pecking order is not enough to meet essential needs, you cannot say that is fair. And if their pay is raised so as to give them enough, does fairness require that all the better-off groups, too, be paid more so as to maintain differentials? Again, think of differentials of another kind. The entitlement of conservative justice to keep what you have is offset by the obligation to contribute in taxes to public expenditure, and that obligation is differentiated according to ability to pay; it is fair that the poor should have less of a burden than the rich.

Conservative and reformative justice are not at loggerheads with each other. Each tries to fulfil a good purpose. Conservative justice assumes that everyone benefits from a stable social order, however imperfect, and so it aims to preserve stability. Reformative justice supplements this good purpose by another, trying to remove the imperfections, redistributing rights so as to make the social order more fair. But in that second purpose there are two elements which do seem to be at loggerheads. Right from the time of the ancient Greeks there have been two, apparently inconsistent, ideas of distributive justice.

The first idea is that justice looks to and matches merit; it claims that people should be given what they deserve. This notion is obviously central to criminal justice, in which liability to punishment depends on guilt. It is not always necessary or right to inflict punishment on those who have broken the law, but before this can even be considered, it must be clear that the person charged is guilty. Any suggestion of punishing the innocent, those who have done nothing to deserve punishment, is an affront to justice. If guilt is established and there are no grounds for waiving the punishment, justice again uses the notion of desert in claiming that the degree of punishment should be proportioned to the seriousness of the offence. Outside the law the notion of punishment is the opposite of reward. This, too, depends on merit or desert. If someone finds a purse and returns it to the owner, he deserves a reward. If someone comes first in a race or competition, he deserves the prize. To award the prize to another competitor who is less deserving would be unfair. When there is a question of an appointment or promotion to a position of responsibility, the aim is to get the best-qualified candidate. It would be unfair to select a less well qualified person instead. In the award of scholarships it is just or fair to go for the most talented student. All such examples illustrate the notion of justice or fairness as a distribution of benefits and burdens or responsibilities on the basis of merit or desert.

The second idea of distributive justice has a different basis. It looks to equality and need. It says that all human beings have equal worth and equal claims. A just treatment is focused upon equality. It is unjust to foster inequality, as for instance by giving special benefits to the talented. They are already exceptionally fortunate to have been endowed by nature with their talent; why add to the inequality, the injustice, by giving them still more benefits? That simply increases the morally offensive gap between the rich and the poor. If all human beings were to act up to the principles of justice, specially talented people would gladly devote their talent to the public good without expecting any special reward. In practice only a few will put aside natural self-interest, and so it is necessary, for economic reasons, to offer the reward. But we should not blind ourselves to its character by calling it justice instead of expediency. Justice calls for equality. Discrimination in favour of some and against others is contrary to justice, with one exception. If you discriminate in favour of the disadvantaged, your aim is to reduce inequality, to bring the needy a little nearer to the level of the better off, and that of course serves the basic egalitarian purpose of justice. So the principle of distributive justice is to aim at equality and to favour the needy in order to reduce inequality.

These two ideas of distributive justice are inconsistent with each other, and yet they both seem to have some persuasive force, reflecting intuitive notions of justice in the general moral consciousness. Some philosophers have tried to present a rational argument for regarding only one of them as genuine. Aristotle gave a (surprisingly weak) argument for rejecting the egalitarian conception of distributive justice. In our own time John Rawls has worked out an ingenious argument for accepting a form of the equality-needs conception and has added a less impressive argument for rejecting the merit conception. I shall discuss these arguments in due course. Meanwhile it is worth noting that both conceptions have remained vigorous elements of practical moral and political thought for two and a half millennia. As in the days of Plato and Aristotle, right-wing political parties tend to stress the merit conception, while left-wing political parties stress the equality conception. A controversy of such long standing in active political life is unlikely to be dissipated by purely philosophical argument.

Philosophical analysis can, however, help to clarify the ideas involved. So can attention to the history of philosophical, and quasi-philosophical, thought about justice. The history of ideas is always enlightening in political philosophy, and not just for historical understanding but for philosophical understanding too. In this instance, the history of the idea of justice shows us that there has been substantial development in thought about justice, especially in its association with the concept of rights; that, despite this substantial change, there has also been a striking stability in basic conceptions, including the opposition between left-wing and right-wing notions of justice in political thought; and that the relationship between ethics, law, and politics is subtly interwoven and can be illustrated most clearly in the concept of justice.

This book does not pretend to be anything like a complete survey of the history of philosophical thought about justice. Such a survey would have to include much about the traditional forms of natural law theory and more about medieval thought than the little I have mentioned. Even with modern philosophers, my selection is somewhat arbitrary, being largely confined to thinkers who wrote in the English language and whose contribution has seemed to me original and significant. The book has grown up from reflection on sources with which I happen to be familiar as the result of upbringing, education, and natural interest. I have no doubt that a study of other sources would yield further enlightenment.

Two of the advisers to the Oxford University Press have expressed surprise that I did not include a chapter on Kant; one of them added Aquinas and the other added Locke and Marx. I did in fact think about all four of these thinkers when I was writing the book, and perhaps I should explain why I did not go further with them.

A chapter on Aquinas would indeed be desirable but I decided that I was not competent to write it. One of his tenets is touched upon in Chapter 6 and I say, both in this introductory chapter and at the beginning of Chapter 6, that a history of the concept of justice should include much more about medieval philosophy than the little I have mentioned. My education has left me pretty ignorant on medieval philosophy and I am too old to try to go into it with any thoroughness now.

I did expect to write a chapter on Kant. My general position in ethics relies heavily on one of Kant's formulations of the categorical imperative, that we should treat human beings as ends and not simply as means. But when I looked at various works of Kant, I was, to my surprise, unable to find any substantial treatment of the concept of justice as such. Perhaps I have missed it, but if so I am in good company. One of the advisers who regretted the absence of a chapter on Kant noted my several references to him and pointed specifically to the chapter on Rawls, who is of course a very important contributor to philosophical reflection on justice and who acknowledges the influence of Kant. When I first read Rawls I wondered why he called himself a Kantian, since Kant does not apply the idea of a contract to the concept of justice, as Rawls does. On going back to Rawls in writing this book, I learned that he regards his theory of justice as Kantian because he is following Kant's doctrine of autonomy; but that seems to me to have little direct relevance to a theory of the concept of justice. If Kant had had more to say about justice as such, Rawls would surely have referred to it.

On Locke and Marx there is no need for apology. Locke receives a fair amount of discussion at the end of Chapter 6. He does not get the full treatment of a separate chapter because there is nothing like enough about justice in his writings to warrant this. That is even more true of Marx. He has very little to say about justice. He takes over the dictum of Louis Blanc, 'From each according to his ability, to each according to his needs', but he does not provide any reasoning or reflective thought to argue for it. Nor does Louis Blanc himself. The thinker who does provide it is Kropotkin. That is why I have written a chapter about him. One should not suppose that, just because Locke and Marx are outstanding political thinkers, they must have had a substantial and distinctive theory of justice.

Nor should one suppose that distinctive conceptions of justice can be found only in the works of political philosophers. Another of the Press's advisers, with his eye on a history of political theory, questioned the inclusion of chapters on the Bible and Aeschylus. I think that both these sources can add to our understanding of the development of the idea of justice. That, not the history of political theory, is the aim of this book.

Part I

ANCIENT ROOTS

Chapter 2

JUSTICE IN THE BIBLE

It is often said that the ethics of the Old Testament concentrate upon justice while those of the New concentrate on love. This way of describing the difference between the two Testaments can be misleading to people who do not know that the two great commandments of the Christian Gospels, to love God and to love our neighbour, are quotations from the Pentateuch. The Old Testament in fact refers far more frequently to love than to justice. Still, it is true that the concept of justice has a prominence in the social ethics of the Old Testament which is not apparent in the New. I hope that this makes it reasonable to confine my discussion of justice in the Bible to passages from the Old Testament.

There are two words in the Hebrew Bible that connote the concept of justice or something like it. One is a legal term, *mishpat*, coming from the same root as the word for a judge. So it means 'judgement', the decision of a judge, but with a normative connotation: it is what a judge ought to decide, what a true judge would decide. The second word is an ethical term, *tzedek*, coming from the same root as a word that means a righteous or upright person, and also connected with a slightly longer form of the word, *tzedakah*, which means righteousness, and later, charity.

A key instance of the second term is Deuteronomy 16: 20, 'Justice, justice, shalt thou follow'. That is the translation of the Revised Version, which renders precisely the form of the Hebrew original. The repetition, 'Justice, justice', is designed to express emphasis. The Authorized (King James) Version seeks the effect by translating, 'That which is altogether just shalt thou follow'; the New English Bible has 'Justice, and justice alone, you shall pursue'.

This quotation comes in the context of an instruction to set up courts of law. The preceding sentences say that the judges must judge the people with 'just (or righteous) judgement', combining the two words together with a hyphen, *mishpat-tzedek*. The text goes on to explain what this means: a judge must not pervert or twist *mishpat* (judgement); he must not discriminate ('show favour') or take a bribe. Then comes the principle: 'Justice, justice, shalt thou follow.'

The meaning is that, in the administration of *law*, the *ethical* concept of 'justice' or 'what is right' must be central. Yet one can see from the passage as a whole that the legal term *mishpat* itself includes the notion of ethically right behaviour. This is apparent from the statement that judges ought not to pervert or twist *mishpat*; if they give a judgement which is ethically at fault by perverting or twisting what is ethically right, it is not a genuine 'judgement' (*mishpat*).

Before leaving the passage, we should note the two ways in which justice in the courts can be perverted, by discrimination ('showing favour') and by bribery. This suggests that the essence of true legal justice is impartiality.

I turn now to another key passage in the Old Testament, one that comes very early, in Genesis 18: 19, 25. It is a dialogue between God and Abraham about the imminent destruction of Sodom and Gomorrah. The first mention of the concept of justice in this story occurs in verse 19, where God decides to tell Abraham of his intention and says that he has made himself specially known to Abraham so that Abraham and his descendants may 'keep the way of the Lord, to do justice and judgement' (*tzedakah* and *mishpat*, translated in the New English Bible as 'what is right and just'). God then speaks to Abraham of the sins of Sodom and Gomorrah. Abraham responds by urging that the two cities should be spared if they contain a few righteous men. He pleads at first for remission if there are fifty righteous men; when that is accepted, he comes down gradually to ten; and God agrees to it all. The implication of the story is that there were not even ten righteous men, for the cities are destroyed—though the angels first bring out Lot and his family, presumably the only ones who have not succumbed to the prevalent sins.

Now when Abraham begins his plea to God, he says, in verse 25, that if there are fifty righteous men, the place should be spared: 'Far be it from thee to slay the righteous with the wicked. Shall not the judge of all the earth do what is just?' The word used for 'just' is *mishpat*: 'shall not the universal judge follow a true judgement?' So here the legal term *mishpat*, judgement, plainly carries the ethical connotation of justice. The same thing applies to verse 19, where *tzedakah* and *mishpat* are joined together as aims for Abraham.

In this particular argument, justice requires that the righteous, the innocent, should not share the punishment due to the guilty. So here the justice of the courts requires that punishment presupposes guilt; or, to put it in another way, it requires that there *should* be discrimination—between the guilty and the innocent.

Both passages concern justice in law or legal process. Both imply that the 'judgement' (*mishpat*) delivered by judges must be just if it is to be true or acceptable judgement. But both passages also spell this out by using the ethical term *tzedek* or *tzedakah* to explain that true or just judgement is one that is ethically righteous.

I suppose that the original meaning of the word *mishpat* may not have necessarily carried an ethical overtone. 'Judgement' was what the judge decreed. But then, when it became an emphatic part of common opinion that courts ought to follow ethical principles, the word *mishpat* came to mean an ethically just judgement.

Let us now look at another place in the Bible where the idea of justice enters into an argument between God and a man, the Book of Job. Job is afflicted although he has not done wrong. We are told in the prologue that God allows this to happen because he wants to prove to Satan that a really good man remains good even if he is unjustly afflicted—which itself raises a problem about the justice of God. But that prologue was added later. The original tale was that Job suffered all sorts of calamities and wanted to know why. His friends, the 'comforters', said it must be a punishment for sin. Job insisted that he had not sinned, and we are given to understand that he was right. So why was he afflicted?

In Job 8: 3, one of the comforters says: 'Does God pervert *mishpat*, does the Almighty pervert *tzedek*?' This recalls Deuteronomy 16: 18–19, 'you shall not pervert (or wrest) *mishpat* . . . a bribe perverts the words of the righteous'. The word used for 'pervert' in Job 8: 3 is not the same as the word in Deuteronomy 16: 18, 'pervert *mishpat*', but it is the same as the word in Deuteronomy 16: 19, 'pervert the words of the just or righteous man'. So this comforter, Bildad, is relying on traditional doctrine: God, the universal judge, will not pervert *mishpat* and *tzedek*.

Well, what answer does Job get in the end? God reminds Job of his omnipotence and indicates that Job does not know what he is talking about. Now Job himself had said earlier that God is all-powerful and all-wise and that therefore a man must not expect to have his arguments answered. But he did also say that one cannot expect justice from God. In his reply, God emphasizes his power, as Job had expected, but he also implies (40: 8) that he *is* just, though man cannot understand that. The sentence, like so much in this particular book of the Bible, is a little obscure. The Authorized Version translates: 'Wilt thou also disannul my judgment? wilt thou condemn me, that thou mayest be righteous?' The New English Bible has: 'Dare you deny that I am just or put me in the wrong that you may be right?' The word in the first half of the sentence is *mishpati*, 'my judgement' or 'my decree'; the word in the second half is *titzdak*, '(in order that) you may be righteous (or just)'. The message presumably is that the justice of God cannot be understood by man.

Throughout these passages there occur together the two terms, *mishpat* and *tzedek*. All the passages refer to legal justice—a just decision, a just punishment.

One other aspect of legal justice in the Old Testament should be mentioned. This is the so-called *lex talionis*. That particular name in fact refers to early

Roman law. There was no actual *lex* called *Lex Talionis*; particular Roman laws were called after the name of the consul who proposed them. But in the early code of the Twelve Tables there occurs, more than once, the rule that, if a man has committed a certain offence, *talio esto*, 'there shall be retribution of the self-same sort'. The general idea is common to a number of early legal systems: that the punishment for a crime against the person should be that the wrongdoer suffer the same harm as he has caused. Exodus 21: 23–5, talking about punishments and compensations, says: 'Whenever hurt is done, you shall give life for life, eye for eye, tooth for tooth, hand for hand, foot for foot, burn for burn, bruise for bruise, wound for wound.' Deuteronomy 19: 21, distinguishing deliberate crime from accidental hurt, says that the former must be diligently punished: 'You shall show no mercy: life for life, eye for eye, tooth for tooth, hand for hand, foot for foot.'

This must have been meant literally at the start, and, as I have mentioned, it is nothing exceptional. The same idea is found in early Roman law, in the Babylonian Code of Hammurabi, and elsewhere. When the ancient Hebrews were settled in the land of Canaan, this *lex talionis* was reinterpreted at quite an early stage so as to require compensation for the victim or his family rather than bodily damage for the wrongdoer, except in the case of murder, and even for that worst of crimes capital punishment became a virtual dead letter in due course. However, the revision certainly did not go as far as the teaching of Jesus in the Sermon on the Mount, as reported in Matthew 5: 38–9 (New English Bible): 'You have learned that they were told, "Eye for eye, tooth for tooth." But what I tell you is this: Do not set yourself against the man who wrongs you. If someone slaps you on the right cheek, turn and offer him your left.' (The Authorized Version is more familiar: 'Ye have heard that it hath been said, An eye for an eye, and a tooth for a tooth: But I say unto you, That ye resist not evil: but whosoever shall smite thee on thy right cheek, turn to him the other also.') This cannot mean that *courts* should turn the other cheek or should ask a victim of crime to turn the other cheek. Jesus is obviously counselling the *individual* to put aside thoughts of personal retaliation and instead to heap coals of fire on the head of an assailant. The Old Testament statements about an eye for an eye refer to punishments inflicted by a court.

Incidentally, the idea that the punishment should be equal to the crime is not a general feature of the Mosaic law. The same chapter of Exodus that says 'life for life', and so on, also prescribes that punishment, including recompense, for theft (a crime against property as contrasted with crime against the person) may be more. Exodus 21: 37 says that, if a man steals an ox or a sheep, and kills or sells it (so that he cannot just return the stolen animal), then he must pay five oxen for an ox and four sheep for a sheep. The multiple penalty is presumably intended to deter. So concepts of punishment in the Old Testament are not simply retributive.

(One might ask why the penalty for stealing an ox was more than for a sheep. I suppose because an ox is more valuable and so the theft of an ox needs a greater deterrent.)

All the passages that I have cited refer to legal or quasi-legal justice, in the decrees of human courts or the governance of the world by God. The Old Testament also contains rules for what we today might call social justice or a sort of welfare state. Leviticus 19: 9–10 says that, when you harvest your crops, you should leave the corners of your field unreaped and you should not pick up gleanings (bits that fall off your wagon). 'Leave them for the poor and the stranger.' This is repeated in Leviticus 23: 22 and is elaborated in Deuteronomy 24: 19–22. When you harvest, don't go back for bits that you have left; they shall be for 'the stranger, the orphan, and the widow'. When you pick your olives, don't go back for a second picking; the leavings should be for the stranger, the orphan, the widow. Likewise when you pick your grapes. Then the chapter ends (verse 22): remember that you were a slave in Egypt. The point of that remark is: you know from past experience what it is like to be poor and downtrodden; have a thought for those who experience it now.

The commands in these passages do not use either of the words for 'justice' to describe their rationale, though the idea behind them is one that was later assigned to the concept of social justice. The major prophets, especially Jeremiah, follow the thought of these passages when they urge that we should think of the poor and the helpless (such as the orphan and the widow). They say that to help the poor and needy is to know God or to do the work of God, but they too do not normally apply the name of justice to this good work. There are, however, a couple of exceptions. Isaiah 1: 17 associates the notion of *mishpat* (but also the more general notion of 'doing good') with giving help to the needy: 'Learn to do well; seek judgment (*mishpat*), relieve the oppressed, judge the fatherless [that is, procure justice for the fatherless], plead for the widow' (Authorized Version). 'Learn to do right, pursue justice and champion the oppressed; give the orphan his rights, plead the widow's cause'(New English Bible). Again, Jeremiah 22: 3 says: 'Execute ye judgment and righteousness (*mishpat* and *tzedakah*), and deliver the spoiled out of the hand of the oppressor: and do no wrong, do no violence to the stranger, the fatherless, nor the widow, neither shed innocent blood in this place' (Authorized Version). 'Deal justly and fairly, rescue the victim from his oppressor, do not ill-treat or do violence to the alien, the orphan or the widow, do not shed innocent blood in this place' (New English Bible).

So much for the actual concept of justice in the Bible. Let us now look in a broader spirit at a couple of the passages I have discussed. Genesis 18 and the Book of Job deal with fundamentally the same issue, the relation between the natural world and our moral concepts, and they both use the same method, a dialogue between a man and God. The subject is the justice of God or the problem that natural disasters raise for a theological interpretation of the universe.

It is quite possible that the writer of the Book of Job had at the back of his mind a recollection of the dialogue between Abraham and God. Earlier parts of the Bible are often recalled by later parts. Obvious examples are found in the sayings of Jesus when he quotes or refers to doctrines of the Pentateuch: for instance, picking out the love of God and the love of our neighbour as the two cardinal precepts of the Pentateuch, or referring to the *lex talionis* when he counsels turning the other cheek. The same sort of thing occurs within the Old Testament itself. For example, Isaiah 58: 5–7 refers to the command in Leviticus to fast on the Day of Atonement and reinterprets it in a spiritual sense as a command to repent and help the poor. A striking recollection of the Old Testament in the New occurs in the language used of Jesus as the son of God. John 3: 16 says that God gave his only begotten son to save the world, and the implication is that the 'giving' was a sacrifice. The language harks back to the story that Abraham was commanded, and agreed, to give *his* only begotten son as a sacrifice (Gen. 22: 2). It is possible that the phrases in the Book of Job about arguing with God are looking back to the argument between Abraham and God. The Book of Jonah seems to recall the destruction of Sodom and Gomorrah when Nineveh is spared after repentance.

Genesis 18 presents the argument as one in which God, through his messengers, first tells Abraham that he is going to destroy the cities of the plain because of their sinfulness, and then hears Abraham's reaction, a plea for justice. If you take the story literally, it implies that of course God knew beforehand that there were no righteous people in those cities (apart from Lot and his family) but he wanted to see if Abraham would react to the news in the spirit of a morally just person. But let us look at the passage with the eye of an anthropologist. The destruction of Sodom and Gomorrah seems to have been some sort of volcanic disaster: it is said that fire and brimstone rained down upon them, and when Lot's wife paused, instead of hurrying on, she was turned into a pillar of salt, which suggests that she died through being covered with volcanic ash or something of the sort. When a great natural disaster of that kind happens, a religiously minded person is moved to ask 'Why did it happen?' And in pre-scientific days the question is taken teleologically: 'For what reason, or for what purpose, did it happen?' The great Lisbon earthquake of 1755 caused Voltaire and others to ask how the God of theism could be held responsible for everything when that must include responsibility for natural disasters.

If you are inclined to interpret the universe in terms of moral theology, the obvious way to deal with natural disasters or misfortunes is to regard them as punishments for wrongdoing (or, in a more primitive theology, as revenge by an angered deity). This is projecting onto the forces of nature the reactions that take place in human relationship and human society. If you hurt or annoy a powerful neighbour, he is liable to hit back. In a more regulated society, if you do something that is forbidden as being harmful to the community, you are punished. Project these reactions onto nature and you have the idea of powerful divinities who retaliate if displeased or who administer just punishment for disobedience to their laws. Hence the destruction of Sodom and Gomorrah is interpreted in the Bible as a punishment for sin. But it is unlikely that every inhabitant of such a city was sinful; so there is still a problem. Natural disasters hit the guilty and the innocent alike. The dialogue between Abraham and God raises the problem and disposes of it by concluding that there cannot have been any innocent people in Sodom and Gomorrah; otherwise God, who is the just judge of all the earth, would not have destroyed them. It seems a simple-minded solution, but there is a degree of sophistication in the story. It looks as if Abraham is naively trying to teach God how he must play the part of God. Yet it is not so naïve; for, to a less credulous age, such as ours, Abraham is indeed putting his own, human, idea of morality into his picture of God, the universal judge. He is moralizing theology, projecting human aspirations onto the power that governs nature.

The writer of the Book of Job is not so easily satisfied. The fact is that natural misfortunes do *not* fit in with ideas of justice; nature is *not* fair. The Book of Job tells us to put away the illusion of a just order of nature. The forces of nature display power, power that goes far beyond what a human being can do; but they do not follow morality—or at any rate human ideas of morality, the only ideas of morality that we can understand. If one is to remain religious, as Job is apparently ready to do, reverence for God must be based on his creative power, not on his justice—or on what we would suppose to be justice.

The Book of Job probably originates from a non-Hebrew environment. Job himself lived in the neighbouring land of Uz (identified by scholars as part of modern Jordan). The sceptical spirit of the book (leaving aside the prologue and epilogue) is more like Greek philosophy than biblical faith. The prologue and epilogue were added later in an attempt to reconcile the story to the general tradition of the Bible: God was only testing Job to show Satan that a righteous man would remain righteous in the face of the greatest misfortunes; and afterwards God made it up to Job by blessing him with greater prosperity than he had had before (though that does not in fact make up for the pains and the losses, including the death of his children). Yet the maturity of the ethical outlook of the Book of Job—as contrasted with the simple faith of Abraham—is not confined to that book. The 'suffering servant' passage of Isaiah 53 contains a recognition that the natural world is not just: so Isaiah produces instead the idea of vicarious suffering; and Amos (3: 2) produces the idea that election by

God is election for the burden of responsibility, not election to be benefited. The recognition by this time that the natural world is *not* just is the reason why the Book of Job could be accepted into the biblical canon as expressing a genuine problem for a moral theology.

When Hobbes relied on the Book of Job to argue that justification of the natural kingdom of God depends on power, and when Spinoza followed him in arguing that morality was man-made, they were both accused of heresy. But their attitude follows out intimations which can already be seen in some later parts of the Bible.

These remarks about moral theology do not apply only to justice. They apply as much to the idea of a loving God. However, the Book of Job fastens upon justice because there is more precision about what justice requires than there is about benevolence.

To come back to the essential points about justice in the Bible. Legal and moral justice are fused together at an early stage, although the different words used for them indicate that they began as independent notions. Ideas of what we would call social justice (a strict duty to help those who cannot easily look after themselves) are prominent in the Bible as moral demands but not, generally speaking, under the rubric of justice.

Chapter 3

AESCHYLUS' *ORESTEIA*: THE DEVELOPMENT OF JUSTICE

Athenian tragic drama was the precursor of Athenian moral philosophy. It was not the same thing, and in so far as it served the same purpose it did not simply do that. Tragic drama had a religious significance, it celebrated a religious festival; and it also fulfilled an aesthetic function—if that can be distinguished, in ancient Athens, from a religious function. Still, part of the religious function is similar to a function of moral (including political) philosophy. I do not mean by this the preaching of moral doctrine, or at any rate preaching pure and simple; I mean rather the giving of expression to moral doctrine in a way that illuminates it. Moral and political philosophy is not moral or political preaching; it is the critical evaluation of moral and political beliefs by means of rational argument and by the clarifying of concepts. It, too, is the illumination of moral and political doctrine.

Some modern moral philosophy (and to a lesser extent some modern political philosophy) puts all the emphasis on the logical aspect of the process. While this is useful as an intellectual exercise, it does not make for outstanding moral or political philosophy. Great moral and political philosophy has used logical argument simply as a means to the end of illuminating doctrine. Plato, Aristotle, Augustine, Aquinas, Hobbes, Spinoza, even Hume, certainly Rousseau, Kant, Hegel, Mill, all had their views of what was sound moral and political doctrine; argument was a means to supporting their views. There are some outstanding thinkers, such as Nietzsche and Kierkegaard (perhaps Rousseau should be included in this group), who do not persuade by means of rational argument but who are nevertheless regarded by many people as philosophers, not preachers, because they present moral and political issues in a novel perspective. I think this is a leading element in all moral and political philosophy that seems outstanding. And this is what we find in tragic drama also— or in a good deal of it.

We find it not only in Greek tragedy but in later tragedy too, in Shakespeare, Corneille, Racine, Ibsen, and in some notable dramatists of the twentieth century, Eugene O'Neill, Gabriel Marcel, Jean-Paul Sartre, Jean Anouilh, Arthur Miller, Samuel Beckett. Marcel and Sartre were avowed philosophers, who deliberately used the medium of drama (as well as the medium of the straightforward treatise) to convey their philosophical views. The others in my list have used drama to present a novel moral perspective without thinking of themselves as philosophers; it simply is a natural function of serious drama. One could say something similar of serious 'comic' drama as well as tragic, but with significant differences. One could also say something similar of certain great novels.

To return to Greek tragedy: I said that it had a religious function. Greek tragedy was a ritual to celebrate a religious festival. But since the ritual was not simply a fixed repetition, like the regular weekly or annual services of religions familiar to us today, it was intended to have novel features, to bring out something different each time. It was also a civic ritual, a religious celebration that concerned the whole citizen body; and so, as with much other religion, it gave expression to and strengthened social solidarity. It was not the kind of religion that consists in the communing of an individual with his god.

A great deal of Greek tragedy holds up before us issues of human life that are hard to deal with, issues that show why we admire some traits of character and despise others, issues that show the dangers and the limitations of human capacity, yet also show how human beings, in facing up to crushing adversity, can display a nobility of character that more than makes up for their limited powers. Fate, nature, the gods—whatever name you give to superior external powers—control the vicissitudes of human life; but when someone like Oedipus insists on finding out the truth, however horrible, or when someone like Antigone insists on doing what she thinks is right, whatever the consequences, they show us the moral heights to which human beings can ascend. The Stoics said that in this respect human beings can equal the gods. One may even say surpass the gods, when one thinks of the moral failings attributed to many of the Greek gods. The gods of Greek mythology symbolize natural power. Whereas the Bible generally (the Book of Job is an exception) shows an ever-increasing attribution to God of qualities that are morally admirable, the reflective religious thought of Greek tragedy in the fifth century BC tended to attribute moral qualities rather to man. Plato in the fourth century moved towards the moral theology that we find in the Bible. He tried to reform the old theology, ascribing moral perfection to a sort of monotheistic God as well as making it an ideal to be aimed at by men. When Plato in the *Republic* criticizes the poets (and his quotations show that he means the tragic dramatists as much as Homer), one of his charges is that the poets describe the gods as signally lacking in moral virtues. But Plato follows the tragic dramatists in concentrating on an illumination of human virtue.

There is, of course, a difference between Greek tragic drama and Greek philosophy in this business of shedding light upon virtues and duties. Philosophy proceeds by explicit argument; drama shows us human beings coping with concrete situations and evokes a natural response, often mirrored for us in the songs of the Chorus. Yet the technique of explicit argument is found to a small extent in Greek drama, with the device known as *stichomythia*, single-line speeches of repartee, which often present question and answer, argument and rebuttal, thesis and antithesis. In the *Eumenides*, the third of the plays that make up Aeschylus' *Oresteia*, there is a trial scene, where *stichomythia* fits the context very naturally as the cross-examination of witnesses and accused. The device is, however, commonly used in any confrontation of opposed attitudes and it is rather like the Socratic method of question and answer that forms the substance of Plato's early dialogues. Plato derived this method from the actual practice of his master Socrates, but he may well have been influenced by the drama too. If he was, he does not stand alone as an example of such influence. Thucydides' history of the Peloponnesian War, the great war between Athens and Sparta in the latter part of the fifth century BC, has the shape of a tragedy and is written in the spirit of tragedy, to teach the Athenians, and all men, not to tempt fate by the proud exercise of power. At times Thucydides uses the device of dialogue, to show vividly the opposed attitudes of different groups, enemies engaged in war or allies in a relation of great power and satellite.

Aeschylus' *Oresteia* illuminates the concept of justice. That is not to say that it is concerned simply and solely with justice; the subject matter of a great work of literary art cannot be confined to one topic enclosed within a firm boundary. My comparison between Greek tragic drama and moral philosophy does not mean that they are two species of the same genus. But it is clear that the main subject of the *Oresteia* is justice, and I think one can call it a quasi-philosophical exploration of the nature of justice. Aeschylus uses the medium of an old myth, as so much (not all) of Greek tragedy did. The tradition is continued in later drama. When Shakespeare wants to show the effects of folly allied to power, and the difference between disinterested love and self-interested calculation, he takes up an old tale of King Lear and his daughters. Racine uses figures from Greek or biblical mythology (Phaedra, Esther, Athalie) or Roman history (Britannicus). Some modern tragedy follows the example of his *Phèdre* by taking up again the themes of Greek myth that are found in Greek tragedy but, like Racine, relating them to a later moral outlook. The reason for locating the action in myth or antiquity is to distance the events from the audience and so to give the theme universality. The idea is not to suggest that this is how things were once upon a time but not today, thank goodness. Rather the device brings the theme close to us while managing to preserve the calm, the objectivity, that aesthetic value demands. If a dramatist portrays some recent tragedy that has been close to us, the real event is too distressing to allow our feelings in the theatre to partake of the tranquillity that Wordsworth ascribed to aesthetic emotion. Herodotus reports that the Athenians fined the tragedian Phrynichus for staging a play about the recent capture of a friendly city, Miletus, by their common enemy the Persians.

The story taken up by Aeschylus is an apt one for illustrating the concept of justice as traditional retribution, the vendetta. A killer must himself be killed. 'What you do shall be done to you'; the phrase occurs twice in the trilogy and is described on its second occurrence as an 'old, old tale'. The murder of a member of one's own family was especially heinous and the guilt was greater if the family connection was a relationship by blood as contrasted with marriage. The first of the great crimes recalled in the *Oresteia* was worse still: it was not simply murder of kinsfolk; it added the enormity of serving up the bodies of murdered children to their father as food.

The series of crimes haunts a family, the house of Atreus. The first crime calls for retaliation, which in its turn calls for further retaliation, so that there is an apparently unending chain. The house is subject to a curse. The series began when the two sons of Pelops quarrelled about the succession to the throne of Argos. One of them, Thyestes, also seduced the wife of his brother Atreus. Atreus exiled him. After a time Thyestes returned and asked for forgiveness. Atreus pretended to grant it but plotted revenge. He killed the children of Thyestes (all but the youngest one, Aegisthus, who was still a baby), cooked their flesh, and served it up to Thyestes at a banquet, supposedly of reconciliation. When Thyestes realized the truth, he cursed the house of Atreus and departed into exile again with the baby Aegisthus. The two sons of Atreus were Agamemnon and Menelaus. They married two sisters, Clytemnestra and Helen. Helen succumbed to the blandishments of Paris, left her husband, and went off with Paris to Troy, giving rise to the Trojan War. When the Greek fleet, under the command of Agamemnon, was prevented by a storm from setting sail, a soothsayer divined that the storm was caused by the goddess Artemis, angry with Agamemnon for some obscure reason; the storm would cease only if Agamemnon were to sacrifice his daughter Iphigeneia to Artemis. Reluctantly he did so. The war lasted ten years, ending in victory for the Greeks.

This is the point at which the action begins in *Agamemnon*, the first of the three plays that form the *Oresteia*. While Agamemnon was away at the war, his wife Clytemnestra had become the lover of Aegisthus, son of Thyestes. Agamemnon returns home from Troy and is murdered by Clytemnestra with the aid of Aegisthus.

Why did Clytemnestra kill Agamemnon? In the play we are given more than one answer. When Clytemnestra first explains and justifies the murder, she says it is revenge for the sacrifice of Iphigeneia (line 1417). A little later (1432), she says she has exacted justice for her child through Fate and the Avenging Spirit. But at this point she adds other things: she talks spitefully about Cassandra, the captive daughter of King Priam of Troy, whom Agamemnon brought back as his share of the booty and who has now shared his death. Clytemnestra talks of Agamemnon having had affairs with other women and seems to imply that he deserved to be killed in revenge for that, too. She also speaks, at this point, of Aegisthus as a shield and as loyal to her. Later still (1498), after the Chorus have talked of a demon afflicting the house of Atreus, Clytemnestra seizes on this and denies that she is responsible for the murder. It is, she says, the divine spirit of vengeance, taking on the shape of Agamemnon's wife, which has killed him in retribution for the sin of *Atreus* in killing and cooking the children of Thyestes. To this the Chorus reply that the avenger of Atreus' crime could be an abettor but not the actual murderer. At 1526 Clytemnestra goes back to her first excuse, the sacrifice of Iphigeneia.

When Aegisthus appears on the scene, he takes it for granted that the murder of Agamemnon is retribution for the crime of Atreus. Aegisthus claims that he planned the whole thing, and when the Chorus accuse him of cowardice, of getting a woman to do the actual killing, he says he had to use guile because he himself would obviously have been an object of suspicion.

So we are given two different explicit motives and there is an implicit suggestion of a third. The two explicit motives are revenge on the part of Clytemnestra for the killing of Iphigeneia and revenge on the part of Aegisthus for the crime of Atreus. The third, implied, motive is jealousy by Clytemnestra of Agamemnon's affairs with other women, including Cassandra. The two explicit motives are, of course, not incompatible. Clytemnestra and Aegisthus could gang up together because each of them wanted revenge. As for the suggested implicit motive of jealousy, it is hard to take that seriously. It would be expected, in that sort of society at that stage of human civilization, that a chief, away at a war for ten years, would have sexual liaisons. His wife, on the contrary, would be expected to have none and to wait patiently for his return (which is not to say that all the women other than Clytemnestra lived up to that expectation). Clytemnestra betrays a sense of guilt about her liaison with Aegisthus, both when she tells the herald early in the play (611–12) that he can assure Agamemnon that she has had no pleasure of other men, and later when she talks of Agamemnon's loves and then says that Aegisthus is loyal to her. This criticism of Agamemnon seems to be just a cover-up for her sense of guilt about her own liaison with Aegisthus.

What about her statement to the Chorus that it was not she who killed Agamemnon, but the divine spirit of vengeance taking on the form of Agamemnon's wife? This idea of transferring uncontrollable passions to a superhuman figure is common in Greek tragedy; it is a way of saying that the passions *are* uncontrollable, so that the human possessor of them is not (or not fully) responsible.

Several aphorisms about justice uttered by the Chorus give us a general impression of the traditional concept of justice in the time of Aeschylus. At 250 the Chorus say that Justice inclines her scales so that learning comes as the result of suffering. It was a common maxim of Greek thought that 'we learn by suffering', by sad experience. The idea here is that this is an aspect of justice, a balancing of evil with good: we suffer evil but we gain the benefit of wisdom.

At 376 the Chorus say that Zeus punishes those who are proud beyond what is just. At 383: riches are of no help to the man who has spurned the great altar of Justice. At 463–4: the Furies, the Avenging Spirits, bring low the man who has prospered unjustly. At 758–75: an iniquitous deed begets more like itself; pride engenders fresh pride and black fate; but justice and righteousness shine out in the houses of the poor.

At 1430 the Chorus say that Clytemnestra will have to pay 'stroke for stroke', an expression of the familiar idea of *lex talionis*. And at 1564 they say it is a fixed decree of Zeus that what you do shall be done to you.

There is an interesting remark at 813, where Agamemnon, on his return, says that he has exacted justice from Troy. There is nothing unexpected about that statement. But he then goes on to say that the gods 'voted' unanimously for the destruction of Troy. This is worth bearing in mind when one comes to consider the significance of the court procedure in the third play of the trilogy, the *Eumenides*.

The second play is the *Choephoroe* (the Libation-Bearers). It gets its name from the character of the first act, in which Electra, the surviving daughter of Agamemnon and Clytemnestra, comes with her companions to the grave of Agamemnon to pour a libation of mourning. Electra yearns for the return of her brother Orestes to avenge their father's murder. Orestes had been sent away by Clytemnestra, ostensibly for his own safety but really to ensure that he should be out of the way when she kills Agamemnon. Orestes does indeed return to Argos for vengeance; he has in fact just arrived when Electra and her companions come to pour the libation and to express their continuing sense of outrage.

Together they form a plan, and Orestes kills first Aegisthus and then his mother. He has to use guile, as she had done, but then that is part of the just requital, as Clytemnestra herself declares: 'By guile we perish, just as we slew' (880). Orestes recognizes that to kill one's mother is a dreadful deed, whatever she has done, and he shows it in several things. First, the long song and dance at the tomb of Agamemnon are a way of rousing Orestes' determination, calling on his father's spirit to help him. Secondly, he insists more than once that the god Apollo has ordered him to do the deed, on pain of being pursued by his father's Furies (avenging spirits) if he shirks it. Thirdly, there is a momentary hesitation when his mother confronts him with the breast that suckled him and asks how can he kill her? Orestes pauses and asks his friend Pylades whether he may spare his mother (having carried out part of the task of vengeance by killing Aegisthus). Pylades reminds him of Apollo's order and says that the wrath of the gods is worse than the enmity of all men. Both in this play and in the final one, Orestes says that Apollo shares the responsibility for what he has done. This is rather like the earlier plea of Clytemnestra that the divine spirit of vengeance was responsible for her murder of Agamemnon, but her claim had less assurance than that of Orestes. She *wanted* to kill Agamemnon; Orestes did not *want* to kill his mother but felt that he *had* to. Clytemnestra brings up the old excuse again in the *Choephoroe* (910), when she says that Fate shares with her the responsibility for Agamemnon's death. Orestes dismisses this brusquely: 'So Fate has provided for your death too.'

It is worth noting in this connection that Orestes has no compunction about killing Aegisthus, as may be seen from 989–90: 'I say nothing of the fate of Aegisthus; he has paid the penalty of a seducer, as the law requires.' But Orestes feels obliged to give a special justification for killing his mother, and so he displays the net she used, so as to show her cunning guile.

In the *Choephoroe*, as in the *Agamemnon*, there are references to the traditional concept of justice. At 121, before Orestes has made himself known, Electra asks if it is righteous to pray for a death in place of a death; the Chorus reply that of course it is righteous to requite evil upon your enemies. At 144 Electra prays for the coming of one who will kill in just requital those who have killed. There are further expressions of the *lex talionis* at 310. The Chorus say: ' "Let hostile speech be answered with hostile speech," cries Justice, exacting what is due; "let murderous stroke be repaid with murderous stroke." ' And they repeat the proverb they had uttered in the *Agamemnon*: ' "What you do shall be done to you," says an old, old tale.' Then again at 400 they say: 'It is a law that drops of blood shed upon the ground demand more blood. For murder calls upon the Avenging Spirit that brings, from those who were slain before, a new ruin added to ruin.' The idea of *just* retribution, as contrasted with the natural *desire* for vengeance, is especially prominent in the *Choephoroe*. It is there in the *Agamemnon* too, but the *Choephoroe* displays less of a crude desire for vengeance and more of the sense of duty to exact retribution.

The change of mood is more striking still in the final play of the trilogy, the *Eumenides*. The term 'Eumenides' means 'the kindly ones', a euphemistic name given to the 'Erinyes', the Furies or Avenging Spirits. The play begins at the temple of Apollo in Delphi, to which Orestes has fled to try to escape persecution by the Furies, who seek vengeance on behalf of Clytemnestra. Apollo promises Orestes his protection and tells him to go to the shrine of the goddess Athena at Athens, where judges will acquit him because, in killing his mother, he was obeying the behest of Apollo. At the trial the Furies put the case for retributive justice, while Apollo argues that no blame can be attached to Orestes. The jurors cast their votes, an equal number on each side. The goddess Athena, who presides over the trial, gives her casting vote in favour of acquittal and appeases the Furies by promising them a new function and a new name: they will be the Eumenides, the kindly spirits, whose blessing will be essential for the welfare of all households.

In the arguments between the Furies and Apollo, the Furies insist on the idea of retributive justice, linking it particularly with the awful nature of the crime of killing someone of your own blood. When the Furies are challenged, both by Orestes and by Apollo, to say why they did not pursue Clytemnestra for murdering her husband, their answer is that this murder was not so terrible, or at any rate was not *their* business, because a husband is not blood kin. Apollo tries to get round this argument with the reply that a mother is not blood kin either, because true heredity comes from the father, the mother being simply a carrier of the father's seed. One might well wonder whether Aeschylus intends us to take this seriously. Even if the view expressed by Apollo was not uncommon, a people so intelligent and inquisitive as the ancient Athenians must surely have included some who reflected on the familiar fact of observation that children resemble their mothers as often as their fathers.

In terms of retributive justice Orestes is caught in a cleft stick. If he fails to avenge his father, he goes against his filial duty and will be pursued by his father's Furies. If he does avenge his father, he goes against his filial duty to his mother and will be pursued by her Furies. Which duty is paramount? Apollo says one thing, the Furies say another.

Apollo also tells the Furies that the bonds of marriage should count for more than other bonds: 'Marriage between a man and a woman, when ordained by fate, is greater than an oath and is guarded by justice' (217–18). We have here the first hint of a wider conception of justice than that of retribution. A more radical expression of the wider conception is voiced by Athena when she enters the stage. Having noted the extraordinary appearance of the Furies, resembling no other beings, divine or human, she breaks off and says: 'But to speak ill of any persons in their presence, even if one is blameless, is far from justice and is shunned by righteousness' (413–14). The notion of justice is being stretched to cover the whole of what is right. This is why the Furies complain of the 'younger gods' with their newfangled ideas. They mean Apollo and Athena: Apollo because he told Orestes to kill his mother and now defends him; Athena because she gives her casting vote in favour of Orestes' acquittal at the trial. The *Eumenides* draws a contrast between the older conception of law and justice, the law of retaliation, and the new, wider, kinder conception of justice that would pardon murderers who have a good reason for their deeds. But it goes beyond a more merciful attitude to what one may call justifiable homicide. The new conception of justice is one of trusting to the judgements of *juries*, of trial, of democratic procedure. It has a political and progressive significance.

The Furies say that they will accept the verdict of Athena. She replies that the issue is too serious for mortals to decide and that it is not right either for her to be the sole judge of a verdict on a murder committed in anger; it needs a combination of judges. So she sets up a court to try murder cases (this is the first case of murder heard by a court, she says); but, because the conflict of duties is evenly balanced and so produces an equal number of votes on either side, she exercises her casting vote in favour of acquittal. Her professed reason for doing so is to follow up the peculiar argument of Apollo that a mother counts for less than a father. As evidence for his assertion that the mother is merely a carrier and that the seed of the father is the generator of the child, Apollo had cited the case of Athena herself, who was supposed to have sprung, fully grown and armed, from the head of her father Zeus. (The point of this myth was presumably to emphasize the *wisdom* of Athena.) Athena now says that, since she had no mother, she thinks the father is all-important.

Are we to take this argument, and Apollo's argument, seriously? I doubt it. Apollo and Athena want to make the idea of justice more humane. But they have to reckon with the Furies, who represent the old order of ideas. When Athena first talks to the Furies, she asks why they pursue Orestes. 'Because he killed his mother.' 'Did he do it from necessity or fearing someone's anger?' asks Athena. The Chorus reply that nothing can compel the murder of a mother. And when Athena says 'Let us hear his side of the story', they answer 'He won't take an oath' (424–9). This shows that Athena is already prepared to think that the murder of a mother could be excusable. In fact Orestes did feel compelled and he did fear the anger of Apollo and of his father's Furies. Athena's first questions suggest that she would be ready to acquit him on these grounds. But she has the Furies to reckon with. As she puts it in the play, she too is faced with a dilemma. Orestes has been purified, so there is no reason to think that he is polluting her temple or city. But if she acquits him, the Furies will afflict Athens. She has to find an argument that will satisfy them. They make their case in terms of the ties of blood kinship. So Apollo, seconded by Athena, says that the relation between child and mother is not one of blood kinship and is less important than the relation between child and father. And when the Furies complain after the verdict, Athena says (795–9): 'You have not been defeated. The votes were equal. But we had testimony (from Apollo) that Zeus had decreed that Orestes should do the deed and not be punished.' Athena is reconciling adherents of the old view to acceptance of the new one.

What is the new view? I suggest that it contains two important elements. First, questions of guilt and of punishment for guilt should be determined by a court, a court of jurors, a rational and a democratic procedure; they should not be determined by sticking to tradition if tradition is harmful. Secondly, if the conflicting claims in a moral dilemma are evenly balanced, then the just solution is to stop the chain of evil. If the old way, represented by the Furies, had been taken, there would have continued an unending series of retaliatory killing. That does nobody any good. In the case of Orestes there was a conflict of duties. The new concept of justice says that this should be taken as an opportunity to put an end to the series of retributive acts.

Professor Sir Hugh Lloyd-Jones in his book *The Justice of Zeus* maintains that justice in early Greek religious thought is the prerogative of Zeus and remains unchanged. If that is so, it cannot be correct to suggest, as I do, that Aeschylus in the *Oresteia* is propounding a new, progressive view of justice. When Professor Lloyd-Jones gives his interpretation of Aeschylus' view of justice, he says:

> The cliché we have heard repeated all our lives, that the *Eumenides* depicts the transition from the vendetta to the rule of law, is utterly misleading. Even in the *Iliad*, the blood feud is regulated by the justice of Zeus administered through kings; even in the law of the Athenian polis in the fifth century, the blood feud and the Erinyes have their allotted place.[1]

I was not consciously familiar with the 'cliché' that Lloyd-Jones recalls, though a glance at my books soon brought an example in D. W. Lucas, *The Greek Tragic Poets*: 'Apollo, who claims that his oracles give effect to the will of Zeus, represents the new order in which civic justice overrides the anti-social rigour of the blood-feud'.[2] My own reading of the *Oresteia* has not depicted a 'transition from the vendetta to the rule of law'. The *lex talionis* has already gone beyond vendetta to law, and I have suggested that in the *Eumenides* the concept of justice is widened, not that the earlier notion is abandoned. Still, my account does depart from Lloyd-Jones's view that the justice of Zeus has not changed in Aeschylus.

One can find some evidence in the trilogy to support the idea that justice does not change. I noted that early in the *Agamemnon* (813) the king says that he has visited retribution on Troy and that the gods 'voted' unanimously for its destruction. It is as if the gods had held a trial and had decided the issue by vote. So the idea of determining justice by trial and votes is not new in the *Eumenides*. Agamemnon is, of course, talking metaphorically, and one might say that he is anticipating the later idea. But still this passage does afford a reason for denying that there is a progression. Another passage that might be cited

---

[1] Hugh Lloyd-Jones, *The Justice of Zeus* (Berkeley and Los Angeles: University of California Press, 1971), 94.
[2] D. W. Lucas, *The Greek Tragic Poets* (London: Cohen & West, 1950), 75.

is the claim of Apollo when he says at the trial (*Eumenides*, 618–21) that his oracle speaks only as commanded by Zeus. This is certainly an indication that Zeus is the source of all justice, including the more lenient kind of justice that Apollo is going to advocate. But the fact that all justice reflects the will of Zeus does not imply that it is unchanging.

In any event, the fact that a proposal has the support of Zeus will not necessarily convince the Furies. They put it to Apollo and to the jury at 641 that Zeus himself failed to honour his father Kronos, whom he displaced. There are also repeated statements by the Furies that they represent the old traditional order of justice, which the 'younger gods' are uprooting. If it is true to say that justice remains the justice of Zeus, perhaps one must also say that the conception of Zeus changes towards that of a deity with a higher and wider moral outlook.

Let me note what the Furies say about the older morality. At 162–3 they complain that the younger gods wield their power 'beyond justice'. At 490–516 they complain again of the harmful consequences if Orestes is acquitted. It will be of no use to appeal to Justice or to the Avengers; 'the house of justice is falling'. At 778–9 they cry shame on the 'younger gods', who have overturned the 'ancient laws'. So the Furies certainly think that the old idea of justice, the old laws, have been replaced, Zeus or no Zeus. And what they treat as most important in the old laws is honouring parents and guests (270–1, 545–9).

When Aeschylus wrote the *Oresteia*, it was already the practice of the court of Areopagus to acquit on a charge of murder if the votes of the jury were equal. So Aeschylus is not telling his countrymen to advance beyond what they were already doing. But he is suggesting to them that *their* political structure, and *their* conception of justice as practised in their courts, mark an advance on an older conception.

Is he also suggesting that there has been an advance in religious ideas too? Athena, the patron deity of Athens, and Apollo, the deity of the temple at Delphi revered by all Greek cities, are described as new or younger gods, subordinate to Zeus and citing Zeus as their authority, but still 'new'. What about Zeus himself? At the beginning of the *Agamemnon* (160–2), the Chorus sing a hymn to Zeus: 'Zeus, whoever he may be, if it pleases him to be called by this name, then I call upon him by it.' They go on to say that they will not call upon Zeus' predecessors, Ouranos and Kronos. This implies a notion of theological change and of ethical progress, because the Chorus describe Ouranos (the Sky) as having been 'mighty, swelling with ever hostile audacity', while Zeus is described as having set up a rule that wisdom comes from suffering.

Whatever may be said about Aeschylus' theology, it seems to me that in the *Oresteia* he puts before us an earlier and a later conception of justice, recommending the latter and associating it with the judicial and democratic procedures of Athens.

Chapter 4

PLATO'S *REPUBLIC*

The full title of Plato's *Republic* is '*Politeia* (Governance) or On Justice'. The main subject matter is indeed governance, the establishment of governed order in society—though in the course of the book Plato relates that topic to all other branches of philosophy or theory—but a central issue in the main subject is justice. The book begins with justice and ends with justice.

Book I was written before the rest. It deals with the historical Socrates. It may or may not report, more or less correctly, an actual conversation that the historical Socrates had with his friends and with the sophist Thrasymachus; but it certainly represents the kind of philosophical discussion that Socrates engaged in. The rest of the *Republic* is different; it represents the views of Plato himself.

Book I is more of a genuine dialogue. Socrates gets other people to give their views and then criticizes them. When asked for his own opinion, his offering is fairly limited. He believes that justice, and virtue generally, has to do with knowledge and brings happiness, but his account is not elaborated and his arguments are not really convincing (an indication that Plato thought Socrates had pointed the way but had not reached the destination). It is characteristic of Socrates to seek definitions, especially definitions of moral virtues, to proceed by negative criticism of definitions offered by others, to profess relative ignorance on his own part, and to believe that in some sense virtue is knowledge.

In the remainder of the *Republic* Plato uses the character of Socrates as a mouthpiece for his own views. The method is still nominally dialogue, but for the most part the other characters are simply asked to endorse or query ideas put forward by the character called 'Socrates'. Far from professing ignorance, as the historical Socrates and the Socrates of Book I had done, the so-called Socrates of Books II–X is remarkably bold in making positive assertions of a far-reaching and interconnected nature.

It is worth spending a little time on proposed definitions of justice in Book I. These are common views held at the time. First we are given the view of

Cephalus, a pious and simple-minded old man, who would not go in for philosophising at all if he were not prodded into it by Socrates. Cephalus follows traditional religious practices; he does not worry about discovering the truth concerning them. As a matter of fact Cephalus himself does not offer a definition; it is put into his mouth by Socrates. Socrates says that we can all learn from old age—that is, from the *experience* of the elderly—and asks Cephalus what does he think is the chief value of his wealth. Cephalus replies that you do not have to fear, when you die, that you have deceived or cheated anyone, or that you have failed to pay your debts to gods or men. The reply sums up his idea of wrongdoing—or rather, of the kind of wrongdoing that it is easy to fall into: deceit or cheating, and failing to pay your debts. He does not speak of greater wrongs such as murder or assault or theft, or more subtle wrongs such as insulting or shaming someone. Cephalus has been a successful businessman; he is conscious of the kind of wrongdoing that can easily arise in business. Socrates takes him to have suggested that 'telling the truth (avoidance of deceit) and paying debts' is a definition of *dikaiosyne* (right action or justice).

Let us pause to say something about that Greek word. It is an abstract term, a relatively sophisticated one. You will not find it in Homer, nor does it occur in the *Oresteia*. The earlier word for justice is a shorter one, *dike*, what is right or just. The word *dike* would commonly imply an idea of order, of balance or redressing disturbance of balance. It is what a judge or juryman, a *dikastes*, must have in mind. A person who conforms to *dike* is *dikaios*, one who does right; he is just or righteous. When reflective people started to think philosophically, abstractly, they coined the word *dikaiosyne*, as the name of the quality, the virtue, manifested by a *dikaios*, a just or righteous man. *Dikaiosyne* can therefore have a wide meaning, righteousness, the quality of acting as one ought.

But it is also distinguished from other virtues, other human qualities that are admired and approved from a moral point of view. In the later parts of the *Republic* Plato speaks of four cardinal virtues, wisdom, courage, self-control or 'temperance', and justice, as if this were a standard view of ethical doctrine. There are in fact some references to three or four leading virtues in poetical literature of the time, but they do not include *wisdom*; its place is taken by piety, that is to say, religious observance. The substitution of wisdom for piety is one of Plato's innovations; he thinks that *philosophy* can do better than traditional religion in giving men guidance on how to live. Cephalus represents unthinking piety; he sacrifices to the gods, pays his debts, does as he has been taught, but has no capacity or desire to ask what lies behind it all. Another point worth noting is that Aristotle (*Nicomachean Ethics*, v.1, 1129^{b}29–30) quotes a line from the poet Theognis which says that all virtue is contained in justice. Plato follows up this notion in the *Republic* when he makes justice the most important of the virtues and also the one that synthesizes the rest. But there is a sense in which he makes wisdom the leading virtue, for it is the virtue of his ruling elite and it is also the virtue of reason, the controlling element in the soul. To allot a primacy to wisdom is to follow up the doctrine of his master Socrates. I shall suggest later that there is a sense in which Plato gives an unwarranted special importance to the virtue of self-control (or 'temperance') and reinterprets justice so as to make it almost identical with 'temperance' or self-control.

The one cardinal virtue that does not in any sense have priority in Plato's scheme is courage. Courage is the virtue especially associated with the second class in his ideal city, the 'Auxiliaries' or the military. The Greek word for courage or bravery is *andreia*, a noun formed from the word for a (male) man. One may compare the Latin *virtus*, derived from *vir*, a male human being. These derivations indicate that, in an early stage of Greek and Roman society, bravery or courage was thought of as *the* cardinal virtue or excellence of the male. The quality of physical courage is most highly regarded in early forms of society because the survival of the society depends upon it.

With a more settled form of society there can be a more general co-operation. There is less continual fear of external invasion. More attention is given to internal order and stability, and so justice, the ordered regulation of behaviour between citizens, gains more importance as the cardinal virtue. We have already seen something of this in Aeschylus' praise of legal justice at Athens.

Plato goes along with this tendency. The fact that the adjective *dikaios* could have the wider meaning of 'righteous' or 'right-acting', as well as the narrower meaning of 'just', enables him to emphasize the centrality and the synthesizing character of the virtue of justice. It also enables him to write as if justice could be a virtue of the individual soul or personality (as wisdom, courage, and self-control can be), although normal usage of the word takes justice to be a social, not an individual virtue, a virtue that concerns the relation between persons, not one that can apply to an individual on his own.

Let us now return to Cephalus. The supposed definition of justice that Socrates has extracted from Cephalus, telling the truth and paying your debts, is soon shown to be too narrow. Socrates interprets 'debts' or 'what you owe' to include things that you have borrowed, and he asks whether it is 'just' (or right) to return a borrowed sword to someone who has gone mad. Cephalus agrees that it would not be right, but he has no head for this kind of thing, so he gladly bequeaths his role in the discussion to his son Polemarchus and goes off to his ritual of religious sacrifice. He is a man incapable of philosophic wisdom; his corresponding virtue is religious piety: don't ask questions, just do what you have been told is right. If we look forward for a moment to Plato's ideal city, Cephalus is incapable of becoming a Guardian, or even an Auxiliary. His natural capacities make him suited for the larger third class of citizens that includes artisans, businessmen, and people practising a profession or skill. He will follow 'right opinion'; he will do as his teachers have told him. He is not capable of finding out the truth of things for himself.

Polemarchus takes over the position of Cephalus and gives it a more generalized expression, found in one of the poets: justice is 'rendering to every man his due'. Among the ancient Greeks, general expressions of practical wisdom in the poets were often cited as authoritative, much as conventionally religious people in modern Western society will cite sayings from the Bible. We may recall some of the general proverbial remarks quoted by the Chorus in the *Oresteia*: we learn by suffering; what you do shall be done to you. It is also worth noting that the statement from the poet Simonides which Polemarchus cites is in fact pretty well identical with what became the standard definition of justice in the Roman law tradition: *justitia est cuique suum tribuere*; justice is rendering to each man what is his (his own, what belongs to him, what is due to him). The main trouble with this definition is that it is too vague. What exactly is 'due' to each man, or 'belongs' to him, or is 'his own'?

Socrates puts this criticism to Polemarchus when he says that the proverbial maxim cannot mean that possession of a sword is due or proper when the owner has gone mad. Yet, in the most obvious sense of *suum*, of what is 'his', what belongs to him, the sword *is* due, does belong, to the man who has gone mad.

The question leads Polemarchus to interpret the proverbial dictum as meaning that one should benefit one's friends and harm one's enemies: you should do good to those who love you or do good to you, and you should do evil to those who hate you or do evil to you. This is a crude statement of the merit or desert concept of justice: return good for good and evil for evil: that is what is 'due', in the sense of being *deserved*.

Socrates challenges this traditional view, and so reminds us of a similar challenge by Jesus in the Sermon on the Mount, but Socrates does so with an unconvincing argument. He says that to harm someone or to do him an evil is to make him worse in terms of human excellence. Justice is a virtue, an *arete*, a human excellence. So if it were true that it is just to harm someone, this would mean that it is the function of justice, a human excellence, to make men unjust, to make them lack human excellence. The argument is fallacious. Granting that justice is *one* human excellence, the reducing of a man's human excellence by harming him does not imply the reducing of *all* human excellences, including justice, in him.

I doubt if Plato expects us to regard this argument as convincing. There is a fallacy of a similar kind in Socrates' refutation of Thrasymachus at the end of Book I. I think that these manifestly fallacious arguments indicate that Plato thought of Socrates' position was not good enough. There is at least one other place in Plato's works (*Crito*, 49) in which the historical Socrates is represented as believing, contrary to popular opinion, that it cannot be right or just to harm those who harm you. So it seems likely that the historical Socrates did hold a more idealistic view of justice than the conventional one. In the *Crito* passage, Socrates speaks with deep conviction but does not give an explicit argument for his view. There is perhaps an implicit argument that it would be self-contradictory if doing an injury (a wrong) were right or just, but the overall theme of the passage is to affirm a basic moral (rather than a logical) principle that it can never be right to do injury or harm, even as requital. The *Crito* depicts Socrates near the end of his life. The Socrates of *Republic* I is somewhat younger and perhaps represented as less mature in his thought.

Having despatched Polemarchus, Socrates is given a much harder nut to crack, first by the sophist Thrasymachus and then, in a more subtle form, by two of Socrates' own supporters, Glaucon and Adeimantus, acting as devil's advocate. The view that they put forward is not an account of the specific virtue of justice but a theory about law and morality in general; it is about justice as meaning the whole system of law. Thrasymachus holds that the system of law is an artificial invention designed to serve the interests of 'the stronger', that is to say, of *de facto* rulers. It is rather like Marx's view that the social 'superstructure', which includes law and morality, is 'ideological', serving the interests of the ruling class—except that Marx also believes, or implies, that there is a genuine 'human' morality which will come to light when classes are abolished. Such a human or genuine morality involves disinterested action to serve the whole community. Thrasymachus would have said that this is illusion just as much as the conventional morality found in actual societies. The only natural way of behaving, according to Thrasymachus, is self-interested; but the majority of men are compelled, by law and its sanctions, to serve the interests of the rulers in order to avoid even greater unpleasantness. Glaucon's reiteration of the essence of Thrasymachus' theory is slightly different in that it regards the system of law and government as the result of a social contract made in order to avoid the worse alternative of being oppressed by a tyrannical regime. Glaucon's hypothesis is rather like Hobbes's theory of a state set up by social contract, while Thrasymachus' theory is more like Hobbes's account of a state set up by conquest. (We shall see in due course that Hobbes is more sophisticated than Thrasymachus; he realizes that even a state set up by conquest must rely on a measure of consent.)

Glaucon says that this kind of view of law and government is popular; he himself does not believe it but he does not know how to refute it. A hard-boiled or 'realistic' theory of law and government always has a wide appeal, because law certainly depends on force, and it is therefore tempting to suppose that its invocation of moral justice is a sham. We all know that in political life the motive of self-interest is very prominent, despite protestations of acting for the sake of ideals, and so it is tempting to go the whole hog and conclude that talk of disinterested action is always a sham.

There is a further reason why the view of Thrasymachus and Glaucon should have seemed plausible to Greeks. The view is a theory about government and law. The Greek word for law is *nomos*, which also means custom. The reason why this word came to describe law as well as custom is that law begins in customary practice. The Common Law of Anglo-American systems was originally custom, just as the legal rules of a primitive society are largely the result of custom. Code systems of law appear superficially to have a different base, but their codes are derived from Roman law, which itself began as customary law and was codified at a relatively late stage. Nearly all systems of law contain ordained statutes which have been added to the base of customary law or code with which they begin, and ancient Greek has words different from *nomos* for individual laws that are the result of legislation (resolutions of the legislative assembly), as it has for rules that were supposedly ordained by the gods. But the body of law as a whole is *nomos*, and it was natural enough, indeed basically correct, to think of law as something that exists as the result of human custom or convention. A number of the sophists (itinerant teachers of rhetoric and philosophy) distinguished between that which was true 'by nature' (the subject matter of natural science) and that which was true 'by convention' or custom (a great deal of human behaviour and rules about human behaviour). The Greek terms that they used for 'nature' and 'convention' were *physis* and *nomos*. So to say that law was artificial, man-made, not natural, was to say little more than the virtual tautology that *nomos* existed *nomōi* (the dative case of *nomos*), that law or custom existed by convention, as a matter of custom.

But because law practically always comes to include, very soon, ideas of moral justice, the easily held view, the virtual tautology, turns into a wider and less obvious theory that justice, and indeed morality as a whole, exists by convention as much as law does. Plato and others objected to this theory, partly because they thought it dangerous (if people believe that morality is simply a matter of convention, they will not take it seriously), and partly because it does present serious philosophical difficulties.

However, since our discussion is concerned with the concept of justice as a specific virtue, and not with conventionalist or relativist theories of morality as a whole, we can now turn from the theory of Thrasymachus and Glaucon to that of Plato himself.

Plato draws a distinction and an analogy between justice 'in the soul', or in the individual, and justice in society. It seems odd to talk about justice in the soul of the individual. Justice concerns relationships *between* individuals, and although it does not have to refer to law or to the way in which a whole society is run, still it must refer to a group, even if only to a small group. There can be justice and injustice within a family (a parent may treat his or her children justly or unjustly, in comparison with each other), or within a group of friends or associates, or within a group consisting of teacher and pupils; but what on earth can it mean for a solitary individual on a desert island to be just? Plato is using the word in its wider sense of righteousness or behaving rightly. You can think of this as a virtue of the individual, perhaps independently of his relations to other people (though one might have some doubts even about that). At any rate Plato wants to stress two things about justice or righteousness as a virtue of the individual. First, he wants to urge that righteousness is not simply a matter of carrying out certain prescribed actions (like Cephalus with performing his due sacrifices and paying his debts); it also involves acting in a moral spirit. Secondly, he wants to urge that righteousness is a comprehensive virtue: although it can be distinguished from courage and wisdom and self-control (and perhaps minor virtues too), it binds them all together, precisely because it expresses the *spirit* of morality, of trying to do the right thing from a sense of duty or a sense of idealism.

Plato's actual characterization of the inner spirit of righteousness or morality is peculiar. He sees it as a balance or harmony among different elements of the soul or personality. Such a balance, with reason in control of the passions, is undoubtedly desirable, but we would not think of it as righteousness or as any specifically *moral* virtue. No doubt Greek ideas of moral virtue were less concentrated on the notion of service to others than are the ethical notions that we have inherited from the Bible. Nevertheless I do not think that Plato's conception should be regarded as typical of Greek thought. It is a spin-off from his concept of justice in society, which is undoubtedly peculiar to himself.

In talking about justice in the *Republic*, Plato has a political as well as a moral purpose. He says that we shall more easily see the nature of justice as an individual virtue if we first look at its larger analogue, justice in society. But his intention, in discussing justice in society, is not simply to use it as an aid to understanding righteousness in the individual. He has a definite view of what a well-ordered society would be and he uses the concept of justice in order to recommend it.

He regards justice in society as a situation in which each person sticks to the one function that suits his natural abilities. We get a first approach to this in Plato's picture of a simple, rudimentary society with a division of labour. An individual *could* do everything for himself but he would have a hard job to keep going. He is not really self-sufficient. Life is much easier and more comfortable if there is a division of labour and an exchange of products. Men need the help of each other. That is why society exists. When Socrates has described this simple form of society, he asks where justice is to be found in it. Adeimantus says (372a), 'I have no idea, unless it be somewhere in their dealings with one another'. Adeimantus is no doubt thinking of the fact that mutual exchange involves a notion of fair dealing. Later theory, building on Aristotle's remarks about justice in exchanging goods, was to talk of commutative justice, justice in exchange, a fair price for a product and a fair value in the product that you get for your money. Plato does not take up the suggestion in this sense and puts the issue aside while the discussion proceeds to describe a more elaborate society.

The first, rudimentary 'city' provides for economic necessities. It does not provide for luxuries. Glaucon says (372d) that the first city is a city fit for pigs. He does not mean that it is disgusting. He means that it simply serves biological needs, the needs that men share with animals. If a society is to cater for specifically human desires and capacities, it will have to go further. And so a city or society of luxury is described. It has its dangers. It offers a temptation to outsiders to invade it for its wealth, and so it will need an army. It also offers the opportunity for its citizens to take things to excess, and so it needs controls to teach them restraint. It can accommodate specifically human virtues or excellences and it also allows for the converse, human failings or vices. So it needs an education system, a set of rulers, and a body of people to enforce the rules if need be. Consequently the economic division of labour, which existed in the first city, is supplemented by a social or political division of classes. There are to be three classes: the Guardians or rulers; the Auxiliaries or military; and the rest, who are to conduct the economic life of the society.

The economic division of labour is the basis of society; it is essential if men are to have a tolerable life. So it is a necessary condition of society, but it is not, strictly speaking, a virtue, because the purely economic form of society allows neither for virtues nor for vices. Virtues are required to maintain the second, ideal city: the Guardians need the virtue of wisdom to carry out soundly their function of governing; the Auxiliaries need the virtue of courage for their specific function of maintaining security and order; and, according to Plato, all three classes need the virtue of temperance or self-control to accept their respective roles; the remaining virtue of justice is the balance or harmony of each class performing its proper role.

When Plato eventually reaches his definition of justice in Book IV of the *Republic* (433), he says that the initial division of labour, applied in the first city, is the clue to the understanding of justice. But he does not say that the economic division actually *is* justice; it is a shadow or semblance of justice. To explain why the economic division is not justice, he says (434) that no great harm will be done if people exchange economic functions (for example, if a carpenter and a cobbler exchange jobs and tools), 'or even if the same man undertakes both' (while justice, it will be recalled, requires one man, one job); but it would be disastrous if there were a change of *social* functions, that is, if there were movement from one social class to another. Plato is not really worried about the possibility that a member of the governing or of the military class might become an artisan or a businessman. He illustrates his thesis by a move from the class of producers and merchants to the class of rulers or to the class of soldiers. What bothers him is the possibility that people whose natural capacity is for production or commerce might aspire to political rule or military security. They are not capable of it and so the society might collapse. When Plato says that movement within the economic class does not matter, he also says it would not matter if one man took more than one job, so long as they were both economic jobs. When he insists that justice requires one man, one job, his concern is to prevent the lower orders, people who lack the virtues of wisdom or courage, from trying to govern or to fight as well as to produce. It is all part of Plato's opposition to democracy. The Athenian democracy prided itself on the fact that it had a citizen army and a citizen parliament. All citizens were judged capable both of helping to defend their country and of helping to run it. Indeed participation in defence, in political decisions, and in the administration of the law, was held to be the glory of a democratic city.

The critics of democracy accused democrats of being busybodies, of *polypragmosyne*, 'meddling in many things', instead of sticking to what was their proper business, their allotted place in society. Plato supports this attitude. He believes in aristocracy. He thinks that politics requires leadership from people with particular gifts. He says that the particular gift needed is wisdom, the aim of philosophy. This is partly because he thought he could be good at it himself, but even more because he resented the condemnation of Socrates by the Athenian democracy. He believed that Socrates, or rather perhaps an idealized Socrates, could have been the philosopher-ruler posited for the Guardian class. In realistic terms, however, the nub of Plato's political position is not so much the particular suggestion that political leaders should be philosophers, but rather his conviction that democracy was responsible for the defeat of Athens in its war against Sparta, an elitist city with a military leadership. Plato did not favour the actual type of government that existed at Sparta. He valued the culture of Athens and so he proposed that the military elite should be subordinate to an intellectual elite. But he did think that Athens had met disaster because it had a democratic regime, in which any Tom, Dick, and Harry could affect political decisions.

All of that is intelligible, but why call the principle of elitism by the name of *justice*? One reason is that the principle of elitism exemplifies the conception of justice as distribution according to merit. This conception says that benefits and burdens, including responsibilities, should be distributed according to merit or worth, and one kind of 'merit' (or better, of worth) is the talent or ability to do a particular kind of job well. But I think that Plato had another reason, too. In his time, at Athens if not elsewhere in Greece, justice had come to be regarded as the leading social virtue, the quality essential to society and the main benefit resulting from society. In a democratic society, however, justice was associated with ideas of equality and universal participation. Plato thought that was misguided. But since the term 'justice' had come to be rated so highly, it would have been swimming against the tide to say that justice, in its popular democratic sense, was a bad thing and should be replaced by a principle of hierarchical order and discipline. So Plato arranged his argument in such a way that the principle of hierarchical order and discipline was virtually identified with the favoured name of justice.

I say this because there is no *substantial* difference between Plato's account of 'temperance' or self-control and his account of justice. Both are said to be conditions in which each of the different elements in the city and in the soul has a specific role in relation to the other elements.

The three classes in the city are compared with three elements in the soul, reason, 'spirit' or ardour, and appetite. The virtue of wisdom in the city, possessed by the Guardian class, corresponds to wisdom in the soul to be attained by the element of reason. Courage in the city, shown by the Auxiliary class, corresponds to courage in the soul expressed by 'spirit'. Unlike the virtues of wisdom and courage, each of which pertains to one particular class in the city and one particular element in the soul, the remaining cardinal virtues of temperance and justice concern all three classes or elements. But, oddly enough, Plato's description of these two virtues makes little distinction between them.

Temperance is established in the city when the wise Guardians rule, the courageous Auxiliaries support them with force of arms, and the third class accepts that rule; justice is established in the city when each of the three classes sticks to its own role—the first of governing, the second of supporting government with force of arms, and the third of accepting the orders of the government. What is the difference? In the soul, temperance comes about when reason, aided by 'spirit', controls the appetites, and when the appetites do not rebel but accept the control of reason; justice comes about when each of the three elements sticks to its own job, reason having the job of controlling the appetites, spirit that of giving support to reason, and the appetites that of accepting subordination. What is the difference? Commentators tell us that there is a subtle difference: temperance describes the situation from the point of view of each element, while justice describes the situation as a whole, as a balance or harmony. Maybe. But essentially we have two descriptions of the same situation.

In ordinary Greek usage, the concept of justice as a specific virtue would apply to society, not to an individual soul or personality. (We have noted this already.) On the other hand, the word translated as temperance or self-control, *sophrosyne*, would apply in ordinary Greek usage to a disposition of an individual's character, not to society. A person is *sophron* if he is self-controlled, prudent, under the guidance of reason. When Plato applies the term to society, he is drawing an analogy between this desirable feature of an individual character and what he regards as a desirable feature of society, namely discipline or settled order, in which potentially unruly elements are kept in check by the strength of law and order, that is, by government and its enforcement agencies. An elitist who believes in discipline might well compare this desired social situation with 'self-control' (the control of passion by reason) in an individual's character, and so might apply the term *sophrosyne* to a well-ordered society.

Let us now look at the passage in Book IV of the *Republic* where Plato reaches his definition of justice (justice in the city, since his account of the virtues in the city comes before their analogues in the soul). He has identified the other three cardinal virtues. His ideal city exemplifies the virtue of wisdom in the nature of the Guardian class and the virtue of courage in the Auxiliary class. When he comes to 'temperance', he does not say, as you might expect, that this is exemplified by the producing and commercial class, who accept their subordinate position and agree to follow the orders of the Guardians. Instead Plato says that temperance is exemplified by all three classes in accepting their respective roles of ruling, supporting, or obeying.

He then comes to justice. His mouthpiece Socrates says that it has been in front of their noses all the time. It is 'something like' the division of labour; it is the principle that everyone should perform the function for which he is best suited. Then Socrates says (433a8 ff.):

'That justice is doing your own job and not being a busybody, we have heard from many others and have often said ourselves.'

'We have,' agrees Glaucon. And Socrates continues:

'Well, it somehow happens to have turned out that doing your own job is justice.'

Why does he repeat it? If it is commonly said that justice is doing your own job, why does Socrates now say 'It somehow happens to have turned out that justice is doing your own job'?

Let us now look at the previous sentence, which is also puzzling: 'We have heard from many others, and we ourselves have often said, that justice is doing your own job and not meddling in other people's business.' *Where* has this been said? If it really were a common Greek view, one would expect it to be mentioned by Aristotle, who, as is his practice, gives an account of common conceptions in the course of providing his own classification and synthesis. In fact Aristotle says nothing of this particular idea of justice. No scholar has produced instances of the idea in other writers before Plato.

Again, what about the statement that 'we have often said it ourselves'? Where is it to be found in the other works of Plato? Scholars have asked the question and, with one exception, they fudge the answer. For instance, F. M. Cornford[1] says, in a note on the passage: 'If "justice" is here taken in the wide sense of "the right way to behave", "right conduct", this has, of course, been stated several times in the *Republic*. But the statement need not refer to any passage in the dialogue.' The last sentence betrays his uneasiness. It is not true that the statement *has* been made several times in the *Republic*. Book II says that people will benefit from a division of labour; it does not say anything about this being the morally right way to behave. *After* our present passage, of course, the definition is often cited; but at this point it is being said for the first time.

James Adam,[2] the best editor of the Greek text of the *Republic*, asks the question, 'Where has this been said?', answers 'Nowhere, so far as I know', and goes on to suggest a possible solution to the genuine problem that is raised. He notes that this definition of justice is given in only one other dialogue attributed to Plato, *Alcibiades I*, a late work, almost certainly not written by Plato himself. The definition of justice there is simply following the doctrine of the *Republic*. Adam supposes that Plato must be referring to conversation, not written work, but he says it is curious that Plato's dialogue *Charmides* speaks in one place of *sophrosyne* (temperance) as 'doing your own job', sticking to your appointed place, and that there is a hint of this idea in another dialogue, *Timaeus*. Adam therefore conjectures that in the *Republic* sentence, 'We have heard from many others, and have often said ourselves, that justice is doing your own job', the word *dikaiosyne* (justice) may be a scribe's error for *sophrosyne* (temperance). This is intelligible enough. A medieval monk, copying the manuscript, comes to a sentence which appears to state that *sophrosyne* is doing your own job. 'Oh,' he says to himself, 'that is a mistake by an earlier scribe. We all know that doing your own job in Plato's *Republic* is *dikaiosyne*.' So he, as he thinks, corrects the error, but in fact introduces an error.

If we accept Adam's emendation of restoring *sophrosyne* in this sentence, the whole passage makes much better sense.

SOCRATES. It seems to me that justice is what we spoke of earlier, or something like it. We said that everyone should do one job, the one to which he is naturally suited.
GLAUCON. Yes, we did.
SOCRATES. *And yet* [the Greek is Καὶ μὴν . . . γε, which sometimes means 'And yet', sometimes 'Moreover'] we have heard from many others, and we ourselves have often said, that doing your own job and not being a busybody is *self-control* (or discipline).

---

[1] F. M. Cornford (trans.), *The Republic of Plato* (Oxford: Clarendon Press, 1941), 124 n.
[2] James Adam (ed.), *The Republic of Plato* (Cambridge: Cambridge University Press, 1902; 2nd edn., with introduction by D. A. Rees, 1963), i. 239, note on 433b9.

GLAUCON. That's true.

SOCRATES. Well, my friend, it somehow happens to have turned out that this business of doing your own job is *justice*.

That makes much better sense, as Adam observed. One can, however, go further and show that it helps us to understand Plato's aim. Adam says that the virtue of *sophrosyne* was not always distinguished from *dikaiosyne* (in that word's wider sense of a general virtue, right-mindedness) and so he takes the passages in the *Charmides* and the *Timaeus* to be expressions of a popular view. But the *Charmides* passage (161b ff.) treats the proposed definition of *sophrosyne* as hardly intelligible if applied to *sophrosyne* in its normal sense of temperance or self-control in the individual. It refers to *sophrosyne* as a desirable feature of society, social discipline. That was not at all a common or popular sense of the word. Moreover, the statement in the *Charmides* that social discipline is a matter of sticking to your own job is made by Critias, a political aristocrat, who tried to persuade Plato to join the oligarchical government that came to be called the Thirty Tyrants. He and Charmides were both related to Plato. In the *Republic* passage, Plato is adopting that aristocratic sentiment but is trying to make it more palatable by giving it the label of justice. That is why his account of temperance or self-control and his account of justice are virtually identical. He is recommending an aristocratic doctrine but tries to make it more popular by giving it the name of the more popular virtue, justice. He is able to do so because the long-standing meritarian conception of justice allows one to say that government should be exercised by those with a talent for it, not by anybody and everybody.

We can see that Plato's definition of justice is *not* a reflection of any usual sense of the term if we look at an argument whereby he tries to show that it is. Socrates says (433e) that in the judgements of the law courts the aim of judges is to ensure that the parties shall not have what belongs to others or be deprived of what is their own, because that is justice. Thus it is generally agreed, he continues, that justice is the 'having and doing' what is one's own. The evidence to which Plato here appeals, the practice of the courts, is that each person should *have* what is his own. This, of course, is a familiar notion of justice in regard to property. But to make it come near to his own definition, Plato has to say the accepted opinion is that justice is 'having *and doing*' what is your own. The maxim about the practice of the courts says nothing about *doing*, and Plato's own definition says nothing about *having*. He has to distort both the common view and his own in order to pretend that they fit, that the common view supports his own. The idea that justice is sticking to your own job comes from Plato and Plato alone.

Chapter 5

ARISTOTLE

Aristotle's thoughts about justice are given most systematically in Book V of the *Nicomachean Ethics*. The treatment is not as clear as one would like. There is, first, the general obstacle presented by the form of Aristotle's works as they have come down to us. The text is apparently a set of lecture notes or something similar, not a finished work written for publication. There are repetitions, insertions, omissions, and perhaps faulty arrangement of passages by early editors. Secondly, there are unnecessary obscurities introduced by Aristotle into this particular discussion. He has a general theory that each of the virtues is a mean between excess and defect, and he tries to apply this to his account of justice, where it does not fit at all well. He is also keen on subjecting his treatment to mathematical formulae whenever he can, and this too turns out to be unhelpful. Aristotle was, for his time, a very good scientist in the field of the life sciences, to which he made important contributions both by way of observation and by way of systematization. He was, in addition, a penetrating thinker on more general problems of theoretical physics (as that subject was seen in his day). His signal contributions to metaphysics and the philosophy of mind were greatly influenced by his scientific understanding. But he was not particularly gifted for mathematics and his would-be mathematical treatment of the concept of justice in the *Ethics* has been described as childish and excessively simple. It does not promote understanding or give one any additional insight into the notion of justice; it simply obscures the view.

One may complain also of Aristotle's discussion that it does not tie up its different elements into a coherent whole and that it inexplicably omits any consideration of the justice of punishment.

Yet despite all these criticisms, there is a world of difference between Aristotle's handling of the subject and Plato's. In Aristotle we have a genuine attempt to approach the matter in a scientific spirit, with a clarification of different branches of justice, a sensitivity to linguistic usage (even though it includes a piece of dubious etymology), and a location of the concept on the map of ethical ideas as a whole. Plato's treatment is much more attractive but Aristotle's conveys more enlightenment, both about ancient Greek thought and as a model for future analysis to follow and refine.

Aristotle begins by drawing a distinction between universal and particular justice. Although he identifies universal justice with *moral* righteousness in general (subject to one qualification) and so reminds us of a leading aspect of Plato's *Republic*, he is led to this concept of universal justice more by his consideration of the law. He says at the start (chapter 1) that the words 'just' and 'unjust' are ambiguous in meaning (1) lawful and unlawful, (2) fair and unfair. This is comparable with the general distinction that we might make today between legal and moral justice. In the law we apply the term 'justice' to the whole of the system of law. Aristotle is thinking especially of the Greek word for 'unjust' (*adikon*), which means 'wrong' as well as 'unjust'. The corresponding word for 'just' (*dikaion*) can also mean 'right', and certainly 'righteous', but the very wide meaning is more obvious with the negative word. If one wants to say in ancient Greek that a man has wronged another, has done what is wrong, has transgressed the law, this word *adikon* and its cognates would naturally be used. One can infer from these linguistic considerations that a *specific* concept of injustice was still emerging, or rather, perhaps, that the linguistic usage preserves an older state of thought in which there was no sharp distinction between legal and moral defect or between wrongdoing in general and more specific kinds of wrongdoing.

Aristotle goes on to identify the legal sense of justice and injustice (what conforms to and what goes against the law) with the idea of moral virtue and vice in general. He draws this conclusion because he believes that the aim of the law is to promote virtue and prohibit vice ('the law bids us practise every virtue and forbids us to practise any vice' (ch. 2, 1130^{b}23–4)).

I do not think we should accept too readily that this is an accurate description of the function of ancient Athenian law. It is an inference which Aristotle himself makes from premises that are more obviously acceptable. He says first that law aims at the common good or at the good of the ruling group. That is sensible enough. He then says that the law requires people to do the acts of a brave man (not to desert his post or run away or discard his weapons on the battlefield), and the acts of a self-controlled man (not to commit adultery or to behave insultingly), and the acts of a gentle or good-tempered man (not to assault or slander), 'and so on with regard to the other virtues and vices' (ch. 1, 1129^{b}14–24).

The *examples* that Aristotle gives could be found in modern law systems too. The prohibition of desertion, flight, or discarding arms relates to the battlefield and will be found repeated in modern military law. But those prohibitions do not imply that the law commands every act that we would include in the virtue of bravery or courage. The code of firemen lays upon *them* a duty to enter a burning house, but no law in modern society requires the rest of us to rescue victims of a fire, although we would all commend the bravery of somebody who did so. No law requires that we bear up when we have lost a loved one, although it is courageous, and so morally virtuous, to do so. There is no reason to think that Athenian law required it any more than modern law, though it is obvious from Greek literature that the Greeks, like ourselves, did not think that the virtue of courage could be shown only on the field of battle.

Again, consider Aristotle's examples to illustrate a failure to show the virtue of self-control; the law, he says, prohibits adultery and insulting behaviour. While adultery is not a criminal offence in modern Western systems of law, it still counts in most of them as a civil wrong, being a ground (or at least evidence of a ground) for divorce. Insulting behaviour can in some circumstances be a criminal offence. There are, however, other actions which show a lack of self-control in regard to other people but which are not prohibited by the law: for example, laughing at other people's weaknesses or being greedy at a party so as to leave others short. Aristotle's third category is the other side of this coin: a gentle or good-tempered man is one who exercises self-control or one who does not need to control his impulses. Here again, Aristotle's examples of prohibited actions, assault and slander, are criminal or civil wrongs under modern law, too; but there is no suggestion that the law therefore requires us to perform all the acts that we should praise morally as gentle or good-tempered, such as turning the other cheek or avoiding angry remonstrances. The ancient Greeks, like us, would have called these the acts of a gentle or good-tempered person and would have regarded them as a mark of the moral virtue on that account, but there would never have been any suggestion that they were required by law.

However, Aristotle does draw the inference that the law aims at promoting all the virtues and restraining all the vices, though he adds that actual laws may do the job more or less well. Having decided that the wider sense of justice, legal or universal justice, can be identified with the whole of virtue, Aristotle adds a qualification. Justice is complete virtue but only in relation to other people. In support, he quotes here (and again later in chapter 6) a phrase that is used by Thrasymachus in Book I of Plato's *Republic* and that no doubt represents a common idea, 'justice is another's good'. Plato himself tries to deny this in the *Republic* because he wants to argue, against Thrasymachus, that justice or righteousness benefits also the person who does the just act. Aristotle's use of the phrase, in order to qualify the identification of justice with the whole of virtue, is more sensible and indicates that among the Greeks, as with us, justice was a *social* virtue. Some moral virtues, certainly in Greek thought, may pertain to the individual alone: prudence, many instances of self-control or temperance, some instances of courage (such as putting up with painful disease). Justice does not, despite Plato's effort to depict a virtue of justice in the individual soul. If we follow up Aristotle's qualification, we can form a more accurate view of the relation between law and ethics. The aim of law is to give effect to *some* of the purposes of ethics, in particular to protect individuals and the community at large from the harmful consequences of the actions of others.

Having dealt briefly with so-called universal justice, Aristotle turns to specific or particular justice. He had first distinguished this as meaning the 'fair', in contrast to his characterization of universal justice as the 'lawful'. The Greek word for 'fair' which he uses, *ison*, literally means 'equal'. Because the one word was used for the two ideas, Aristotle does not distinguish sharply between them. Instead he describes the fair or the just as the 'proportionately equal'.

He says there are two species of particular justice, distributive and corrective justice. Distributive justice is concerned with the distributing of honour or money or other things. Sir David Ross, writing his book *Aristotle* in the early 1920s, has a comment which is itself indicative of changes that take place in the application of the concept of justice. Ross says: 'The account of distributive justice sounds somewhat foreign to our ears; we are not in the habit of regarding the state as distributing wealth among its citizens. We think of it rather as distributing burdens in the form of taxation.'[1] In the 1920s, one did not hear anything about the 'welfare state', though Lloyd George had introduced a scheme of national insurance for low-paid workers to be entitled to unemployment benefit and old-age pensions. Nowadays we are so used to the idea of social-security measures that it is Ross's comment which sounds strange. At the same time it reminds us that the concept of distributive justice is to be applied at least as much to the distribution of burdens as of benefits. It applies to taxation policy no less than to social-security charges and benefits; and in terms of the effect on *politics*, taxation policy is probably the more important.

Ross goes on to repeat the view of another scholar, that in ancient Greece 'the citizen regarded himself . . . as a shareholder in the state rather than as a taxpayer'. There was from time to time a distribution of public property, such as the land of a new colony, and there was also some welfare-state provision for the poor. Ross notes that one of Aristotle's examples shows that he is thinking also of the just distribution of profits in a business when he says that it should be in proportion to the amount of capital that each partner has contributed. We can see from Aristotle's discussion of justice in the *Politics* that when he talks of the distribution of honour, he is thinking of political power as much as anything else. So we should not take the notion of *distribution* as always meant literally. It covers also the just *arrangement* of benefits and responsibilities. The point is mentioned briefly in the *Ethics* too, when Aristotle says (ch. 3, 1131^{a}25–9) that

---

[1] W. D. Ross, *Aristotle* (London: Methuen, 1923; 4th edn., rev., 1945), 210.

distribution in accordance with 'merit' or 'worth' is interpreted by democrats in terms of the status of a freeman, by oligarchs in terms of wealth or of noble birth, and by aristocrats in terms of 'virtue' or 'excellence' (*arete*).

According to Aristotle, a distribution of goods is just if it conforms to 'proportionate equality'. He calls it equality because the word for 'fair' (which he has said describes particular justice altogether) also means 'equal' and because his formal account of it states an equivalence of ratios. But really that formal statement tells us nothing more than that benefits are distributed justly if distributed in accordance with 'worth'. If A has more worth or merit than B, he should receive more benefit. This has the implication that if, and only if, the merit or worth of the potential beneficiaries is equal, then their share of benefit should be equal (cf. *Politics*, III.9, 1280^a).

Many political theorists still think that this basic principle of Aristotle is a correct account of distributive justice: equal shares to equals, unequal shares to unequals. Aristotle recognizes that democratic ideas about distributive justice differ from the ideas of aristocrats and oligarchs. I would say that democrats have an egalitarian conception of justice while the non-democrats have a meritarian conception. Aristotle thinks that all three groups have a meritarian conception but differ in the kind of merit or 'worth' that they make crucial.

He makes his case in an odd way; it comes out when he explains it in more detail in the *Politics* (III.9, 1280^{a}23–5, and v.1, 1301^{a}29–37). He says that democrats suppose that since citizens are equal in one respect, freedom (he means that they have the status of a freeman as contrasted with the status of a slave), they are equal in all respects; and that supporters of oligarchy suppose that since men are *un*equal in one respect, wealth, they are unequal in all respects. This account of Greek political attitudes is most implausible. The women of Athens, like the men, were either free or enslaved, but the Athenian democrat did not think that a free woman was equal to a free man in being entitled to participate in government, jury service, and so forth. Nor is there any reason to suppose that a supporter of oligarchy believed that the wealthiest people were also the cleverest or the physically strongest.

It would have been more sensible for Aristotle to refer to his discussion in *Politics*, III.12, about the quality or capacity that is *relevant* for exercising political power. He says there that, when flutes are distributed, the best flutes should be given to those who have the best talent for flute playing; this makes for the most efficient use of the flutes. Applying the analogy to politics, Aristotle argues that since the *polis* (the organized political community) exists for the sake of the good life, it needs to be governed by those who know about and practise the good life, namely the virtuous. By means of this argument Aristotle gives his support to the *aristocratic* concept of distributive justice, namely that eligibility to participate in government should be distributed according to virtue. But he does not say that aristocrats mistakenly suppose that those who are unequal in the one quality of virtue are unequal in all respects.

The real question is what quality is thought to be *relevant* for participation in government. Oligarchs say wealth. They think that the wealthy have more of a stake in political society than the poor; they have more to lose; and therefore they, and they alone, should participate in government. The reasoning is the same as that applied in later times by those who said that a property qualification was necessary in order to have a vote. One may compare also the position of those who said that a certain level of education was necessary, in order to understand what it was all about. When the democrats of ancient Athens said that all free men were entitled, as a matter of justice, to participate in government, they believed that all the free adult males of their society were *competent* to participate—not so much because they were free but because they did not have the defect of ability which the Athenians, and Greeks generally, attributed to slaves, women, and children. If you were to grant that some groups are congenitally or institutionally defective (instead of women and slaves, let us say idiots and imprisoned criminals), you would be left with the proposition that all others—all normal people, so to speak—have the ability to take decisions. In short, you would have a qualified egalitarianism. The Greek democrat did not think that equality of freedom implied equality in all respects. He simply thought that those people who were not handicapped by reason of immaturity (children), sex (women), or social status (slaves) were all equally capable of forming a judgement about the common interest.

A further point that needs to be taken up concerning Aristotle's concept of distributive justice is the notion of 'merit' or 'worth'. In modern discussion we tend to think of the concept of distributive justice in terms of merit or desert, and we then raise questions about what is to count as merit. Does it depend on our own efforts, or on achievements even if little effort is involved? Or is it really a question of what benefits society? Aristotle does not go into such questions in his discussion of justice in the *Ethics*, but in the *Politics* he gives, as examples of what is accounted 'worth', the status of a freeman, wealth, virtue, and a talent for playing the flute. The examples show that his notion of worth does not coincide with what we mean by 'merit'. There is nothing meritorious in being a freeman; the freeman is just lucky to have been born free and not a slave. There *can* be merit in possessing wealth, but that depends on whether the wealth has been earned by hard work rather than inherited. There *is* merit in moral virtue, at least if it is the result of effort and difficult choice, but perhaps not if it is simply the result of a happy disposition and fortunate home circumstances. As to a talent for playing the flute, that is a matter of luck, though if the flute-player has worked hard to develop his talent, he may be counted as meritorious.

Aristotle is not bothered about these questions because his conception of choice did not include a clear concept of free will. The word that he uses, *axia*, is best translated 'worth' and he is able to include in it both the kind of worth that is earned and the kind that is not.

Aristotle's second species of particular justice is corrective or rectifying justice. He is not talking about retributive justice or about any concept of what we now call criminal law. He is talking about a feature of what is now called civil law, namely the making good of breaches of contract and the paying of damages for torts. He distinguishes between voluntary and involuntary transactions; what he has in mind is that when contracts are made, both parties act voluntarily, while in the case of a tort the person who suffers harm or damage has not been in any way a voluntary agent in the relationship. Aristotle's distinction is not really significant, however, since in the case of breach of contract the person who suffers damage is not a voluntary party to breaking the contract, and that is what matters; the fact that he was a voluntary party to making the contract is not relevant to the requirement of justice that the wrong be rectified. Aristotle's distinction is merely a way of indicating that two branches or categories of (what we call civil) law are involved.

What Aristotle has to say about this species of justice is curiously insubstantial. He makes much of a mathematical relationship of equality between the gain to the offender and the loss to the victim, and says that the duty of the judge is to render the now unequal positions of the two parties equal to what they were originally. In the course of these remarks Aristotle tries to support his position by an appeal to etymology, which happens to be unsound. He says that the just, *dikaion*, is a half, *dicha*, 'as if one were to pronounce the word "*dichaion*"', and that the judge, *dikastes*, is a bisector or halver, *dichastes* (ch. 4, 1132^{a}31–2). He also refers to the practice of calling the judge, in a civil dispute, a mediator, and says this is because the judge produces a mean, intermediate between the claims of the two parties.

All this arises from Aristotle's desire to uphold his general theory that justice is a mean, like other virtues, and that corrective justice is a matter of equalizing. Modern philologists, with greater knowledge of etymology than Aristotle had, tell us that *dike* and *dikaion* have nothing to do with the words for 'half' (*dicha*) and 'halving' (*dichazein*). As for calling a judge a mediator, the point of this is not that his award stands in the middle of the two claims but that he himself stands between the two opposed contestants and makes it possible for their hostile relationship to become a peaceful one.

The upshot of Aristotle's account of corrective justice is that the gain or advantage which is taken away from the offender is equal to the loss which the victim has suffered. What does this imply in concrete terms? Does it simply mean that the offender must restore what he has taken or, if it cannot be restored, must make up its equivalent in compensation? Sir David Ross[2] says that Aristotle's doctrine goes further than that; 'it takes account of "moral and intellectual damages" as well as of physical or financial injury'; but although he places the words 'moral and intellectual damages' within inverted commas, Ross does not give the source of the quotation. W. F. R. Hardie[3] adds a little enlightenment by referring us to the *Magna Moralia*, 1.33 ($1193^{b}37$–$1194^{a}3$), where Aristotle (or whoever wrote that work) says that a wrongdoer should suffer more than the hurt he has inflicted because 'he was the first to begin and did a wrong, and is in the wrong in both ways'. Even so, we are not much wiser, since we are not given any statement of just how much the reparation should be or how it should be calculated.

Aristotle's account of corrective justice is far less informative than his account of distributive justice. What is clear is that corrective justice is different from distributive; it is not a matter of arranging things according to 'proportionate equality', that is to say, according to merit or worth. Aristotle says that corrective justice is a matter of arranging things in terms of equality or 'arithmetical proportion'. He wants to maintain that both species of justice are forms of 'proportion' (*analogia*), though modern mathematicians would not call the second by the name of proportion at all. Corrective justice is concerned with a straightforward equality. The two parties are considered as having been equal before the wrong was done, and they must be restored to that position of equality. Their different merits or worths are ignored by the judge.

So one point to note is that the justice of the civil law, unlike the political justice of distributing benefits and positions, ignores merit or status and treats all parties on a basis of equality. A second point, which Aristotle does not stress in his comments but which is implied in the name of corrective or rectifying justice, is that the function of the court is to *restore* the status quo that existed before the wrong was done. This form of justice is restorative and aims at preserving an existing structure. Aristotle does say that the judge restores a presumed earlier state of equality, but he stresses the idea of equality more than the idea of restoration.

He next turns to an alternative view, which he attributes to the Pythagoreans and which he criticizes. It is that justice is 'reciprocity' or 'requital'. The Greek term, *antipeponthos*, literally means 'suffering in return', and so one would expect the Pythagorean view to be a form of the *lex talionis*, saying that justice requires a wrongdoer to suffer the same hurt as he has inflicted. This is explicitly confirmed in the version of Aristotle's discussion given in the *Magna Moralia* (1.34, $1194^{a}20$–30). It is implicitly confirmed in the version of the *Nicomachean*

---

[2] W. D. Ross, *Aristotle*, 211.
[3] W. F. R. Hardie, *Aristotle's Ethical Theory* (Oxford: Clarendon Press, 1968), 193.

Ethics when Aristotle says that people want to identify the notion of reciprocity with 'the justice of Rhadamanthus: "if one suffered what one has wrought, true justice would be done"' (ch. 5, 1132^{b}25–7; the quoted verse is from Hesiod). In Greek mythology Rhadamanthus was one of the judges of the dead in Hades; so the Pythagorean view must have been a theory about the justice of punishment, which means that it concerned the public law of wrongdoing, what we now call criminal law. Strangely, in the *Nicomachean Ethics* Aristotle treats it as if it were an account of the justice of civil law, corrective justice, or even as if intended to cover both corrective and distributive justice.

He does not bother to show that it will not fit distributive justice (although one can in fact argue that the distribution of goods, including rewards, in accordance with merit, implies a similar distribution of evils, including punishments, in accordance with demerit). He does show that it will not fit corrective justice because, he says, corrective justice does not always require simple reciprocity or requital, and he gives an example. If an *archon* (one of two public officials in charge of political proceedings) strikes a citizen, it is not just for the *archon* to be struck back in return. On the other hand, if a citizen strikes an *archon*, it is not enough for the *archon* to strike back; the citizen should be punished in addition. Aristotle is presumably thinking of a situation in which a citizen has become unruly at a meeting of the Assembly (or something of the sort) and the *archon* is acting in an official capacity as a disciplinary officer. If the *archon*, having told the citizen to be quiet, but without success, reinforces his instruction with a blow from his official stick or baton, the citizen is not entitled to hit back. But if the citizen, annoyed at being told to keep quiet, hits the *archon*, then the *archon* is not only entitled to hit back but can also summon the citizen before a court and ask that he be punished.

This is an unsatisfactory way of dealing with the Pythagorean view of justice as requital. The Pythagoreans were probably thinking of the moral basis of the vendetta, the precursor of criminal law. Aristotle supposes that their view was intended to apply to the corrective justice of private or civil law; and then, having observed that there are circumstances in which the civil law does not allow for requital, adds that there are also circumstances in which criminal law applies as well. Even the first part of his example, where the *archon* strikes the citizen, brings in public law, because the immunity of the *archon* from being struck in return arises from the fact that he acts as a public official and not as a private citizen.

It is strange that Aristotle should give no account at all of the justice of punishment. One would expect it to follow from his reference to the popular connection between requital and the justice of Rhadamanthus. The omission is all the more surprising since Plato more than once (for example, *Republic*, Book X) suggests a reformative theory of punishment, and we might have expected Aristotle to react to that, one way or the other. We should, of course, remember that categories which seem obvious to us will not have been obvious to Aristotle. He was a pioneer in systematizing the concept of justice in the light of legal and common usage, and the division of Athenian law into public and private branches did not correspond closely to the division of modern systems of law into criminal and civil branches. Still, it does seem that in arranging his thought about the relevant facts he was unduly influenced by preconceived theory in terms of equality and of a mean.

There is, however, one bonus that follows upon Aristotle's unsatisfactory criticism of the Pythagorean theory of reciprocity or requital. It leads him to say something about the justice of exchange. His earlier account of corrective justice had included compensation for breach of contract, where a notion of equality comes in. He now considers a different kind of equality as forming the justice or fairness of *making* a contract. In consequence, Aristotle produces a piece of economic theory which is strikingly perceptive in a pioneering analyst. Plato had spoken, in *Republic*, Book II, of the importance of a division of labour for improving the standard of life, but this little excursion into elementary economics had said nothing that was not obvious. Adeimantus, when asked about the role of justice in the situation, had suggested that it might be involved in exchanges, but Plato had not followed this up. Aristotle by contrast thinks hard about the justice or fairness of exchange, realizes that it depends on a concept of equal *value*, and then produces a theory that the real measure of economic value is *demand*. That marks a real advance in economic analysis.

Aristotle appreciates that, if you say that the required equality of value in goods exchanged depends simply on the judgements of the parties involved, you will not get far. A party may change his mind about the value, taking one view before he agrees to the exchange and another afterwards. The private interests and desires of the two parties may differ, so that you cannot easily find a common measure of value there. In practice, he continues, one has a concept of money prices. If a house costs five minae (about the annual earnings of a professional man) and a bed one mina, then the value of a house is equal to the value of five beds. (The example may seem to give a house a surprisingly low value relative to a bed, but one must remember that a house in ancient Greece was a simple affair, with not much comfort and built quite quickly.) Now money, Aristotle says, simply symbolizes demand. If people did not want beds and houses, there would be no value in having them available on offer. Money 'serves as a surety of exchange in the future' (ch. 5, 1133^{b}10–12). You have a house to dispose of, but you do not want any beds or other goods at present. You exchange your house for money, which you can exchange for other goods in the future when you do want them. Aristotle goes on to say that money is liable to fluctuation of demand, like other goods, and so its purchasing power varies, but as compared with other goods its value tends to be pretty constant. It therefore serves as a measure. But the ultimate measure is demand. So equality of value, which constitutes the fairness or justice of a commercial transaction, depends on the relatively objective factor of public demand, not on the subjective factor of one individual's wishes at a particular moment.

Aristotle then distinguishes briefly between political justice, justice in the *polis*, and domestic justice, justice within the family. He makes the point that the concept of justice presupposes some sense of equality of status between the parties. He adds that this equality may be 'proportionate' or 'arithmetical', so as to allow for the discriminatory system of status that obtains in aristocratic and oligarchic regimes; otherwise he would have to admit that political justice can exist only in a democracy. He does admit that there can be no justice in a tyranny because the tyrant thinks only of his own interests and does not regard his subjects as having equal status in any sense. In both the *Ethics* (VIII.10) and the *Politics* (III.8), Aristotle compares the relationship of a tyrant to his subjects with the relationship of a master of a household to his slaves. There is no notion of equality between a master and his slaves, and therefore, Aristotle says in *Ethics*, V.6, there can be no question of injustice in the treatment by a master of his 'chattel', meaning his slave. A man's chattel, or his young child, is like a part of himself; and since you cannot be unjust to yourself or part of yourself, you cannot be unjust to your slave or to your young child. Aristotle allows that there can be relations of justice and injustice in the treatment by a husband of his wife, but this does not imply that they are 'arithmetically' equal. Aristotle would say that there is a 'proportionate equality' between husband and wife, as there is between rulers and subjects in an aristocratic *polis* (*Ethics*, VIII.10, 1160^{b}32–3); the husband has a higher status or 'worth', but the wife does have some.

It is worth nothing that, at one point in the *Ethics* (VIII.11, 1161^{b}5–10), Aristotle says that a man might have relationships of friendship and justice with his slave '*qua* man', though not '*qua* slave': 'for there seems to be some room for justice in the relations of every human being with every other that is capable of participating in law and contract, and therefore friendship too is possible with anyone so far as he is a human being. Hence . . . there is most room for friendship and justice in democracies, where the citizens, being equal, have many things in common.' This is virtually an admission of the falsity of Aristotle's view in the *Politics* that some men are slaves 'by nature', and it is also close to an admission that the equality of democracy is based on a notion of the common humanity of all human beings.

Aristotle next distinguishes, in Book V, chapter 7, between natural and conventional justice. He acknowledges that a great deal of law, and so of justice, is conventional and differs from one society to another, unlike the workings of physical events, which are the same everywhere ('fire burns both in Greece and in Persia, while rules of justice vary', 1134^{b}26–7). Nevertheless he insists that there are some rules of natural justice, but he does not give us any definite examples. We can perhaps form an idea of what he thinks when we look at his two examples of *analogous* natural tendency.

First, he says that the right hand is naturally stronger than the left but it is possible for any man to make himself ambidextrous. Secondly, he says that measures of corn and wine differ in different societies but they are always larger in wholesale than in retain markets. (I suppose he means that in wholesale markets people buy and sell in larger quantities than in retail; for example, they buy and sell milk by the pint in retail markets, by the gallon in wholesale.) These two examples are of general tendencies found among all men or in all societies, despite variations from individual to individual or from society to society. It is worth noting that he does not say of his first example that right-handedness is 'natural' because a *majority* of people have a stronger right hand. His point is that the natural bent is not a necessity; it can be varied by human practice; anybody can make himself ambidextrous. But the natural *tendency* is for the right hand to be stronger. Likewise, with the economic example, it is not necessary for wholesale markets to use larger measures, but it is a general tendency. I think we can infer that the sort of examples which Aristotle would have given of natural justice are laws which *tend* to be found in societies generally: for example, treating murder and assault as serious wrongs, with murder being more serious and calling for a more severe penalty. Even though murder carries different penalties, both of kind and of severity, in different societies, it is a feature of natural (that is, universally practised) justice that murder should be reprobated and punished—and more severely than assault.

A further important topic in Aristotle's discussion of justice is his account of the distinction between justice and equity, reflecting the procedure of the courts. The distinction is one that is made in modern legal systems too, and Aristotle's description of the relation between the two concepts has influenced the thought of later theorists. Aristotle notes that justice and equity are connected but not identical. Equity, he says, is a 'rectification of legal justice' (ch. 10, $1137^{b}12$–13). Equity comes in when the strict letter of the law produces an unfair result and so the court relaxes the strict letter in order to reach a fair judgement. In modern law, courts will say that they are appealing to natural justice or equity in order to mitigate the inflexibility of an established rule of code, or common law, or precedent. Aristotle says that 'law is always a universal statement, yet there are cases which it is not possible to cover correctly in a universal statement'. The material with which the law deals, human conduct, does not lend itself to rigidly inflexible rules. So when a case arises which is an exception to the general rule, the court should decide 'as the lawgiver would have decided' if he had known of this sort of case. Equity, Aristotle concludes, is a 'kind of justice', not an altogether different category.

It is worth noting that, whereas the Latin word *aequitas* and the derived English word *equity* originate from the concept of equality, the Greek word for 'equity' is different. The Greek work for 'fair', *ison*, as I have mentioned earlier, literally means 'equal'; but the word for 'equitable' in the technical legal sense is *epieikes*, which literally means 'fitting' or 'suitable'. It is a broader term than the Greek for 'justice' or 'right-doing'. But like the modern concept of fairness (and unlike equality, which could imply some rigidity), the Greek term for equity indicates a certain flexibility, which is indeed what the concept is used for. It is also something that Aristotle indicates, both in his general remarks and in his apt analogy with the 'leaden rule' of the Lesbian builders, who used the flexible material of lead to deal with moulding that had to follow the particular shape of a particular piece of stone.

Despite the defects of Aristotle's treatment of corrective justice and the curious absence of any account of criminal justice, Book V of the *Nicomachean Ethics* is a penetrating piece of analysis. Some later treatments, which had the advantage of learning from predecessors, contain sounder theory; but, considering how early this one comes in the history of philosophic thought on the subject, it outstrips the others as a human achievement.

Chapter 6

JURISTS AND THEOLOGIANS

A history of the concept of justice would include much of interest from Roman law and from patristic and scholastic philosophy. I know little of those fields of learning but I must mention a few salient points.

The corpus of Roman law that was consolidated by direction of the Emperor Justinian includes a dictum of the jurist Ulpian (third century AD) that had become the standard definition of justice: *Iustitia est constans et perpetua voluntas ius suum cuique tribuendi* ('Justice is the constant and permanent will to render to each person what is his right').[1] Earlier instances of the idea speak simply of *suum cuique tribuere* ('rendering to each person what is his'); Cicero uses the phrase on several occasions. Ulpian's definition summarizes the task of a judge in disputes of civil law, and I imagine that this is what was originally intended. One can, however, stretch the shorter formulation to cover the judicial task in criminal trials, too, if one understands *suum* ('what is his') to mean 'his due' and to include 'what he deserves' as well as 'what is owed to him'. The definition is, of course, a bare form. If it is a sound definition it will embrace all instances of justice, but it does not tell us how it is to be applied: it does not specify what makes a particular good (or a particular evil as a punishment) the *suum* of a particular individual in such and such circumstances. Still, it serves a useful purpose in encapsulating the judge's function within a concept that analyses the simple, vague term 'justice'.

The definition of justice in the Justinian Code is followed by another traditional dictum that links the notion of *suum cuique tribuere* with two further principles as a summary of the demands of *ius*, what is right or legally required: *Iuris praecepta sunt haec: honeste vivere, alterum non laedere, suum cuique tribuere* ('The precepts of what is right are these: to live uprightly, to do no harm to others, to render to each person what is his'). The term *ius* is wider than *iustitia*, but in later discussion among philosophers of law the threefold formulation was apt

---

[1] Justinian Code, *Digest*, i.1.10, and *Institutes*, i.1.

to be taken as a comprehensive definition of justice. This is partly because the term 'justice' can be applied to the system of law as a whole and partly because of the influence of patristic and scholastic philosophy.

Giorgio Del Vecchio, in his study of the concept of justice,[2] tells us that several of the Church Fathers (Lactantius, St Ambrose, St John Chrysostom, St Augustine) held that justice was a comprehensive virtue that included all the rest. This was a continuation of the Platonic and Aristotelian concept of universal or general justice, associated with a recollection of the broad sense given to justice in some passages of the Bible. The influence of the Greek concept is even more marked in the scholastic philosophers, especially St Thomas Aquinas. These philosophers followed Aristotle not only in distinguishing general from particular justice but also in dividing particular justice into two species corresponding to Aristotle's distributive and corrective (or rectifying) justice. As we have seen in Chapter 5, Aristotle's account of corrective justice is a little confusing, and the scholastics made things worse by calling it commutative justice. They did so because Aristotle says that this species of justice is concerned with rectification 'in transactions of exchange' (as well as the rectification of torts). The scholastics took the Greek word for 'rectifying' (*diorthotikon*, putting right) to mean 'directing' (putting on the right path), and they also supposed that the phrase 'in transactions of exchange' applied to the whole of Aristotle's discussion under this head. So 'diorthotic' or corrective justice became 'commutative' justice. Aquinas reports the view of Aristotle in these terms: 'It is called by the Philosopher "commutative justice" in that it is directive of exchanges or mutual dealings'; and again, 'The Philosopher posits two species of justice and says that one is directive in distributions, the other in exchanges.'[3]

That is not the end of the story. Del Vecchio notes that Leibniz (seventeenth-eighteenth century) 'formulates a tripartite division of justice ... and to the three degrees of justice (*justitia commutativa, distributiva* and *universalis*) he makes correspond the three legal precepts derived from Roman sources (*neminem laedere, suum cuique tribuere, honeste vivere*) ['to harm no one, to render to each person what is his, to live uprightly'] but understood by him in a still wider sense'.[4] Leibniz, then, identified 'commutative' justice with the Roman law precept of doing no harm to others. To make sense of this strange conclusion we have to put aside the literal meaning of *justitia commutativa* ('the justice of

---

[2] Giorgio Del Vecchio, *Justice: An Historical and Philosophical Essay*, trans. Lady Guthrie, ed. A. H. Campbell (Edinburgh: Edinburgh University Press, 1952), chs. 4, 6.

[3] Aquinas, *Summa Theologiae*, 1a.21.1: 'haec dicitur a Philosopho, "justitia commutativa", vel directiva commutationum sive communicationum'; 2a2ae.61.1: 'Philosophus ponit duas partes justitiae, et dicit quod una est directiva in distributionibus, alia in commutationibus.'

[4] *Justice*, 25–6. Cf. Ch. 8 below.

exchanges') and recall that Aristotle's corrective justice, which had come to be known as commutative, deals with the rectifying of all wrongs to individuals, not solely in transactions of exchange. That view was continued in the jurisprudence of Grotius and Pufendorf. Grotius indeed dropped the name 'commutative' precisely because the major part of rectifying justice has nothing to do with the rights acquired from contractual exchange. He described this species of justice as *expletrix* because it 'fills up' the place left absent by depriving a person of an existing right. Pufendorf went back to the older name of commutative justice to cover all 'perfect rights', whether issuing from contract or directly from the law of nature.

Del Vecchio himself is happy to accept the identification of particular justice with the two legal precepts *suum cuique tribuere* and *alterum non laedere* ('to render to each person what is his' and 'to do no harm to others'). He writes of an 'inter-subjective correlation which constitutes the essence of justice' and says that the two legal precepts 'express more or less completely either the positive or the negative side of this correlation'.[5] He thinks that the essence of justice consists positively in the protection of each person's rights and negatively in the prohibition of harm, which he takes to mean a breach of rights. In an earlier part of his book Del Vecchio says that the legal maxim *suum cuique tribuere* was understood as an inheritance of the Aristotelian doctrine of distributive justice:

Particularly did the concept of distributive justice, which, as the highest type of justice, in a way epitomizes all its characteristics, remain unchanged in the formula of proportional equality according to merit; this was the meaning given to the maxim that to everyone must be assigned what belongs to him, the maxim which was laid down as the basis of Jurisprudence. It is hardly necessary to recall the famous definition of Ulpian: 'Justitia est constans et perpetua voluntas jus suum cuique tribuendi.'[6]

Del Vecchio regards this as an example of a 'remarkable . . . convergence . . . between Greek speculation and Roman experience in the subject of law'.[7] But A. H. Campbell, the editor of the English translation of Del Vecchio's book, felt obliged to add a note of reservation to this last statement. He observes that another scholar, Fritz Schulz, in a more recent book on *History of Roman Legal Science*, had urged that 'Greek philosophy had little or no influence on the practical work of the professional Roman jurists . . . "Roman legal science . . . stuck to its last and left philosophy to the philosophers" '.[8]

It is indeed not easy to see why the Roman jurists should have identified the precept of 'rendering to each person what is his' with Aristotle's concept of distributing benefits and responsibilities according to worth. The former principle goes back beyond Aristotle. We saw in Chapter 4 that it is mentioned twice in

[5] *Justice*, 112.   [6] Ibid. 55.   [7] Ibid. 56.   [8] Ibid. 73–4.

Plato's *Republic* as a familiar conception of justice. In Book I Polemarchus quotes a traditional maxim from the poet Simonides when defining justice as 'rendering to everyone his due'; and in Book IV Plato's own mouthpiece, 'Socrates', says that the aim of judges is to see that the parties to a lawsuit should not have what belongs to others or be deprived of what is 'their own', because that is justice. Later philosophical tradition associated *suum cuique tribuere* with Aristotle's concept of distributive justice, but there seems little reason to suppose that the Aristotelian doctrine had anything to do with the crystallization of juridical practice in the maxim of Ulpian.

A less conspicuous consequence of the interweaving of ancient traditions is the gradual emergence of the concept of 'social justice', which came to full fruition in the nineteenth century. It began with thoughts about the relation of justice to charity. As we have seen, patristic philosophers retained the Greek concept of universal or general justice embracing all the virtues. Some of them made special mention of the virtue of charity because it has a central role in the Bible and is at times associated with justice, as when Isaiah (1: 17) says: 'Learn to do good; seek justice, relieve the oppressed, judge [i.e. procure justice for] the fatherless, plead for the widow.'[9] A more explicit connection is made in a sentence of St Augustine about the four cardinal virtues, in which he speaks of 'what justice does in helping the wretched' (*quod agit iustitia in subveniendo miseris*).[10] Elsewhere Augustine follows the traditional Roman law definition of justice as *cuique suum tribuere*. But his statement that justice is concerned with helping the poor was reported by a theologian of the twelfth century, Peter Lombard, as if it were a definition of justice: *Augustinus ait: 'Iustitia est in subveniendo miseris'* ('Augustine says "Justice consists in helping the wretched"').[11] Peter Lombard's collection of *Sententiae* became a textbook for Christian thinkers of the thirteenth century. One of the questions that exercised them was how to reconcile two quotations from Augustine in Peter Lombard: the first was the characterization of justice as helping the poor; the second was a statement that 'almsgiving is a work of mercy' (*Est enim eleemosyna opus misericordiae*).[12] The standard doctrine that emerged, and was endorsed by St Thomas Aquinas, was that almsgiving by the rich from their superfluity to relieve those in extreme need was an act of justice or strict duty, while almsgiving that was made from the

---

[9] Cf. Ch. 2 above.   [10] St Augustine, *De Trinitate*, XIV.ix.12.

[11] Petrus Lombardus, *Sententiae*, III.33.1.2 (3rd edn. (Grottaferata: College of St Bonaventura, 1981), ii. 188).

[12] St Augustine, *Enchiridion*, xx.76, correctly quoted this time by Peter Lombard, *Sententiae*, IV.15.5.1 (op. cit., ii. 330). The history of attempts to reconcile the two texts as given by Peter Lombard is described by Odon Lottin, 'Notes sur la vertu de justice et deux devoirs connexés', included in his collected papers, *Psychologie et morale aux XIIe et XIIIe siècles* (Louvain: Abbaye de Mont-César, 1949), iii. 283 ff.

donor's own necessities went beyond strict duty and was a meritorious act of charity or mercy.

Jewish theologians taught rather more emphatically that charity was a requirement of justice owed virtually as a debt to the poor, who therefore had a moral right to it. The Hebrew word *tzedakah* (righteousness, allied to *tzedek*, justice) came to be and is still used as the normal term for charity. The Jewish doctrine is reflected in a work of the philosopher Philo (first century AD),[13] who says that charity is a debt due to all men, and this might perhaps have been known to Augustine. So far as I am aware, the Jewish doctrine was not accompanied by any distinction between the use of superfluities and necessities.

The theme of superfluity and necessity came up again, however, in another branch of medieval Christian thought, that of canon law. In this context the contrast was not between superfluities and necessities in the possessions of the rich but between the superfluities of the rich and the needs of the poor in times of necessity. The doctrine was evolved by thirteenth-century theorists of canon law, commenting on the twelfth-century *Decretum* of Gratian, which was a basic text for them in the same way as the *Sententiae* of Peter Lombard was for the theologians. The discussion of the canon law jurists was conducted in terms of property rights rather than of justice, but since it turned on the notion of what is and what is not 'one's own', it clearly affected the understanding of the traditional concept of justice as rendering to each person what is 'his own'. Gratian's *Decretum* attributed to St Ambrose the statement, 'No one may call his own what is common'. Joannes Teutonicus, commenting (about 1216) on this text, took the expression 'what is common' to mean what should be shared 'in time of necessity': a man could appropriate as his own what was required to meet his needs, and indeed he could keep superfluities too, so long as others were not in need; but in time of necessity the superfluities of the rich had to be regarded as common property, to be used for securing the needs of the poor.[14]

The doctrine of these medieval Christian thinkers, theologians and canon lawyers alike, depended upon the premiss that God has given the earth and its produce to mankind as a whole. They therefore limited the right of private property in order to cater for meeting the needs of the poor. A version of this tradition is continued in John Locke's *First Treatise of Government* (section 42) at the end of the seventeenth century. Locke's statement contains a distinction of some interest. He is ready to speak of the needy as being endowed with a right or title to have extreme want relieved by means of the superfluity of the rich, but he is not prepared to assign this right to the category of justice. It is, he

---

[13] Philo, *De Caritate*, 17–18.
[14] For the information in this paragraph I am indebted to Brian Tierney, *Medieval Poor Law* (Cambridge: Cambridge University Press, 1959), 34–5.

says, a right of charity; justice is concerned simply with the right or title of those who have earned their wealth by 'honest industry' or have acquired it by inheritance.

But we know God hath not left one man so to the mercy of another, that he may starve him if he please: God the Lord and Father of all, has given no one of his children such a property, in his peculiar portion of the things of this world, but that he has given his needy brother a right to the surplusage of his goods; so that it cannot justly be denied him, when his pressing wants call for it. . . . As *Justice* gives every man a title to the product of his honest industry, and the fair acquisitions of his ancestors descended to him, so *Charity* gives every man a title to so much out of another's plenty, as will keep him from extreme want, where he has no means to subsist otherwise.

This sounds half-hearted, giving with one hand and taking away with the other. If the relief of need is a function of charity and not of justice, what is the point of calling it a right? In defence of Locke we can say that he was following the tradition of the canon law jurists, who described the relief of need in terms of a right, but not in terms of justice as the theologians did. Scholars who are expert on those thirteenth-century discussions are careful to explain that even the theologians, in speaking of justice, did not mean either that the duty of almsgiving was juridically enforceable or that it required organized social action as the modern concept of 'social justice' would imply; they simply meant that the moral duty of individuals to help the poor could, in some circumstances, become a strict duty, what was later to be called a duty of perfect obligation.[15] By the time the doctrine had reached the natural jurisprudence of Pufendorf in the 1670s, the idea of a perfect obligation to help the poor had gone by the board; the duty of charity was one of imperfect obligation, and the potential recipient was said to have an 'imperfect right' to it. But in these circumstances what is the point of talking about rights at all? The duty is discretionary, the time and place of its fulfilment depend entirely on the choice of the donor, and the potential beneficiary has no say in the matter. Adam Smith, in his lectures on jurisprudence, justifiably said that so-called imperfect rights are not rights at all: 'when we use the word right in this way it is not a proper but a metaphorical sense.'[16]

When Locke assigned the 'right' of the needy to charity as contrasted with justice, presumably he too implied that this right was not juridically enforceable, as were the rights of justice to the fruits of one's labour and to inherited property. Still, we must suppose that he included the right or title of the needy among his natural rights. He summarizes these in his *Second Treatise* as rights

---

[15] e.g. Tierney, 37, referring to articles by O. Lottin (see n. 12, above) and E. Lio.
[16] Adam Smith, *Lectures on Jurisprudence*, ed. R. L. Meek, D. D. Raphael, and P. G. Stein (Oxford: Clarendon Press, 1978), LJ(A) (delivered in 1762–3), i. 14–15, at p. 9.

to life, liberty, and estate. The right to life is mainly a right not to be killed, but I imagine that Locke would say it covered also the right not to be starved by the inaction of a rich neighbour whose superfluities could relieve the extreme want of the poor.

Part II

Modern Shoots

Chapter 7

THOMAS HOBBES

Modern political philosophy begins with Hobbes, as modern epistemological philosophy begins with his contemporary, Descartes. Both men were truly revolutionary thinkers (while inevitably owing something to past tradition) and both are ranked among the greatest of philosophers for the depth of their insight, the subtlety of their argument, and the novelty of their perspective. The political philosophy of Hobbes is set out in three different works, *The Elements of Law* (written about 1640), *De Cive* (Latin version, 1642; English version, 1651), and *Leviathan* (English version, 1651; Latin version, 1670). The general tenor of his theory remains unchanged in all three books but there are important differences of detail. *Leviathan*, in its original English form, is the best known of these works and is undoubtedly the most enjoyable to read. Although one or two Hobbes scholars have claimed that *De Cive* is the real key to understanding his political thought, many of the changes in *Leviathan* reflect a more considered and more defensible view, intended by Hobbes to replace the earlier versions. His account of justice is not a prominent element of his political theory, but its actual role and its subsequent influence are considerable, reflecting the acute, innovative intelligence that helped to make him a great philosopher.

Hobbes has a distinctive view of justice. His most explicit statement of it comes at the beginning of chapter 15 of *Leviathan*, where justice is identified with the third law of nature, '*That men performe their Covenants made*'. In making the identification Hobbes does not immediately speak of definition: he says, in the English version, that 'the Fountain and Originall' of justice consists in the third law of nature, while the Latin version abbreviates 'Fountain and Originall' to 'natura'. A couple of sentences later, however, it is plain that for Hobbes these terms are tantamount to, or include, the notion of definition; he says that 'the definition of INJUSTICE, is no other than *the not Performance of Covenant*. And whatsoever is not Unjust, is *Just*.'[1]

---

[1] Thomas Hobbes, *Leviathan*, ed. C. B. Macpherson (Harmondsworth: Penguin Books, 1968; hereafter cited as *L*.), 202.

If we were to follow everyday usage of the word 'definition' and suppose that the definition of a common word gives its normal meaning, we should find Hobbes's statement puzzling. To say that 'justice' means the performance of covenants (that is, promises and contracts) seems not only excessively narrow but positively untrue. The categories of action to which we apply the terms 'just' and 'unjust' do not even include the keeping or breaking of promises and contracts. We would say that the breaking of a promise or contract is 'wrong' but we would not naturally use the word 'unjust'. We would say that there is an 'obligation' to keep a promise but we would not naturally say that it is a requirement of 'justice'.

J. S. Mill evidently thought otherwise. In chapter 5 of *Utilitarianism* he analyses six classes of action to which the term 'justice' is commonly applied, and one of those six is the keeping of promises (or of faith). I do not think that Mill reached this view from attention to actual usage; it is not borne out by the classifications of the *Oxford English Dictionary*, which are genuinely based on a survey of usage. Mill probably reached his view because he was arguing towards the conclusion that the idea of the just always connotes the idea of a right, and it is easy to suppose (I have done it myself in the past) that the two ideas are coextensive in their application. It is indeed the connection between justice and rights that led Hobbes to his distinctive view of justice, and it is possible that Hobbes's account, which certainly influenced Hume, may have had some influence in leading Mill to assume that the concept of justice includes the keeping of faith within its ambit even though the two cannot simply be identified, as Hobbes had argued.

Hume is more circumspect. His complex analysis in the *Treatise of Human Nature* does not treat the keeping of promises as a species of just action, but it does, more reasonably, regard the two as being closely allied so that the analysis of promises can shed light on the nature of justice. There is, I think, no doubt that, consciously or unconsciously, Hume was stimulated to this line of inquiry, and to his characterization of both justice and promise keeping as 'artificial virtues', by Hobbes's argument that 'Humane Justice'[2] is not 'natural justice' but depends upon convention in the form of covenant.[3]

---

[2] The term is used, to distinguish human from natural justice, in Thomas Hobbes, *A Dialogue between a Philosopher and a Student of the Common Laws of England*, ed. Joseph Cropsey (Chicago: University of Chicago Press, 1971; hereafter cited as *D*.), 73.

[3] John Laird, *Hobbes* (London: Benn, 1934), 286–7, noted that Hume's theory of artificial virtue, and especially of justice, was 'intentionally Hobbian'. In an article, 'Obligations and Rights in Hobbes', published in *Philosophy*, 37 (1962), I suggested (p. 351) that the distinction which I found in Hobbes between natural and artificial obligation was 'the source from which there arose, consciously or unconsciously, in Hume's mind the idea of a distinction between natural and artificial virtue. Both philosophers treat the obligations of justice, and especially of promise-keeping, as artificial, and artificial in the special sense of depending upon a *verbal formula*.' I repeated this briefly in my book *Hobbes: Morals and Politics* (London: Allen & Unwin, 1977), 100.

After giving his definition of justice in chapter 15 of *Leviathan*, Hobbes goes on to argue that, although covenants can be made in the condition of nature (that is, before a political order has been set up), they are invalid until and unless backed up by the coercive power of a state; consequently there cannot 'actually' be injustice or justice in the absence of a state. He then adds that this conclusion can be drawn also from 'the ordinary definition of Justice in the Schooles', namely that '*Justice is the constant Will of giving to every man his own*'.[4] Hobbes takes the term 'own' to mean property and recalls that in the condition of nature every man has a right to all things, so that there is no property, no exclusive right that assigns a thing to one man and excludes other men from it. Hobbes accordingly regards it as immaterial for practical purposes whether justice be defined in terms of covenant, as he defines it, or in terms of property, as he understands the traditional formula to define it.

Hobbes's explicit definition of justice as the performance of covenants appears only in *Leviathan*. The corresponding passages in *The Elements of Law* (1.16.2) and *De Cive* (3.3) touch lightly upon one half of it, the identification of unjust action with the breach of covenant or contract. Even then the mention of injustice is secondary to the definition of 'injury', which Hobbes regards as synonymous with unjust action. The point that Hobbes chiefly wants to make is that injury is action *sine jure*, without right, and can therefore be connected with a previous renouncement of natural right, leaving the renouncer 'without right'. As for an explicit definition of the positive term 'justice', *De Cive* simply accepts, in the Epistle Dedicatory, the traditional view that '*Justice . . . signifies a steady Will of giving every one his Owne*'.[5] So does the later *Dialogue between a Philosopher and a Student of the Common Laws of England*.[6]

The point of Hobbes's definition of justice in terms of covenant is twofold. In the first place, it brings out Hobbes's view that 'human justice' exists by convention and not by nature. The new definition, however, is not essential for this purpose. The point is made quite clearly without it in the Epistle Dedicatory to *De Cive*, where Hobbes conducts his argument from the traditional definition. He says that when he thought about natural justice, he was led by the 'very word *Justice* (wich signifies a steady Will of giving every one his *Owne*)' to consider the idea of 'one's own' (property) and 'found that this proceeded not from Nature, but Consent'.[7]

---

[4] L. 202.

[5] *De Cive*, ed. Howard Warrender (Oxford: Clarendon Press, 1983), English version (hereafter cited as *DCE*), p. 27; cf. Latin version, p. 75, where, however, 'his own' is rendered 'Ius suum', and not 'suum' simply, as in the usual formulation.

[6] D. 58. In *A Dialogue* Hobbes says, incorrectly, that the traditional definition, 'giving to every Man his own', is Aristotle's. In fact it comes from Ulpian's *Digest*; cf. beginning of Ch. 6 above.

[7] *DCE* 27.

The second purpose of Hobbes's definition is to support the absolute authority of the sovereign. Hobbes wishes to argue that the sovereign has a right to do whatever he thinks fit, so that his commands are never a breach of justice. Since justice depends on covenant and since the obligation of subjects to sovereign arises from the social contract (in a 'commonwealth by institution', that is, a state set up by agreement) or from an implicit covenant (in a 'commonwealth by acquisition', that is, a state acquired by conquest), the subjects can be guilty of injury or injustice, but the sovereign cannot because he has not made any promise under the social contract or in response to an implicit covenant undertaken by his subjects.

The scope of Hobbes's conception of justice is therefore much wider than it looks at first sight. John Laird[8] wrote that Hobbes had both a narrower and a wider sense of justice and that he confused the two. The narrower sense was that given in *Leviathan*, chapter 15, the performance of covenant; the wider sense, according to Laird, was 'whatever was done "with right" ', and this Laird professed to find in the corresponding passage of *De Cive*, 3.5, where Hobbes distinguishes two uses of 'just' and 'unjust', one applied to persons, the other to actions. Of the latter Hobbes writes: 'When they are attributed to Actions, *Just* signifies as much as what's done with Right, and *unjust*, as what's done with injury.'[9] This is not in fact a wider definition or meaning than the one given in *Leviathan*, chapter 15. Hobbes explains in all three statements of his political theory that action 'with right' and action 'without right' (injury) involve covenant or contract, so that for him a definition of justice in terms of covenant and a definition in terms of a right come to the same thing. Laird might have done better to refer to a slightly later passage in the *Leviathan* chapter itself (para. 9), where Hobbes repeats the distinction between the justice of persons and the justice of actions that he drew in *The Elements of Law* and in *De Cive*. In the *Leviathan* formulation of this distinction, the terms 'just' and 'unjust' are said to mean 'Conformity, or Inconformity to Reason',[10] which might well be called a wider meaning than a definition either in terms of covenant or in terms of a right. It is probable, however, that Hobbes did not intend a wider scope; he says here that the justice (or righteousness) of a man is the conformity to reason of his 'Manners, or manner of life', while the justice of an action is the conformity to reason of that particular action. What he wants to stress is the distinction between a tendency and a particular instance; the use of the word 'reason' is of no special consequence in this passage.[11]

---

[8] Laird, *Hobbes*, 183.

[9] *DCE* 64. The Latin version, p. 110, defines just action as 'quod iure factum' and unjust action as 'quod *Iniuriâ*'. [10] *L*. 206.

[11] As F. C Hood, *The Divine Politics of Thomas Hobbes* (Oxford: Clarendon Press, 1964), 113, observes, Hobbes writes loosely here but his meaning is clear enough. He is thinking of the third

There is, then, no confusion of a wider and a narrower meaning, but rather a deliberate extension by Hobbes of what in other hands would be a narrow meaning. Hobbes links *effective* justice with the social contract or with the implicit covenant that takes the place of the social contract in a commonwealth acquired by conquest. In consequence, effective justice covers the whole field of positive law. This does indeed give justice a wide sense, but still tied to the idea of covenant. Although Hobbes's actual discussion of justice is brief, the concept itself has a vital role in his ethical and political doctrine, and it is an advantage for his theory to show that an apparently narrow definition turns out to give justice a wide range. The resulting wide scope of the term has the added advantage of conforming to common usage; we often apply the term 'justice' to the system of law as a whole, as when we speak of the courts of justice.[12]

Hobbes's definition of justice in terms of covenant has a further consequence of capital importance for his theory of obligation. He points out an interesting logical feature of promise breaking and then uses it to portray the obligation of promises, and of justice, as having a different character from the obligation of natural law. A. E. Taylor was led by some of Hobbes's remarks about obligation into suggesting that Hobbes's 'ethical doctrine proper . . . is a very strict deontology, curiously suggestive . . . of some of the characteristic theses of Kant'.[13] That judgement, in my opinion, mistakes a part for the whole, but it is true that Hobbes indicates a radical distinction between prudential obligation and a form of non-prudential obligation which shares something of the logical features of Kant's conception of moral obligation. Hobbes's notion, however, does not apply to the whole of moral duty but to that large part of it which can be assigned to justice. Nor does it have the kind of absolute metaphysical status that Kant gave to the claims of morality. On the contrary, non-prudential obligation for Hobbes is to be contrasted with the more fundamental obligation of natural law. It is the result of convention and so can be classed with the notions of the ancient sophists. But it has a distinctly original feature in fastening upon logic and language as being responsible for the formation of this peculiar kind of

---

law of nature and so speaks of the performance of covenant as conforming to reason, but does not imply that this is the only kind of action that conforms to reason (i.e. to a law of nature). My comments on Laird can be applied also to the more guarded criticism of Hobbes's usage made by Howard Warrender, *The Political Philosophy of Hobbes* (Oxford: Clarendon Press, 1957), 132.

[12] The lawyer in *A Dialogue* defines a just action as 'that which is not against the Law' (*D.* 72). The philosopher does not himself adopt this definition but uses it to argue that law must be logically prior to (human) justice.

[13] A. E. Taylor, 'The Ethical Doctrine of Hobbes', *Philosophy*, 13 (1938), 408 ff.; repr. in Keith C. Brown (ed.), *Hobbes Studies* (Oxford: Blackwell, 1965), 37 ff.

obligation. I believe we are justified in calling it artificial obligation.[14] It foreshadows Hume's notion of artificial virtue.

Hobbes makes the initial logical point about promises by comparing injury or injustice to 'absurdity', that is to say, self-contradiction.[15] In *The Elements of Law* he says flatly that 'there is in every breach of covenant a contradiction properly so called',[16] and in *De Cive* that it is 'no lesse contradiction' than denying what has previously been affirmed.[17] In both places Hobbes's ground for the assertion is that the making of a promise is willing an action in the future, while breaking the promise is willing the omission of that action in the present. The result, says Hobbes, is that the promise-breaker has willed the doing and the not doing of the same action at the same time. In *Leviathan* Hobbes is more cautious and restricts himself to saying that injury is 'somewhat like' absurdity; 'to contradict what one maintained in the Beginning' is compared but not fully equated with 'voluntarily to undo that, which from the beginning he had voluntarily done'.[18] Even if the facts were as Hobbes represents them, a willing or a doing of mutually exclusive actions is not the same as self-contradiction, the utterance of mutually exclusive statements. Perhaps Hobbes realized this when he came to write *Leviathan* and therefore confined himself to a comparison with self-contradiction. However, the facts are not as Hobbes represents them. While the precise characterization of promising is notoriously difficult, promising is certainly not the doing or the willing of the action promised; if it were, promise breaking would be impossible, for an action that has been done cannot be literally undone.

Nevertheless there is a logical peculiarity about promises and it seems likely that this is what caught Hobbes's attention. The making of a promise is the voluntary creation of an obligation by the use of words. To promise is to undertake an obligation. Consequently the statement that a person is obliged to do what he has promised is an analytic statement (one made necessarily true by the meaning of its words), so that the denial of that statement would be a self-contradiction. Since incurring the obligation is voluntary, breaching the obligation is a voluntary act that opposes or cancels (one might metaphorically say that it 'belies') the earlier voluntary act of promising.

---

[14] I used the term 'artificial obligation' in my article, 'Obligations and Rights in Hobbes' (published in 1962) to describe covenantal obligation, which Hobbes distinguished from '*naturall obligation*' in *De Cive*, 15.7. In ch. 10 of *The Divine Politics of Thomas Hobbes* (published in 1964), F. C. Hood, quite independently (for he knew nothing of my article at that time) and more elaborately, described a distinction in Hobbes between natural and artificial obligation, associated with a distinction between natural and artificial rights and justice.

[15] *The Elements of Law*, 1.16.2; *De Cive*, 3.3; *Leviathan*, ch. 14, para. 7.

[16] *The Elements of Law*, ed. F. Tönnies (London: Simpkin, Marshall, 1889: hereafter cited as EL), 82.

[17] DCE 63.   [18] L. 191.

The *Leviathan* (ch. 14) version of this logical feature of promise breaking is followed by a characterization of the bond or obligation that is produced by promises or similar acts.

And the same are the BONDS, by which men are bound, and obliged: Bonds, that have their strength, not from their own Nature, (for nothing is more easily broken than a mans word) but from Feare of some evill consequence upon the rupture.[19]

A similar remark is made in chapter 18 (para. 4): 'Covenants being but words, and breath, have no force to oblige, contain, constrain, or protect any man, but what it has from the publique Sword.'[20] In *The Elements of Law* (II.3.3) Hobbes had drawn a distinction between the 'natural bonds' of chains or imprisonment and the 'verbal bonds of covenant'.[21]

The verbal act of promising produces a verbal bond or obligation, one that does not have the force to 'oblige' in the sense of 'constrain' a man. It is not a real bond or chain in the actual world of things and actions. When Hobbes says in chapter 18 of *Leviathan* that covenants 'have no force to oblige', he is using the word 'oblige' as synonymous with 'contain' and 'constrain', while when he says in chapter 14 that 'men are bound, and obliged' by the bonds of covenant, he is using the term 'obliged' in a different sense to mean a verbal or metaphorical bond that is 'easily broken'. He tries to bring out the difference between the two kinds of obligation in a note to *De Cive*, 14.2, where, having distinguished between contracts, which 'oblige', and laws, which '*tie* us fast, being obliged', he proceeds to this explanation:

To be obliged, and *to be tyed being obliged*, seems to some men to be one, and the same thing, and that therefore here seems to be some distinction in words, but none indeed. More cleerly therefore, I say thus, That a man is obliged by his contracts, that is, that he ought to performe for his promise sake; but that the Law tyes him being obliged, that is to say, it compells him to make good his promise, for fear of the punishment appointed by the Law.[22]

Hobbes's comparison of the verbal bond or obligation of a promise with the verbal bond or necessity of logic is apt. Logical necessity, too, can be contrasted with the effectively forceful necessity of the real world. If a person contradicts himself, one might object: 'You cannot say that.' Logically or rationally he cannot (or, in 'more correct' speech, he *may* not). Physically, however, he *can* say it; he has just done so. Anyone *can* use language arbitrarily, but in the interests of communication, the main point of having a language, there are rules which we are told we 'cannot' violate. 'Cannot' means 'should not'; the rules lay obligations upon us. These obligations, however, do not have the power to constrain us physically; they do not remove our ability to break the rules.

---

[19] Ibid. 192.   [20] Ibid. 231.   [21] *EL* 128.   [22] *DCE* 169–70.

The full implications of the comparison between promise breaking and self-contradiction are not brought out, and were probably not realized, by Hobbes himself. But there are certain straws in the wind which are worthy of notice. In chapter 17 of *Leviathan* (para. 12) Hobbes calls covenant an 'Artificiall' agreement in contrast to the 'Naturall' agreement or sociability of bees and ants.[23] Then, in chapter 21, he writes of liberty, and in the course of doing so he discusses the relation between liberty and necessity. This involves an understanding of different kinds of necessity. There is natural or physical necessity and there is the different necessity or bond of laws. Hobbes describes civil (that is, positive) law as 'Artificiall Chains' that men have made by mutual covenants (para. 5). He then repeats what he has said earlier about the intrinsic weakness of such covenantal bonds: 'These Bonds in their own nature but weak, may neverthelesse be made to hold, by the danger, though not by the difficulty of breaking them.'[24] The marginal heading to the paragraph summarizes its content as 'Artificiall bonds, or Covenants'. The artificial bonds or chains of covenant and civil law are plainly to be contrasted with the natural bonds of real chains or imprisonment. They are also to be contrasted with the constraining or persuasive power of natural laws.

In the first sentence of the Introduction to *Leviathan*, Hobbes contrasts Nature with Art. Nature is the art of God. Human art or artifice is an imitation of nature. The state is an artificial man. The natural man is made by God; the artificial man is made by human beings in imitation of the natural man. So, too, the laws of the state are artificial chains or bonds, made by men, in imitation of the natural chains of the laws of nature. Although Hobbes does not say so explicitly, I think that the verbal or logical bond or obligation which he attributes to covenant is a form of artificial bond or obligation, to be contrasted with the natural obligation of natural law.

The obligations of natural law have a genuine force. If we go against the precepts of natural law, we find ourselves in trouble; we get into the competitive condition of war, in which we are liable to lose our lives. Laws of nature are for Hobbes rules of a prudential morality. The artificial laws of the state acquire their constraining power from the sanctions of 'the publique Sword', that is, from enforcement by a system of authorized officers and punishments. Without the sanctions, either of natural consequences or of civil penalties, the obligations of law and covenant would be ineffective. Yet, from a *logical* point of view, there are (verbal) bonds or obligations created by covenants. They are not effective on their own but need to be backed up by the force of the penal system. They make up a logical system of duties and so they constitute a system of morality, the code of justice. They differ from the system of morality made up

---

[23] L. 226.   [24] Ibid. 263–4.

by the laws of nature. The obligation of the laws of nature is fundamentally an obligation of prudential morality: this is what you ought to do in order to preserve your life. The covenantal obligation of the system of justice is an obligation of logic, comparable with logical necessity, depending on rules about the use of words. If you say that S is P, you may not combine this with the statement that S is not P; if you express a will to do X, you may not combine this with a will to refrain from doing X.

Although the artificial system of morality, built on covenant, is intended to be an imitation of the natural system, there is a significant difference which Hobbes appears to have overlooked. The obligations of natural law, as Hobbes understands them, are not obligations towards other men, with correspondent rights, in the sense of claims, held by the other men against those who are obliged. The obligations of natural law are obligations to act for the sake of one's own interests. Even if they are treated as commands of God, the fundamental reason for obedience is still self-interested, an acknowledgement of the power of God to preserve our lives or to end them. Natural right for Hobbes is divorced from natural obligation. It is a right, not in the sense of a claim on others, but a liberty-right, an entitlement to act as you please, a *freedom from any obligation* to do (or to refrain from doing) one particular sort of action. The artificial obligation created by covenant, however, is not merely an obligation to do a specified action, and so a curtailment of the natural right to do whatever one thinks fit. It is an obligation *to* the person with whom one has covenanted, and in consequence that person has a claim-right against the covenantor that the action be done.

Hobbes tries to confine his use of the noun 'a right' to liberty-rights and to describe the possession of claim-rights by the different expression 'has it as due'. He does not altogether succeed in this endeavour, but that is by the way. However, a necessary feature of his conception of justice as depending on covenant is that the artificial obligations and rights which are created by covenant are obligations to other persons and claim-rights possessed by those other persons. Hobbes's failure to perceive this is responsible for his error in saying that injury is acting *sine jure*, 'without right', that is to say, without a liberty-right, without being entitled to act thus. The original meaning of the Latin word *injuria* seems to have been acting contrary to what *is* right or just; but if we think of the developed conception of injury in relation to the concept of 'right' used as a noun, we must say that injury is acting so as to invade or breach another person's claim-right.

Despite this lack of congruence between artefact and the natural system that it is supposed to imitate, Hobbes's account of justice and covenant is clearly of much theoretical interest. His own concern, however, in entering upon political philosophy is not simply theoretical but practical. If the logical obligation of covenant or justice has no force to make people act, what is the point of it? The answer to that question is to be found in understanding the point of Hobbes's social contract. It used commonly to be said that Hobbes's political theory expressed the doctrine that might is right, putting all the emphasis on the role of force. In particular it was said that the social contract was superfluous in his theory. He describes two ways in which a state can come into existence, by 'institution' (agreement and contract) and by 'acquisition' (conquest). Since, being a realist, he acknowledges that states usually arise by the latter method, there is no point (it was said) in his hypothesis of a social contract, which has no real application. In a state that comes into existence by conquest, force is all that matters.

This is a serious misunderstanding of Hobbes's position. Hobbes certainly does stress the necessity and the importance of force and of the fear of force in politics. His grim picture of the condition of nature concentrates on the fearful prospect that we face in the absence of a settled organized state. Again, he emphasizes more than once, as I have noted earlier, the fact that law and contract are ineffective unless they are backed by the force of a strong political authority. Nevertheless, this is not the core of Hobbes's doctrine. Hobbes's greatness as a political philosopher lies in his perception that, although physical power is necessary, it is not enough.

When Hobbes describes the setting-up of a state by conquest, he asks us to imagine the victor standing over one of the vanquished with a drawn sword, in a position to take away his life. If the victor spares the life of the vanquished, we must suppose, Hobbes says, that the vanquished has implicitly promised obedience in return for having his life spared; and having made this promise, the vanquished individual becomes a subject, bound by the same obligations of covenant as apply to the citizens of an instituted commonwealth, who covenant together by a social contract to vest authority in a sovereign and to obey him. The purpose of the unreal hypothesis of a social contract is to bring out clearly the nature of the moral obligation of covenant that the subjects of a state have incurred. Without the supposition of an implicit covenant made by the vanquished to the victor, Hobbes maintains, the members of a vanquished group would not be subjects but captives. They could be held in fear by chains and weapons but they would not be under any moral obligation to obey.

You may ask, what does it matter? Since Hobbes agrees that force is essential and that the subjects of a state must be faced with the prudential obligation of being moved by fear of force, why should he set so much store by an additional obligation of non-prudential morality depending on a promise? The reason is that the sovereign cannot be exerting his physical power on all his subjects all the time. Hobbes compares a captive to a slave and a subject to a servant. Captives or slaves will take the opportunity to escape if the immediate threat of swords or guns is removed or if they are not kept in chains or prisons. Subjects or servants, on the other hand, can generally be trusted to obey the rules, though there had better be sanctions in the background to remind everyone that there will be trouble for any person who breaks the rules. A sovereign must have the willing obedience of at least a good many of his subjects if his exercise of power is to be effective. It is not possible, even in a totalitarian state, to rely simply on force and fear.

This is why Hobbes stresses the importance of covenant and of the morality of justice, depending on covenant, as a necessary addition to the exercise of force and the threat of force. The purely moral obligation of a covenant, a verbal bond of logical consistency, will not be effective unless the force of the state is there to back up the requirements of the law when the law is broken. But the whole system depends on the fact that for most people, most of the time, the exercise of force is not necessary. It depends on their willing obedience. According to Hobbes, it depends on their acceptance of the moral obligation of an implicit promise to obey the law.

The weakness of Hobbes's theory is that his moral, non-prudential obligation is made to depend on a mythical promise. Some citizens—naturalized immigrants, volunteer members of the armed forces—do promise obedience to the law and loyalty to the state. But most people do not undertake voluntarily the obligations of a citizen. They are born in a particular jurisdiction and automatically acquire both the obligations and the benefits of citizenship. Hobbes would have done better to think of a different basis for a moral obligation to obey the law. The most obvious candidate is the notion of utility for the general interest. It is obvious when we think of Hobbes's picture of the condition of nature. Hobbes did not turn to the idea of the general interest because he started off with an egoistic psychology. (He does not retain a completely egoistic psychology in *Leviathan*, but enough of his original view remains to make it virtually impossible for him to think of people being motivated by regard to the general interest rather than their own interest alone.)

There is also the fact that Hobbes did perceive a peculiarity in the logic of promises, and so he thought that the idea of covenant and contract could serve his purpose. One can see from *The Elements of Law*, II.3.3, that this purpose was in Hobbes's mind right from the start when his attention was drawn to the logical character of covenantal obligation. In that passage he describes covenantal obligation as a 'verbal bond', to be contrasted with the 'natural bonds' of chains and imprisonment. He uses the distinction to explain the difference between a servant, who is trusted, and a slave, who is not. All this is intended to illustrate the main subject of the chapter, 'dominion, or a body politic by acquisition' (II.3.1).[25]

---

[25] *EL* 127.

So much for Hobbes's distinctive definition of justice. It is worth noting, by way of supplement, what Hobbes has to say about traditional ideas of justice. I have already discussed the relation of Hobbes's definition in *Leviathan* to the traditional definition that he accepts in *De Cive* and in *A Dialogue*. Hobbes does have something to say about other traditional doctrines concerning justice.

In the first place he criticizes the traditional classification, derived from Aristotle, of commutative and distributive justice. Commutative justice is said to require equality of value in the exchange involved in a contract. Distributive justice is said to be the award of benefit in accordance with merit.

Hobbes rejects the stock idea of commutative justice, pointing out that it is not unjust to sell at a higher price than one buys. Value depends on the desire of those who agree to a contract, so that any kind of agreement can be just or fair so long as it is made voluntarily. Hobbes obviously has a point here. The merit of Aristotle's discussion of 'commutative' justice lies in his giving an *explanation* of what constitutes economic value, and not, as Aristotle himself originally intended, in giving a *justification* of one kind of exchange rather than another. The fairness of a contract does indeed depend on the wishes of the parties, provided that they each have a reasonable knowledge of what is involved and provided that they really are free agents. In the *Leviathan* statement of his position (ch. 15, para. 14), Hobbes goes on to say that commutative justice, properly speaking, is simply the justice of a contractor, that is, the keeping of covenants made in a contract for the exchange of goods. This assimilates commutative justice to Hobbes's own definition of justice as the performance of covenant. But he did say, earlier in this paragraph, that the 'just value' in a contract is what the parties 'be contented to give';[26] so he has there implicitly admitted an idea of 'the just' as meaning 'the fair' and not simply the performance of covenant.

He criticizes the stock concept of distributive justice, again in the *Leviathan* statement, on the ground that to give people benefits because of their merit is not justice at all but 'grace'; it is a matter of free gift and not of obligation. Distributive justice, in Hobbes's view (para. 15), is to distribute to every man 'his own', as the traditional definition of justice requires. More properly, he adds, this is to be called equity.

Hobbes draws a firm distinction between justice and equity. Justice, the performance of covenant, is assigned to the third law of nature in *Leviathan*, corresponding to the second law in *De Cive*. Equity, equal or impartial treatment by a judge, is assigned to a separate law of nature, the eleventh in *Leviathan* and the tenth in *De Cive*. In *Leviathan*, chapter 15 (para. 15), Hobbes says that distributive justice is 'the Justice of an arbitrator', whose function is 'to distribute to

---

[26] L. 208.

every man his own: and this is indeed Just Distribution, and may be called (though improperly) Distributive Justice; but more properly Equity',[27] a separate law of nature. There is in fact a difference between this formulation of distributive justice or equity and the later formulation of equity as the eleventh law of nature in paragraphs 23–4.[28] The earlier formulation is not confined to equal distribution; it follows the traditional definition of justice as the distribution or rendering to each man of what is 'his own', which might be an equal or an unequal distribution, according to circumstances. The later formulation fixes upon equality; it says that a judge or arbitrator must '*deale Equally*', must not be 'partiall in judgment', must produce 'equall distribution to each man, of that which in reason belongeth to him'. This is partly because Hobbes thinks of *aequitas* as meaning equality, and partly because he disagrees with Aristotle's meritarian (and so inegalitarian) account of distributive justice. As a matter of fact Aristotle does not use the term 'distributive justice' to refer to the just (impartial) treatment of litigants by a judge. For Aristotle, equal or impartial treatment by a judge is an element of 'corrective' or 'rectifying' justice.[29]

Having distinguished between justice and equity, Hobbes is able to say, in *Leviathan*, chapter 18 (para. 6), that a sovereign 'may commit Iniquity; but not Injustice, or Injury in the proper signification'.[30] This is because the sovereign has, like any man, a natural obligation to obey the laws of nature, including the law that prescribes equity, but he has no covenantal or artificial obligation towards his subjects as the result of their social contract or implicit covenant of obedience. To be sure, the sovereign has a natural obligation to obey the third law of nature that prescribes the performance of covenant; but the covenants made in the course of instituting or acquiring a commonwealth are all covenants undertaken by the subjects; the sovereign has not bound himself by any promises to them. Consequently the sovereign has absolute authority, retaining the original natural right to do whatever he thinks fit. So if the sovereign orders a citizen to be arrested and executed, he does no injustice or injury since he has the full right to do it. But he may be acting inequitably. If the citizen has not broken any law or, in breaking a law, has not done anything that merits so severe a penalty as death, then the sovereign, in his capacity as supreme judge of the state, is not dealing equitably with that citizen as compared with others. The sovereign is bound by the laws of nature, which prescribe measures to avoid slipping back into the condition of war. He therefore has a natural duty of equity, but no obligation of justice, to refrain from treating the citizen thus.

Hobbes does not explain how the earlier remarks on distributive justice, which he thinks should be called equity, fit in with his later account of equity. In the later passage (*Leviathan*, ch. 15, paras. 23–4), we are told that a judge or arbitrator

---

[27] Ibid. [28] Ibid. 212. [29] Cf. Ch. 5 above. [30] *L*. 232.

should deal with people equally or impartially; that is equity. But Hobbes goes on to say that equity is also 'the equall distribution to each man, of that which in reason belongeth to him'. This is plainly related to the traditional definition of justice which Hobbes interpreted as being concerned with property. But it is not at all clear why the distribution of 'that which in reason belongeth' to a man should be an equal distribution. Hobbes has told us in chapter 13 that all men are roughly equal in natural powers, and here in chapter 15 he says that the ninth law of nature requires men to acknowledge their natural equality. But he cannot think that the possession of property should always 'in reason' be equal. He simply does not explain what he thinks.

Before leaving the eleventh law of nature, prescribing equity or distributive justice, we should note two corollaries of it, which Hobbes gives as the twelfth and thirteenth laws (eleventh and twelfth in *De Cive*). The twelfth says that, if goods cannot be divided, they should be enjoyed in common because equity requires it. And the thirteenth says that, if goods can neither be divided nor enjoyed in common, then they should be allocated by lot. Both of these provisions are egalitarian, but Hobbes interprets the idea of lot as allowing for a right of primogeniture and a right of first possession.

One other feature of Hobbes's political theory that is relevant to justice is his view of punishment. He does not call this an aspect of justice, which he wants to confine to the performance of covenant. He deals with the matter first in enunciating the seventh law of nature (sixth in *De Cive*), which requires '*That in Revenges* (that is, retribution of Evil for Evil,) *Men look not at the greatnesse of the evill past, but the greatnesse of the good to follow*' (*Leviathan*, ch. 15, para. 19)[31] In consequence, Hobbes says, punishment must have for its purpose the 'correction of the offender, or direction of others'. He is putting forward a reform plus deterrence theory of punishment, and this is elaborated in *Leviathan*, chapter 28, a valuable discussion of the nature and justification of punishment. Although Hobbes does not consider this to be a part of his account of justice, the chapter does in fact make a significant contribution to the subject of criminal justice.

Hobbes there (para. 1) defines punishment as '*an Evill inflicted by publique Authority, on him that hath done, or omitted that which is Judged by the same Authority to be a Transgression of the Law; to the end that the will of men may thereby the better be disposed to obedience*'.[32] This is a deterrence theory but not a straightforward consequentialist theory; for the definition of punishment requires that it can be inflicted only for a breach of the law, so that the infliction of such an evil on the innocent would be contrary to the definition. When Hobbes comes to explain this part of his definition (para. 22),[33] his grounds for

---

[31] *L*. 210. [32] Ibid. 353. [33] Ibid. 359–60.

it are partly consequentialist, partly not. He gives three reasons: (1) harming the innocent cannot be useful to society; (2) harming the innocent goes against the natural law of gratitude, which requires a requital of good for good and of evil solely for evil; (3) it goes against the natural law of equity, which requires 'an equall distribution of Justice', that is, impartiality. The second and third reasons are non-consequentialist. They are also reasons which we should normally assign to the concept of justice, and indeed Hobbes himself here refers to equity as 'an equall distribution of Justice'.

Western political thought about justice has always included two distinct and potentially conflicting ideas of what fairness requires, one egalitarian, the other meritarian. The egalitarian conception made its way into natural law doctrine as the normative principle that all men 'are by nature' (meaning that they are entitled to be) free and equal. When Hobbes gives his version of the natural law doctrine of human equality, he changes it from a normative idea to a positive one: all men are roughly equal in power, so that no one man is strong enough to dominate all the rest. Yet he derives from this a normative rule, a law of nature, that the equality of all men should be acknowledged; and he pokes fun at Aristotle for saying that men are unequal by nature, some being fit to rule and others unfit, the fit ones being philosophers like Aristotle himself. From this and from Hobbes's account of equity and its corollaries, it is clear that he follows the egalitarian conception of human entitlement and rejects the meritarian. But he does not assign these ideas to the notion of justice, because he wants to use that notion to support his chief aim in political theory, namely to show that power in politics is essential but not enough.

Chapter 8

G. W. LEIBNIZ

Leibniz discusses the concept of justice in a number of his writings, usually at no great length and simply repeating the essential features of his view with little in the way of argument. There is, however, one sustained essay on the topic, *Méditation sur la notion commune de la justice*, written about 1703 but not printed in his lifetime. The text is to be found in Georg Mollat, *Rechtsphilosophisches aus Leibnizens ungredruckten Schriften*; an English translation is provided by Patrick Riley in *Leibniz: Political Writings*.[1]

The essay does not present a systematic exposition of the concept of justice. It sketches a novel perspective and gives the impression that Leibniz would have liked to develop the sketch into a detailed theory. One may doubt, however, whether he had, in this field of thought, the sort of penetrating insight that he showed in mathematics and general philosophy. Another reason why the essay on justice does not get far is that Leibniz is less interested in the concept of justice itself than in the metaphysical status of ethics as a whole.

He begins with the problem of Plato's *Euthyphro*, whether piety is loved by the gods because it is intrinsically good or whether it becomes good and obligatory because it is loved by the gods. Leibniz reformulates the problem in terms of the will of God: is that which God wills good and just because God wills it, or does God will it because it is good and just? 'In other words,' he adds, 'the question is whether justice and goodness are arbitrary or whether they belong to the necessary and eternal truths about the nature of things, as do numbers and proportions.'[2]

He maintains, contrary to Descartes, that the necessary truths of mathematics

---

[1] Georg Mollat, *Rechtsphilosophisches aus Leibnizens ungredruckten Schriften* (Leipzig: Verlag J. H. Robolsky, 1885), 56–81; Eng. trans. Patrick Riley, *Leibniz: Political Writings*, 2nd edn. (Cambridge: Cambridge University Press, 1988), 45–64. I have in general followed Professor Riley's translation and am much indebted to it, but in some of my quotations I have differed a little from his rendering of the French text.

[2] Riley, 45; Mollat, 56.

are independent of the will of God and that this applies to justice and goodness also. So far as justice is concerned, he makes his case mainly by drawing out implications of its meaning. God is praised for acting justly; if justice meant whatever God wills, the word 'justly' would add nothing to 'acting' and the praise would be pointless. Further, the view that will justifies (*stat pro ratione voluntas*[3]) is the motto of a tyrant and would make God indistinguishable from the devil. Leibniz is ready to add to these philosophical arguments an appeal to the evidence of scripture, where God is represented as justifying himself against complaints.

On this topic of the status of justice, Leibniz takes his prime opponents to be Thrasymachus, as represented in Plato's *Republic*, and Hobbes. He places these two in the same boat because Thrasymachus says that justice is the interest of the powerful and because Hobbes says that the unlimited right of God is derived from his irresistible power. Leibniz does not appreciate that there is in fact a considerable difference between the positions of Thrasymachus and Hobbes. Thrasymachus speaks of justice and law in human societies; but when Hobbes says that the right of God is implied by irresistible power, his purpose is to show that this cannot be true of any human power. Then again, Hobbes's concept of natural right is unrelated to justice: a right is a liberty to act or forbear, that is, an absence of impediment to acting as one thinks fit, while justice is tied to the obligations of covenant. Although the view of Thrasymachus on justice is subsequently connected by Glaucon with the idea of a social contract, neither of them is really concerned, as Hobbes is, with the concept of justice as one segment of ethical thought. Thrasymachus and Glaucon are talking of law in general and of what is counted as right or obligatory in general. And that is what interests Leibniz in his basic question whether ethics is dependent on the will of God or carries its validity in itself.

Leibniz goes on to say that the meaning of justice must in principle be the same whether it is applied to God or to human beings. The undoubted difference between the infinite, perfect justice of God and the finite, imperfect justice of men is a difference of degree, not of kind. Otherwise we would not know what we are talking about when we speak of either; the term 'justice' would be meaningless. This reasonable point is used by Leibniz later to align the concept of justice in human affairs with that which is attributed to God in the scriptures.

---

[3] This looks like an altered quotation from Juvenal, *Satires*, vi.223: *hoc volo, sic iubeo, sit pro ratione voluntas* ('This I will, thus I command, let will be in place of a reason'). But Hobbes had recalled the verse incorrectly in *Human Nature* (i.e. *The Elements of Law*, I), 13.6, defining command as the expression of a desire 'for reason contained in the will itself: for it is not properly said, *Sic volo, sic iubeo*, without that other clause, *Stet pro ratione voluntas* ("Let will stand. . .")'. Cf. *De Cive*, Latin version, 14.1. Leibniz's *stat* ('stands') suggests that he has Hobbes in mind, as so often in this essay.

Meanwhile, however, he supposes that it enables him to reject Hobbes's view of God, and in this he mistaken. Hobbes does not give a different meaning to natural right when ascribed to God and when ascribed to men. It means the same thing in both instances, a freedom from impediment upon acting as one thinks fit. But because God has irresistible power, his freedom from impediment is absolute, while the limited and roughly equal power of men implies that their freedom to act is impeded by the competing power of others.

After these preliminaries, Leibniz declares summarily that the essential nature of justice is obvious. 'Justice is nothing else than that which conforms to wisdom and goodness joined together.'[4] He gives no serious argument at this stage, but thinks the conclusion is obvious because an unjust law is one in which the power that maintains the law lacks wisdom or good will. The premiss is no more obvious than the conclusion, and the inference from the one to the other is slipshod. In any event the proposed definition of justice is intolerably vague.

Later, however, after a digression on the justice of God in ordering the universe, Leibniz gets down to some detailed analysis. He begins with a 'nominal definition', which he thinks will be generally accepted, that 'justice is a constant will to act in such a way that no one has reason to complain of us'.[5] The term 'constant will' no doubt comes from the traditional juridical definition, 'a constant will to render to each man what is his', but the main content of Leibniz's definition is novel. Even more novel is his own filling out of the substance of this nominal definition. He says, very reasonably, that his initial definition is inadequate without specifying what are good reasons for complaint; and that, while everyone will accept the definition in its general form, there will be differences of opinion about the reasons that are admissible. Some will take a restricted view that would limit the object of justifiable complaint to the doing of harm and the deprivation of possessions; they would not include the doing of positive good or even the prevention or removal of evil. Such people 'believe, in a word, that one can be just, without being charitable'. Others take 'larger and finer views' and 'would not wish that anyone complain of their lack of goodness'. Leibniz himself shares this outlook and repeats a formula that he has previously given in the preface to his *Codex Juris Gentium*: 'justice is nothing other than the charity of the wise man, that is to say, doing good for others in conformity with wisdom. And wisdom in my sense is nothing other than the Science of Happiness.'[6]

We can see now that the earlier vague definition of justice as 'that which conforms to wisdom and goodness joined together' was pointing towards the more specific and more striking formulation that justice is 'the charity of the wise man'. Leibniz goes on to connect the distinction between restricted and extended

---

[4] Riley, 50; Mollat, 62.   [5] Riley, 53; Mollat, 67.   [6] Mollat, 67; cf. Riley, 54.

concepts of justice with the different branches of justice distinguished in philosophical and juridical tradition; and he also makes constant appeal to the rationality of the Golden Rule in explaining both the narrower and the wider concepts. But the leading feature of his account is the principle that justice is the charity of the wise man, and it is for this, I think, that he would wish it to be remembered.

As it stands, it is an enigmatic formula. Leibniz explains it as follows. By 'wisdom' he means prudence, a prime regard to one's own interest and to the general interest. That is why he says, in the quotation given above, that wisdom is the science of happiness. He takes wisdom ('which is the knowledge of our own good'[7]) to be basically a prudential concern for one's own interest. When he comes to socially just principles that appear to be independent of self-interest, he relates them to a concern for the public interest based on a rational (well-informed) pursuit of self-interest.

He reaches this position by considering what is implied by his initial definition of the common concept of justice. Why is it reasonable to complain of the doing of harm? Or, in other words, why do we have a duty to refrain from doing harm? The 'most pressing' reason is the fear that others will do the same to us. But then, Leibniz goes on, do we not have reason to fear also that others will hate us if we fail to help them, when we can do so without inconvenience, by preventing or removing an evil that threatens them from another source than ourselves? You may say that you are content if others refrain from doing you harm; you ask no more from them and you offer no more to them. But if you were to find yourself in great trouble that could be easily removed by someone else, would you not think that his refusal to help gave you reason to complain? Once that is granted, think of the next step, the procuring of positive good for others. This seems a more radical advance, enabling an objector to say that it goes beyond the scope of duty. 'Someone will say: I am not at all obliged to make you better off; everyone for himself, God for all.'[8] It seems a difference of kind, but Leibniz treats it as still a difference only of degree. He divides it into two stages, each of which contains a similarity to its predecessor. Suppose a great good is coming to you but then an impediment appears, one that I could easily remove. Would you not think that you had a right to ask me to do so, pointing out to me that I would ask it of you if our positions were reversed? And granting that, how can you refuse to do a great good for another which you can easily do, even though it is not a matter of removing an impediment?

In the course of this progression from the negative refraining from harm to the positive procuring of good, Leibniz twice refers to the Golden Rule, first in its negative form, 'Do not do to others what you do not wish to be done to you',

---

[7] Riley, 57; Mollat, 71.   [8] Mollat, 67; cf. Riley, 55.

and then in the positive, 'Do as you would be done by'. He calls it 'the principle of Equity or, what is the same thing, of Equality or of the same reason, which requires us to give what we would want in similar circumstances, without claiming to be privileged against reason or to be able to adduce our will as reason'.[9] This underlies his initial 'nominal definition' of justice in terms of having a reason to complain. The definition does not state a supposed psychological fact, that everyone (or almost everyone) *does* complain if harmed or not benefited; for that is not true. It is a normative statement that we are entitled to complain. Leibniz (characteristically in the light of his general philosophy) phrases this in terms of 'having a reason', meaning a good or adequate or justifying reason, or (as he himself writes in one place) having a right, to complain. One can ask *why* an alleged reason is a good or adequate reason, and Leibniz thinks that the principle of having the same reason supplies the answer: if any potential agent were in the position of the person affected by the possible action, he would think he had reason to complain.

But that answer is insufficient. The objector pictured by Leibniz can still ask why he should act as the Golden Rule prescribes. 'I grant that if our positions were reversed, I would wish to be helped. But fortunately for me, our positions are not reversed. Why should I be moved by the thought of a hypothetical situation that is quite different from my actual situation? As Leibniz has already said on my behalf, I am not at all obliged to make you better off; everyone for himself, God for all.' The objection is made from a standpoint of self-interest, and so Leibniz takes in that standpoint when referring to the Golden Rule. In requiring that we do as we would be done by, the rule, he suggests, reminds us that we are all vulnerable to the same needs. He says that the most pressing reason for refraining from harm is the fear that we ourselves may be harmed. He implies that if I refrain from harming others I shall thereby induce them to refrain from harming me. And when he comes to reasons for doing positive good to others, he says 'there is the hope that others will do the same for us'.[10] Thus far, charity in conformity with wisdom means charity for the sake of prudent self-interest understood as a direct requital of benefit to the agent.

Some just actions, however, require a wider view of prudential self-interest in relation to the public interest. Leibniz considers criminal justice and distributive justice. His purpose is not to show that we must go beyond self-interest, but rather to deal with the objection that the Golden Rule does not fit these branches of justice. First, criminal justice. The Golden Rule as Leibniz has described it, says the objector, would give criminals a just claim to be pardoned, since the judge too would wish to be pardoned if he were in the criminal's place. Leibniz answers that the judge's duty is to think of himself in the place, not only

[9] Mollat, 70; cf. Riley, 56.   [10] Riley, 57; Mollat, 71.

of the criminal, but also of the rest, whose interest is to see crime punished. The decision must rest on 'the preponderance of good',[11] allowing the general interest served by punishment to outweigh the criminal's interest (his wish to be pardoned). Second, distributive justice. Here the objection is that the Golden Rule requires the same treatment for all, while distributive justice requires unequal treatment in accordance with merit. Leibniz answers again that we must not think of ourselves in the place of the individual who is less well treated than others; we must think of ourselves in the position of everyone, each consulting his own interest, but we must also think of each of them as doing so in an enlightened way, realizing that the reward of merit serves the interest of all.

Leibniz's intention is to show that the Golden Rule still applies to these branches of justice, despite appearances to the contrary. He patently fails to do so. The Golden Rule itself says nothing about self-interested (or any other) reasons for compliance. It is simply a general commandment, interpreted in biblical doctrine as a summary of the whole of the moral law. It has no particular reference to justice and, on the face of it, is concerned with personal rather than social ethics. Leibniz's real aim is to defend his own rationalist theory that the requirements of morality depend on 'having the same reason' and, like many philosophers, he thinks that virtue must be squared with self-interest.

He does not, however, stop there. Having said that justice must have the same meaning when applied to God or to man, Leibniz now asks whether the account he has given of human justice and its aim can fit the justice of God. In practising justice, God has nothing to fear or hope for himself. His motive is simply his own perfection. Even so Leibniz feels obliged to add, as a link with what has gone before, that we may think of God's perfection as his pleasure, pleasure being 'nothing other than the feeling of perfection'.[12] Leibniz then says that this motive can be found also 'in men of true virtue and generosity, the supreme degree of which is to imitate divinity, so far as human nature is capable of it'.[13] It is still prudence since it brings the satisfaction of an inner harmony and of the beauty of divine perfection. But prudence or wisdom now has a wider compass. Leibniz has at last answered the egoistic objection, 'each for himself, God for all'.

Leibniz concludes by distinguishing different senses of justice. Justice may be contrasted with charity; this is because it is given a narrow interpretation, the *jus strictum*. The narrow sense, strict justice, may also be contrasted with equity, the wisdom of judges and legislators, but their function is described as the administration of justice, which aims at the general good, though not always attaining the particular good. Both of these senses of justice may be contrasted with universal justice, which contains all the virtues and is based on the imitation of God.

---

[11] Mollat, 71; cf. Riley, 56.   [12] Mollat, 72; cf. Riley, 57.
[13] Mollat, 73; cf. Riley, 57–8.

Leibniz identifies these three senses of justice with the three precepts of Roman law, *neminem laedere* ('to harm no one'), *suum cuique tribuere* ('to render to each person what is his'), and *honeste vivere* ('to live uprightly'), which he reasonably renders as *honeste* (*hoc est probe, pie*) *vivere* ('to live uprightly, that is, righteously, dutifully'). He also identifies them with the three senses of justice distinguished in the philosophical tradition that stemmed from Aristotle: commutative justice, distributive justice, universal justice. It seems odd to identify the precept 'to harm no one' with commutative justice, as we noted in Chapter 6 above. Leibniz probably did this because Pufendorf had linked commutative justice with the 'perfect rights' corresponding to strict duties.

Leibniz's attempt to tie up his own thoughts with the traditions of jurists and earlier philosophers is no doubt commendable as an exercise in synthesis, but it does not really bring enlightenment to the subject. The Greek philosophers could think of universal 'justice' as embracing all the virtues because Greek usage (especially of the adjective *dikaion*, meaning 'right' as well as 'just') called for it. But in the eighteenth century it was confusing rather than helpful to return to such a wide sense of justice and to define the concept as a form of charity. That definition seems at first sight to forward the embryonic idea of social justice found in Philo and Augustine, but it is in fact rather different. Leibniz's concern is to show that there is no firm line of distinction between justice and charity: both are required by the moral law, and a truly virtuous person takes both to be duties. That hardly needs argument, but it is a truth about morality as a whole rather than justice. It does not try to show that the duty to be charitable is owed to the needy as members of a common fellowship. Leibniz's argument is based on self-interest or at best on the claim of self-perfection. The latter may be the acme of ethics for some, but it has nothing to do with the social justice.

Chapter 9

DAVID HUME

Hume set out his ethical theory in Book III of *A Treatise of Human Nature*, published in 1740, and then restated it less elaborately in *An Enquiry concerning the Principles of Morals*, first published in 1751. His account of justice has a vital role in his ethical theory, and his ethical theory as a whole is the most important example of empiricist moral philosophy. One would therefore expect his discussion of justice to make a signal contribution to elucidating the concept. In fact, however, it fails to do so. This is because Hume's idea of justice is curiously narrow. It is largely confined to the rights of property and the obligation of promises. (In the *Treatise*, Hume treats the keeping of promises as an obligation closely allied to justice rather than included in it. In the *Enquiry*, however, he says that promise keeping 'is itself one of the most considerable parts of justice'.[1]) On these two matters Hume does indeed advance understanding with the kind of subtle thought and novel outlook that we find in his theory of knowledge. But although property rights are a major segment of the subject matter of justice and cover more than one might think at first sight, they certainly do not take up the whole of it. And while the obligations and rights of promises and contracts form a network essential to social life, they are not normally thought of as part of the concept of justice. It is of course true that the rights of contract, like those of property, are protected by the civil law and so come under the aegis of the system of legal justice; but that does not make them part of the concept of justice proper.

Protection by the law is not even a guarantee that a legal right conforms to a sense of justice. We may agree that most legal rights are just or fair, but we may also question the justice of some traditional legal rights, such as giving preference

---

[1] David Hume, *Enquiry concerning the Principles of Morals*, app. iii: in Clarendon critical edition, ed. Tom L. Beauchamp (Oxford: Clarendon Press, 1998), 98, §7; in David Hume, *Enquiries concerning the Human Understanding and concerning the Principles of Morals*, ed. L. A. Selby-Bigge (Oxford: Clarendon Press, 2nd edn., 1902; 3rd edn., rev. P. H. Nidditch, 1975), §257.

in heredity to sons over daughters or to the oldest child over all the rest, practices that may have (or once have had) the backing of utility but not of justice or fairness. Likewise we may question the justice of a particular law in prescribing duties: for instance, a duty of all, whether rich or poor, to pay the same rate of expenditure tax on necessities such as food and fuel.

Hume says nothing about the possibility of querying the fairness of positive law. He does use the word 'equity' from time to time, tending to couple it with 'justice' as if it were virtually a synonym.[2] He never considers what is the relation between the two or whether the rights established and protected by law can be criticized as falling short of equity or fairness. He does briefly mention egalitarian ideas and dismisses them as impractical and socially harmful; he seems to have no sense of the appeal of equality as an element of justice. Even when he writes of making 'an equal partition of bread in a famine', he simply takes this to be a proper suspension of the usual 'rules of equity and justice' and does not think of the equal partition as being itself just.[3]

Hume also says virtually nothing, in his discussion of justice, about the criminal law and the sense of justice associated with the punishment of crime. In the one place where he does mention it,[4] he writes, as with the equal partition of bread in a famine, of 'the ordinary rules of justice' (that is to say, normal rules about rights) being 'suspended'. He adds that it becomes 'equitable' to inflict the punishment for reasons of utility; there is no suggestion that it is equitable because merited. In fact Hume says little in any context about the notion of merit or desert as a prime element of the concept of justice. As with equality, he briefly mentions the ideal of distributing possessions to accord with merit (or 'virtue') and dismisses it as impractical.[5] Elsewhere he tends to use the term 'merit' as a synonym of 'worth'. He disagrees with the common view that restricts 'merit or moral worth' to moral virtues as contrasted with natural abilities or talents,[6] and so, in the *Enquiry*, he uses the term 'personal merit' to cover both.[7]

Merit or desert is, in common usage, consequential upon deliberate choice

---

[2] In one place, *Treatise of Human Nature*, III.iii.1 (ed. L. A. Selby-Bigge (Oxford: Clarendon Press, 1986; 2nd edn., rev. P. H. Nidditch, 1978), 578), Hume includes equity in a list of *natural* virtues, as if it were definitely different from the artificial virtue of justice. Yet in *Treatise*, III.ii.1 (Selby-Bigge, 483) he writes of 'the laws of equity', evidently using the term as a simple synonym for the laws of justice. There are various other places where he treats justice and equity as synonyms.

[3] *Enquiry concerning Morals*, III.i (Beauchamp, 15, §8; Selby-Bigge, §147).

[4] Ibid. (Beauchamp, 16, §10; Selby-Bigge, §148).

[5] Ibid. III.ii (Beauchamp, 19–20, §23; Selby-Bigge, §154).

[6] *Treatise*, III.iii.4 (Selby-Bigge, 606–9); *Enquiry concerning Morals*, appendix iv (Beauchamp, 102–5, §§1–6; Selby-Bigge, §§261–5).

[7] *Enquiry concerning Morals*, I; IX.i; app. iv (Beauchamp, 6–7, §10; 72, §1; 102–5, §§1–6; Selby-Bigge, §§138, 217, 261–5).

and that is why it is not applied to natural abilities. When Hume belittles the distinction between moral virtues and natural abilities, he denies that it can depend on attributing freedom of choice to the former. Apart from his belief that free will is a myth, he notes that some virtues (courage, for instance) are no more voluntary than natural dispositions. As for those virtues that are voluntary, he gives a determinist and utilitarian explanation of praise and blame, reward and punishment. Natural abilities are more or less unchangeable, but tendencies to moral or immoral action can be encouraged or checked by praise or blame, reward or punishment; that is why moral virtues and failings are (mistakenly) supposed to be attended by freedom of choice. This ingenious suggestion, which has been revived and elaborated by Professor P. H. Nowell-Smith in our own day,[8] is sketched only briefly by Hume in a later section of the *Treatise* about natural abilities and is not mentioned at all in the lengthy discussion of justice. He does not seem to have appreciated the prominence of desert in the concept of justice or the need to include the justice of the criminal law in his account. In the circumstances it will suffice to indicate with equal brevity some difficulties facing his suggestion.

The suggestion does not explain why a specific moral connotation is attached to praise and blame, reward and punishment. There are other types of pleasant and painful measures that are used to promote socially useful dispositions and to check socially harmful ones. An obvious example is education, found pleasant by some, painful by others. Sermons are in the same boat. Quarantine for people with a contagious illness is rather like imprisonment in depriving them of freedom of movement in order to avert public harm. But these things differ from praise and blame, reward and punishment. They are indeed adopted because thought to be useful and efficacious, but they are not also thought to be deserved. In Samuel Butler's *Erewhon*, people who are ill are reprobated and their treatment is felt to be shameful. But then *Erewhon* is the topsy-turvy country where sickness meets with blame and crime with compassion. Unlike Hume and Nowell-Smith, Samuel Butler thinks that the punishment of crime is misguided because it does not accept determinism. Hume and Nowell-Smith think that the practice is perfectly sound but is misunderstood. Hume suggests that the misunderstanding is in the minds of modern philosophers and that the distinction between moral virtue and other admirable qualities is purely verbal. He notes that the philosophers of Greece and Rome had no qualms about including prudence among the cardinal virtues. That is a fair argument against a narrow view of moral virtue. But Hume should also have noted that the thought and language of the ancient

---

[8] P. H. Nowell-Smith, 'Freedom and Moral Responsibility', *Mind*, 57 (1948), 45 ff.; *Ethics* (Harmondsworth: Penguin Books, 1954), ch. 20, §4.

world, as of the modern, make a special link between desert and the particular virtue of justice.

We have seen in earlier chapters of this book that ideas of equality and desert are deeply ingrained in the concept of justice. The neglect of them in Hume's discussion is a serious deficiency. I can suggest reasons why he gave special attention to the rights of property and to promises and contracts. It is, however, surprising that his interest in jurisprudence and in moral psychology should not have led him to say more about justice in the criminal law.

So much for Hume's omissions. Let us turn now to what he does say. In the *Treatise of Human Nature*, he presents justice as the foremost example of 'artificial virtue', other examples being promise keeping, political allegiance, adherence to international law, and the strict standards of chastity and modesty required of women. He contrasts artificial with natural virtues, the chief examples of the latter being 'greatness of mind' (including heroism) and 'goodness and benevolence' (including 'generosity, humanity, compassion, gratitude, friendship, fidelity, zeal, disinterestedness, liberality'). Natural virtues spring from motives that arise naturally in human beings. The motivation of artificial virtues is more complex; it depends on a convention that grows up in the course of social experience. The initial impetus to form and follow the convention comes from the simple motive of self-interest, but then a sympathetic appreciation of the general benefit produces a secondary motive of moral approval. Sympathy in the *Treatise* is connected with the imagination and the association of ideas; it differs from natural benevolence, which is limited and does not embrace mankind at large.

Hume's account of justice in the *Enquiry concerning the Principles of Morals* is more straightforward. His aim in this work is to find the 'origin' of morals by analysing all forms of 'personal merit' and he concludes that the object of praise is always that which is agreeable or useful to ourselves or to others. He begins with the two main 'social virtues', benevolence and justice. There is no difficulty in showing that benevolence is praised, at least partly, for its social utility, and Hume deals with that quite quickly. He then turns to justice and says that the value of this virtue is wholly due to social utility, a thesis that is not at all obvious and needs extensive argument. Nothing is said about the notion of artificial virtue, but in an appendix Hume briefly recalls one statement of the *Treatise* discussion, namely that the term 'natural' has several senses. Justice can properly be called natural if that word is opposed to the unusual or the miraculous; but if the natural is opposed to the artificial, 'perhaps' justice cannot strictly be called natural.[9] Likewise nothing is said in the *Enquiry* about the moral approval of justice being a secondary motive added to the initial motive of self-interest; Hume simply says that utility pleases through a natural

---

[9] *Enquiry concerning Morals*, app. iii, n. 2 (Beauchamp, 99, shown as n. 64; Selby-Bigge, §258).

sentiment of humanity (he sometimes calls it fellow feeling, sympathy, and even benevolence).

It looks at first sight as if Hume has substantially revised his theory in the *Enquiry*. The *Treatise* gives prominence and priority to the doctrine that justice is an artificial virtue, while the *Enquiry* dismisses this question as a 'merely verbal' dispute and concentrates on the utility of justice. The *Treatise* also implies a distinction between benevolence, a simple 'passion', and sympathy, a complex process with a wide range, while no such distinction is apparent in the *Enquiry*. I think, however, that the change is in emphasis and presentation rather than one of real substance. The *Treatise* was written for readers with a knowledge of and capacity for philosophy; the *Enquiry* was written for a wider audience and so, while still being a philosophical work, it avoids abstruse arguments and distinctions that would mystify the lay reader and obscure the general picture. Even sophisticated readers of the *Treatise* misunderstood the main point of Hume's thesis that justice is an artificial virtue depending on convention; he probably hoped there would be less misunderstanding if instead he were to emphasize utility as the reason why certain conventional practices arise and then become the rules of justice.

The artificiality of justice is not the only topic that is given priority in the *Treatise* and relegated to a subordinate place in the *Enquiry*. The structure of Book III of the *Treatise* is as follows. Part i deals with the question whether moral distinctions are derived from reason or from a moral sense (that is to say, feeling). The general subject matter of Part ii is justice and injustice, beginning with the claim that justice is an artificial virtue and eventually going on to discuss additional artificial virtues. Finally Part iii turns to 'the other virtues and vices', meaning those that are natural, including natural abilities. Hume presumably felt that he had good reason to start with the dispute about reason and moral sense, and then to proceed immediately to the further disputed question whether justice is natural or artificial. In the *Enquiry*, both these questions are relegated to appendices. The reason for giving them priority in the early work is to be found in the history of philosophy and especially of recent philosophy. The reason for removing this prominence in the later work is that these topics would be of less interest to the wider audience for whom the *Enquiry* was written.

When Hume was composing his first and greatest philosophical work, the *Treatise*, in the 1730s, he had been much influenced by the writings of Francis Hutcheson, at that time Professor of Moral Philosophy in the University of Glasgow. The two books of Hutcheson that Hume knew (they in fact contain Hutcheson's best work) were *An Inquiry into our Ideas of Beauty and Virtue*, first published in 1725, and *An Essay on the Passions and Affections. With Illustrations on the Moral Sense*, first published in 1728. Professor Kemp Smith, in a penetrating study of Hume's philosophy,[10] maintained that Hutcheson's ethical theory was the primary influence on Hume's thinking, first giving rise to Hume's own ethical theory and then enabling him to transfer a key idea from that to the theory of knowledge. The key idea was Hutcheson's view that virtue, like beauty, is partly a projection of the feelings of a spectator: the virtuous motive is an objective fact, but the quality of virtue attributed to it is in the eye, or rather the heart, of the beholder, being a projection of his feeling of approval. Hutcheson called the capacity to feel approval a moral sense, comparing it to the sense of beauty and recalling Locke's usage of 'inner sense' to mean sensation or feeling.

Hutcheson's theory was criticized by rationalist philosophers who held that moral qualities are objectively present in actions and motives, perceivable not by sense-perception but by rational insight. For empiricists like Hutcheson and Hume, the rationalist theory was unsatisfactory because, instead of relying on the experience of sense and feeling, it posited occult qualities that were said to resemble mathematical entities. Hume followed and developed Hutcheson's view in his own ethical theory and then (according to Kemp Smith) realized that he could explain causation in a similar way. Like virtue, the necessary connection of causation is not an object of sense-perception. But whereas rationalist philosophers said it is perceived by rational insight, just as they did with moral qualities, Hume suggested instead that the idea of causation is the result of observed regular succession together with a notion of necessity that is not observed but is projected onto the observed facts from the feeling of compulsion that spectators have when they expect the first element of a regular succession to be followed by the second.

Kemp Smith's view about the origin of Hume's theory of causation is a brilliant conjecture but only a conjecture. The influence of Hutcheson on Hume's ethical theory, however, is solid fact. It had both a positive and a negative effect.

When Hutcheson put forward the moral sense theory in his first book, he was not concerned to provide an alternative to rationalist ethics. He wanted to refute the claims of iconoclastic thinkers such as Hobbes and Mandeville who held that moral action and moral approval are at root self-interested. Hutcheson marshalled arguments and examples to show that both the motive and the praise of virtuous action are essentially disinterested. Traditional rationalist thinkers had also attacked Hobbes but not only for his egoism; they were even more perturbed by Hobbes's view that right and wrong, justice and injustice, would not exist in a state of nature but were the effect of human agreement. While welcoming the strength of Hutcheson's arguments against egoistic theory, the rationalists felt that he had sold the pass to Hobbes in conceding that ethical values were not objectively real but were an outcrop of human experience.

---

[10] Norman Kemp Smith, *The Philosophy of David Hume* (London: Macmillan, 1941).

Hutcheson replied to their criticism in *Illustrations on the Moral Sense*, the more important of the two essays that form his second book. He concentrated his attention especially on Samuel Clarke and William Wollaston.

Hume was clearly much impressed by Hutcheson's arguments in the *Illustrations*. The first part of Book III of the *Treatise* takes up the controversy whether moral distinctions are derived from reason or from a moral sense. Hume had no doubt that Hutcheson was right but thought, justifiably, that he could improve upon the presentation of Hutcheson's arguments and could add others. It is worth noting that he follows Hutcheson in concentrating his fire on Clarke and Wollaston. He refers explicitly to Wollaston in an amusing long footnote about the theory that all immoral action is a form of lying. As for Clarke, Hume's references to 'eternal fitnesses and unfitnesses of things' are plainly directed against Clarke and echo the section in Hutcheson's *Illustrations* that names Clarke as its main target. In addition, Hume's (now famous) final argument, that 'ought' cannot be deduced from 'is', breezily says that he has found the move in every system of morality that he has met, but obviously that cannot be true; I have found it only in Samuel Clarke. Since Clarke's exposition of ethical rationalism was by far the most influential statement of that doctrine, it was not too wild an exaggeration for Hume to say, tongue in cheek, that a small attention to his point would 'subvert all the vulgar systems of morality'.

Having disposed of rationalist theories, Hume goes on in the next section to argue that moral distinctions are derived from a moral sense. That is how he describes the subject matter in the heading, and it indicates general support for the stance of Hutcheson. But the heading is the only place where he uses the term 'moral sense'; in the body of the section, and throughout the subsequent discussions of Book III, he instead writes of 'sentiment' or 'feeling', which helps to put some distance between his theory and Hutcheson's. The term 'moral sense' can mislead in suggesting a close analogy with the external senses. More important, Hutcheson's description of the moral sense as disinterested approval of the disinterested motive of benevolence was too simple. Hume thought that he could give a more explicit account of the special character of the feeling of approval and an explanation of its origin. He also thought that Hutcheson was mistaken in subsuming the whole of virtue under one common form, benevolence. Even taken in a wide sense, benevolence accounted for only part of virtue, what one might call natural virtue, since it was motivated by a natural bent to altruism. Other forms of virtuous action were motivated by a sense of duty or honesty, a readiness to follow the rules of morality without being prompted by kindness, sometimes even in opposition to it. To mark the difference Hume called such virtues artificial. He gave notice of the distinction in the section about the moral sense and then went on in the next section, the beginning of Part ii, to ask whether justice is a natural or an artificial virtue.

Hume may well have felt that the controversy about reason and moral sense was the most prominent topic of discussion among moral philosophers in the 1730s. He certainly felt that Hutcheson had made an important advance but one that was nevertheless deficient and so needed to be modified and developed. That would explain why he began his own treatment of moral philosophy with the dispute about reason and moral sense or sentiment. Having allied himself with Hutcheson on that issue, Hume no doubt felt it incumbent on him to show immediately that Hutcheson's theory was too simple. Rationalists had criticized Hutcheson for giving insufficient attention to the notions of right and wrong, duty and obligation. It is easy to suppose that ethics is purely a matter of feeling if you think only of the approval of benevolence (each of which, Hutcheson said, is a form of love); but judgements of right and wrong, and actions motivated by such judgements, by the thought of what one ought to do, cannot be regarded as simply emotional reactions. Hutcheson dealt briefly, but inadequately, with the objection in *Illustrations on the Moral Sense*. Hume took it further in his discussion of artificial virtue, where he contrasted 'natural motives' with the motives of acting from a sense of justice or honesty or duty.

Why did he put the main emphasis on justice? Hutcheson had said virtually nothing about the concept of justice as such, but he had said quite a lot about rights, following up the special interest that his teacher and predecessor at Glasgow, Gerschom Carmichael, had taken in the jurisprudence of Pufendorf. The distinctive feature of Hutcheson's theory of rights was a novel form of utilitarian thought. Hutcheson's theory of virtue as approved benevolence turned into the first explicit statement of utilitarianism when he reflected that benevolence aims at the promotion of happiness and the reduction of unhappiness, so that 'that action is best, which procures the greatest happiness for the greatest numbers'.[11] When he came to deal with rights, he realized that, although a right can be the ground for obligatory action, that action may not be the most useful one that could be done. Nevertheless he linked rights with his utilitarian cast of thought by saying that the validity of rights comes from their tendency to promote the general good if *universally* followed. This formula justifies the practice of law in insisting on a universal application of its rules even though that sometimes leads to hard cases (as the lawyers call them). Hutcheson's theory of rights is an early expression of what has come to be known as 'rule utilitarianism', but Hutcheson had the good sense to apply it only to rights, that is to say, to the justification of legal practice.

Hume's account of the utility of justice is a development of Hutcheson's theory of rights. He too expounded a version of rule utilitarianism and he too

---

[11] Francis Hutcheson, *Inquiry concerning Virtue*, iii.8; in D. D. Raphael, *British Moralists 1650–1800* (Oxford: Clarendon Press, 1969; repr. Indianapolis: Hackett, 1991), §333.

sensibly restricted it to actions that involve rights, instead of extending it, as modern rule utilitarians do, to all actions that are morally right or obligatory. Hume's theory of justice, however, is not simply a repetition of Hutcheson's theory of rights. Hume saw that the relative complexity of the moral ground of rights shows the limitations of Hutcheson's general theory of ethics, which supposed that all moral value could be explained by naturally arising esteem for naturally arising benevolence. This led Hume to reconsider the case for saying that a substantial part of morality, much of it comprised in the concept of justice, is conventional. His account of the convention was more realistic than the hypothesis of a social contract used by earlier conventionalists. In the course of working this out, Hume perceived a novel, puzzling problem about promises, which he solved in a way linked to his explanation of the conventions of justice.

Hume's thoughts on these matters were influenced by Hobbes as well as Hutcheson. There is ample evidence that he had a considerable respect for Hobbes. The very title of the *Treatise of Human Nature* follows a phrase, 'that *Treatise of Human Nature*', used by Hobbes to describe his first work (published under the title *Human Nature*); and Professor Paul Russell has shown that there is a striking similarity of structure between Hobbes's *The Elements of Law* (originally published as *Human Nature* and *De Corpore Politico*) and Hume's *Treatise*, and that Hume clearly 'borrows' from this and other works of Hobbes in a number of examples and key phrases.[12] In Chapter 7 I have given reasons for thinking that Hume derived the idea of artificial virtue from Hobbes's distinction between nature and art as applied to law and covenant. Hobbes calls covenants artificial bonds and the rules of positive law artificial chains, imitating the compelling force of natural law. I suggested that Hobbes thinks there are two systems of morality, one natural and built on a prudential regard to self-interest, the other artificial and built on covenant. Hume agreed with Hutcheson and other critics that Hobbes had overstated the role of self-interest in human conduct, but he was less ready than they were to reject Hobbes's revival of the doctrine of the ancient sophists that justice exists by convention, not by nature. Although Hume dismissed as a myth and a self-contradiction the idea of instituting justice by a social contract, he realized that this was not the nub of the position of the sophists and Hobbes, and he also saw that Hobbes was on to something important in his remarks about the obligation of promises and its artificial character.

I think there was also some lesser influence, mainly negative, from the work

---

[12] Paul Russell, 'Hume's *Treatise* and Hobbes's *The Elements of Law*', *Journal of the History of Ideas*, 46 (1985), 51 ff. I think that Russell exaggerates a little, at least in respect of Book III of the *Treatise*, when he claims that the structure of Hume's work is actually modelled on that of Hobbes, but his case for extensive influence is thoroughly convincing. In the preface to my *British Moralists 1650–1800* I noted that Hume probably took the title of the *Treatise* from Hobbes.

of Locke. When Hume criticizes ethical rationalism in the *Treatise*, he writes of the 'opinion very industriously propagated by certain philosophers that morality is susceptible of demonstration' and says that 'this science may be brought to an equal certainty with geometry or algebra'.[13] Locke was on the side of the angels in the theory of knowledge since he initiated the revival of empiricism, but in ethics he accepted the traditional rationalism of natural law theory. His unpublished *Essays on the Law of Nature* were of course unknown to Hume. There is, however, a short passage about ethics in Locke's *Essay concerning the Human Understanding* which uses almost the same words as Hume. The paragraph is headed *Morality capable of demonstration* and then speaks of placing 'morality among the sciences capable of demonstration' by deducing necessary consequences from self-evident propositions. It gives two simple examples, one said to be 'as certain as any demonstration in Euclid', the other as certain as any proposition 'in mathematics'. Even more to the point, the first example virtually identifies justice with the rights of property. The proposition to be demonstrated is 'Where there is no property, there is no injustice', and the demonstration proceeds by giving definitions that make the proposition analytic: property is 'a right to any thing', while injustice is 'the name given' to 'the invasion or violation of that right'.[14] It seems to me very likely that Hume had this in mind both when he wrote of the opinion that morality is susceptible of demonstration and when he fastened upon the rights of property as the essence of justice. (In *An Enquiry concerning Human Understanding*, published in 1748, Hume reproduces Locke's proposition almost exactly, as an example of a supposed demonstration which is really no more than an imperfect definition.[15])

It is worth recalling also that Locke's advocacy of natural rights in his *Second Treatise of Government* includes a natural right to property, the existence of which he tried to prove by saying that everyone owns his own body and so the work of his hands, and that one acquires ownership of something in a natural state by mixing one's labour with it. Hume's theory that justice, interpreted as the rights of property, is not a natural but an artificial virtue, is (among other things) an implied criticism of Locke's natural right to property. He criticizes Locke's proof directly and effectively when he comes to the detailed grounds of property rights and deals with first possession, known in law as 'occupation'. He points out that some instances of this right have nothing to do with joining one's labour to the object acquired, and that in any case the idea of joining one's labour is only a metaphor for altering a thing by one's labour, so that there is no real extension of a pre-existing ownership of one's body.[16]

[13] *Treatise*, III.i.1 (Selby-Bigge, 463).
[14] John Locke, *Essay concerning the Human Understanding*, IV.iii.18.
[15] Hume, *Enquiry concerning the Human Understanding*, XII.iii (Selby-Bigge, §131).
[16] *Treatise*, III.ii.3 (Selby-Bigge, 505–6).

Hume's argument for his view that justice is an artificial virtue is somewhat elusive and unconvincing. It runs as follows. The merit of a virtuous action lies only in its motive. That virtuous motive cannot be a sense of duty, since this would entail reasoning in a circle: the virtue of the action lies in 'a regard to the virtue of the action'. So, although the motive of an act of justice or honesty, such as paying a debt, may be a regard for justice or honesty, that cannot constitute its virtue; the virtue must come from some antecedent natural motive. This cannot be self-interest, or a regard for the public interest, or private benevolence (that is to say, a desire to benefit the person to whom the debt is owed). Hume gives sound reasons for rejecting each of these possibilities. It appears then, after all, that there is no motive for acting justly other than a regard for justice. And we can avoid the charge of reasoning in a circle only if we allow that the sense of justice is not a natural motive but arises 'artificially, tho' necessarily', from human conventions.[17]

Three steps in this argument are puzzling. First, why should we agree that the merit of a virtuous action lies only in its motive and owes nothing to 'the external performance'? Hume says, correctly, that if a person, exercising a virtuous motive, fails to do what he ought through some unforeseen circumstance, we do not blame him. This does show that merit and demerit, praise and blame, do not depend on the external performance alone, but it does not show that external performance is irrelevant. We can ask *why* certain motives are praised and others blamed. It is not just a matter of chance that we are prompted to praise kindness or courage, for example. It is because these motives aim at helping other people and usually succeed in that aim. If on occasion they fail through inadvertence or ill luck to produce a benefit that we would expect, we still think well of them because we know that the failure was exceptional; the motives continue to produce good results in most instances. It is true that we do not consciously reflect on the beneficial tendency when we praise an example of kindness or courage; the praise comes naturally. Hutcheson was therefore able to compare the love (esteem) of benevolence with the love (admiration) of beauty. But he also noted that the esteem of benevolence is appropriate because benevolence aims at promoting happiness. Although Hutcheson does not say so, it is reasonable to infer that the natural reaction of approving benevolence has arisen because benevolence usually promotes happiness.

It is surprising that Hume should not have taken account of this when he wrote that the merit of a virtuous action owes nothing to the external performance. When he explains the moral approval of artificial virtue, he says it arises from our sympathy with the general happiness produced by these virtues. He even says in one place that the scheme of law and justice, once established by

[17] Ibid. III.ii.1 (Selby–Bigge, 477–84).

convention, 'is *naturally* attended with a strong sentiment of morals; which can proceed from nothing but our sympathy with the interests of society'.[18] He also says in that section of the *Treatise* (and repeats in the *Enquiry*) that the approval of many natural virtues, too, can be explained similarly as arising from sympathy with beneficial effects. All this counts against the initial argument that the praise of virtue depends entirely on the motive and owes nothing to the external performance.

That initial statement is singularly inappropriate for justice. It is at first sight reasonable to say that the merit or praise of benevolence depends only on the motive. But can one reasonably say the same thing of justice? Justice is a moral end or ideal to be pursued. A particular instance of justice, even in Hume's narrow interpretation of the term, is not the expression of a specific kind of motive but a relationship between persons in relation to things. The ancient Greeks included justice among the cardinal 'virtues', but the word translated as virtues means excellences, forms of moral value, not necessarily qualities of a person, though the word for justice, *dikaiosyne*, can mean a personal quality, righteousness, as well as a set of relationships. We too think of righteousness or conscientiousness as a virtue, and this is what Hume has in mind when he writes of acting from 'a regard to virtue' or a sense of duty. Undoubtedly this differs from what he calls natural virtues, motives like benevolence. But it would be absurd to say that the merit of conscientiousness owes nothing to the external performance. It is not even true to say that blame is always withheld from the production of bad results if the motive of the action was a sense of duty; the sense of duty in some people (from Hitler downwards) can lead to an outrageous breach of the rights of other people, and that cannot be condoned by pleading the normal merit of a sense of duty.

The second dubious step in Hume's argument is the brevity of his list of eliminated possibilities for an antecedent natural motive. His example of a just action is the payment of a debt and he considers the possible motives of self-interest, regard for public interest, and private benevolence. He has no difficulty in showing that none of these can serve as a regular natural motive for paying a debt. Are there no other possible candidates for the role of a natural motive for justice? I cannot think of any as a natural motive for paying a debt, but then no one would want to suggest that a system of credit and debt is other than an artificial construction. If, however, we think of criminal justice, we can suggest that resentment of injury and the desire to retaliate form a natural motive antecedent to the notion of just punishment. And even if, like Hume, we confine ourselves to the rights of property, Locke's erroneous argument about the work of one's hands can be made more plausible. A child who has constructed something

---

[18] *Treatise*, III.iii.1 (Selby-Bigge, 579–80).

from materials available to all, a sandcastle for instance, thinks of it as his creation and his possession: seizure by someone else is felt, not only by him but by others generally, to be unfair. Again, children seem to have a naturally arising feeling of unfairness if some are left out in the distribution of desirable things by parents or guardians. The apparently natural sense of what is fair and unfair seems to serve as a foundational motive for some aspects of justice.

A third and final reason for puzzlement with Hume's argument concerns the conclusion. He says that, since there is no antecedent natural motive for paying a debt, the merit must after all lie in the motive of a sense of duty. As for his earlier statement that this would involve reasoning in a circle (the virtue of the action lies in a regard for the virtue of the action), he now says that we can avoid attributing a sophistry to nature if we allow that justice is not natural but arises 'artificially though necessarily' from human conventions. We avoid attributing a sophistry, circular reasoning, to nature. But does the sophistry, the reasoning in a circle, still exist, attributed to (or at any rate the result of) human artifice? If so, is that a satisfactory outcome? Does it not imply that justice is a sham?

Or have we avoided the circular reasoning because the initial premiss was that the merit of a virtuous action must lie in a *natural* motive? But if we no longer insist on that premiss, where do we now think that the merit of justice lies? Hume is going to show later that the rules of justice grow up because they are generally useful, that they are adopted in the first instance for reasons of self-interest, and that this non-moral motive is then seconded by moral approval arising from sympathy with the general interest. How does this stand in relation to the initial argument that justice must be an artificial virtue? Since it is a virtue, its merit must still lie in a motive. The virtuous motive is evidently not self-interest but the later accretion of moral approval for social utility. According to Hume, that is not a natural but an artificial motive, one that arises from human conventions. However, he does say that it arises 'necessarily' and, as we noted earlier, he is ready to say that, once justice is established by convention, the sentiment of morals from sympathy with the public interest comes 'naturally'.[19] So maybe Hume ends up with a moral motive that is artificial but quasi-natural.

It is a tortuous business to reach an interpretation that makes reasonable sense. One cannot help feeling that Hume would have done better to omit the initial argument for the view that justice is an artificial virtue and simply give his account of the way in which the rules of justice arise. This is what he does in the *Enquiry*, where he highlights the thesis that justice depends wholly on social utility. He says in both books that justice (meaning property rights and rules for specifying them) arises from the combination of two factors, one in the character of human beings,

---

[19] See n. 18; and cf. *Treatise*, III.ii.3 (Selby-Bigge, 500): 'Tho' this progress of the sentiments be *natural*, and even necessary . . .'.

a dominant selfishness alongside confined generosity, the other in the natural environment, a relative scarcity of goods to satisfy human desires. If nature had supplied everything that we need or desire, there would be no point in thinking of things as owned by particular individuals, or in being bothered when someone else took what I was about to use or consume; a substitute would always be at hand. Property rights would likewise be otiose if we all loved our neighbours as we love ourselves; we would as a matter of course help others to meet their needs and would treat material things as available for use by all and to be tended as a common resource.

Hume reinforces the general argument with some telling illustrations. A few good things, such as water and air, are so abundant in many places that the idea of private property in them does not arise; but there are circumstances in which water is scarce and so becomes subject to private ownership and a source of strife (Hume refers to a biblical tale of quarrelling about a well in the desert). The effect of an enlarged benevolence can be seen in many a marriage and in the occasional idealistic community where possessions are held in common. The poetic myth of a golden age includes the two hypotheses described in the preceding paragraph, a bounteous nature and unselfish human beings, with the consequence of unalloyed happiness and no need for rules of justice. The philosophic myth of a state of nature reverses the second of these fictions by picturing human beings as utterly selfish, with the consequence of unalloyed misery and no possibility of following rules of justice. A realistic example of that situation befalls a man who encounters brigands and must think only of self-preservation with no regard for the rules of justice. And a realistic example of the reverse of a bounteous nature is provided by a famine, where again the usual rules of justice (meaning ownership) must be disregarded.

So justice is made necessary and possible because of natural scarcity and a dominant (not an absolute) human selfishness. The scarcity can be remedied by co-operation, with a division of labour and mutual aid. A blind selfishness is turned into a rational pursuit of self-interest as people recognize that co-operation is useful for all. It grows up from practices that are obviously useful (such as two men each taking an oar to row a boat) and so become conventional. Such co-operation can relieve scarcity. But it does not eliminate selfishness, which gives rise to another problem, the lack of stability in the possession of material goods. Many material goods can be seized and so pass from the possession of one person to another. Here again a rational form of self-interest recognizes that it would be useful for all if they could agree on rules for stability of possession, that is to say, rules for property, ownership, an exclusive right to use, consume, or retain a thing, as contrasted with mere possession, having it in your hands, perhaps only for the time being. The particular rules for the acquisition of property rights that we find in the law have grown from conventions of different kinds but all aimed at general utility. In some particular instances, following a rule may not be the most useful action possible, but the overall utility of a strict adherence to the whole body of rules outweighs the deficiency that may occur in particular cases; this is endorsed by the moral approval which comes from sympathy with the general interest and which forms a moral obligation to obey the rules.

The first steps in this account are persuasive in giving a socio-psychological explanation of property rights. It is, however, less satisfactory in its treatment of the particular case that goes against utility. The account is supposed to show both that 'public utility is the *sole* origin of justice, and that reflections on the beneficial consequences of this virtue are the *sole* foundation of its merit'.[20] The origin of justice is a matter of speculation, but reflections on the ground of its 'merit' or moral validity are available for anyone to discover in his own thoughts and in the reports of other people. Almost everyone would agree that the rules of justice, taken as a whole, have beneficial consequences. But when a particular instance of a claim of justice runs counter to utility, we do not think that its moral validity would and should be upheld by reflecting on the contribution of justice generally to public utility. A defence in terms of utility is unnecessary and irrelevant. The moral claim of justice stands on its own feet and is thought to be independent of the claim of utility. Hume tells us that this is due to association: the moral value of justice arises from sympathy with the general happiness, but the approval then becomes attached to the rules of justice so that we feel obliged to follow the rules without thought of the ultimate consequences. He assumes that this sense of duty is attached to following a rule as such. But when we are confronted with an instance of justice that runs counter to utility, the claim of justice is not simply one of following a rule; it is usually an idea of something due to one or more individual persons as a matter of prior engagement, or else an idea of fairness as between different individuals or groups.

To illustrate the first of these, let us take Hume's own example in his initial argument for the artificiality of justice: the obligation to repay a loan at a stated time to a creditor who is in no special need, so that one could do more good with a different use of the money. Hume says the reason we would give for paying the debt is a 'regard for justice' or 'honesty'. We can surely say more than that: in borrowing the money the debtor gave an undertaking to the creditor that he would repay the loan at the stated time. The obligation is an obligation *to* a specified individual, set up in a transaction between the two. The reason for repayment is not just a general regard for justice but the personal responsibility of the debtor in having given an undertaking to that specified individual.

Incurring a debt is of course a form of contract, and my criticism of Hume's

---

[20] *Enquiry concerning Morals*, III.i (Beauchamp, 13, §1; Selby-Bigge, §145).

discussion of debt applies also to his account of promises, which in other respects is enlightening. Hume says that promising is a form of words invented for binding oneself to perform an action. Promising is 'in effect' expressing a resolution to perform and subjecting oneself 'to the penalty of never being trusted again in case of failure'.[21] That misses out an essential point. The penalty of not being trusted again is indeed a probable consequence of inveterate failure to keep promises, as it is of inveterate lying, though not necessarily of a single instance of either; and that consequence can be seen as a (self-interested) reason to keep one's word. But it is not the essential reason, the one involved in using the device of promising. As Hume himself has just said, the device of promising has been invented for 'binding' oneself. The bond is an obligation to act but it is also a bond with the person or persons to whom the promise is made. Hume's concentration on consequences overlooks the specific interpersonal character of this sort of obligation. No doubt the system of practices is adopted for its social utility, but the notion of justice involved in the practices is not simply an aspect of that utility; it can act as an alternative value placing a restraint on social utility.

I turn next to acts of justice that run counter to utility on grounds of fairness. In the *Enquiry* Hume refers to the effect of war in replacing the laws of equity and justice, no longer useful, by the laws of war, which are calculated to be useful in those circumstances. He is speaking of relations between the warring parties, but no doubt he would say that the same principle applies to changes in the internal law and policy of a nation at war. Well, here is an example to show that in war, as in peace, justice and utility can conflict and that, while the weight of their respective claims can change, neither is replaced by the other.

In Britain during the Second World War, conscription was introduced but applied with certain exceptions. One was for suspension or postponement of call-up for men in 'reserved occupations', jobs deemed to be essential to the war effort. Unfair but useful. There were other discriminatory measures too, for instance between male students of science and technology and those of the humanities or social studies. The former group were encouraged to complete (shortened) courses and then to choose either to do useful research in industry or to accept a commission in a technical branch of the armed forces, while the latter group were allowed one year of study and were then called up. Unfair but useful. When the war drew to its close, it was necessary to plan a gradual demobilization of the armed forces. One possible policy was to follow the pattern of the reserved occupations scheme and give early release to men with skills needed for urgent tasks of reconstruction, such as building and repairing houses. The alternative, vigorously advocated in Parliament, was a strict adherence to

---

[21] *Treatise*, III.ii.5 (Selby-Bigge, 522).

the principle of 'First in, first out', fairness before utility now that the extreme exigencies of the war had passed. The government reluctantly decided that it must modify that principle with a limited priority for skilled building workers.

It might be said that the policy adopted, both on call-up and on release, illustrates Hume's view that justice is replaced by utility in a war situation. In fact, however, there was still some regard for fairness even in the call-up, for example in allowing humanities students one year of study. As for the policy on demobilization, it would be absurd to say that the increased concern for fairness was a reversion to unreflective, habitual following of a rule that rests on its general utility. 'First in, first out' was explicitly recognized as running counter to social utility and was insisted upon simply as a claim of fairness, all the more compelling because it had given way to an unfair utility earlier. Yet no one denied that utility still had a strong claim.

The claim of fairness sometimes rests on merit, sometimes on equality. I have noted earlier that Hume neglects the role of merit in the concept of justice but does mention briefly the views of idealistic egalitarianism, only to reject them as impractical. There is one other place[22] where he connects justice with equality. He sets out the hypothesis that human beings might be intermingled with a species of creatures who resembled men in being rational but differed in having very little strength so as to be incapable of resistance or of making men feel the effects of their resentment. Hume says that we would be obliged by humanity to treat these creatures gently, but not by justice since justice presupposes society and society presupposes 'a degree of equality'. He draws analogies with the relation of men to animals (those having some degree of reason), with the temptation of Europeans to forget justice and even humanity in their treatment of American Indians, and with the quasi-slavery of women in many societies. The examples are sound sociological evidence of actual behaviour. What is remarkable is Hume's belief that the only sort of equality relevant to justice is equality of strength. It is reminiscent of Hobbes's conception of equality in a state of nature. Hume was himself an exceptionally humane man and would undoubtedly have been moved by humanity 'to give gentle usage' to creatures of inferior strength. But he does seem to have had a blind spot in his sense of justice.

---

[22] *Enquiry concerning Morals*, III.1 (Beauchamp, 18, §§18–19; Selby-Bigge, §152).

Chapter 10

HUME'S CRITICS: KAMES AND REID

Hume's view of justice was criticized by three other notable Scottish philosophers, all of whom nevertheless recognized his pre-eminence as a thinker. Lord Kames and Thomas Reid both attacked Hume's thesis that justice is artificial. Adam Smith said nothing about that but criticized the view that justice depends on utility, clearly having Hume in mind but without naming him.

Henry Home, Lord Kames, a kinsman of Hume, reached distinction as a judge and jurist, and some reputation as a moral philosopher. His *Essays on the Principles of Morality and Natural Religion*, first published in 1751 with a revised second edition in 1758,[1] include a chapter (Essay II, ch. 7) on justice and injustice, designed to refute Hume's view in the *Treatise* that justice is an artificial virtue. Surprisingly for a judge, Kames begins by defining justice almost as narrowly as Hume: 'Justice is that virtue which guards property, and gives authority to covenants.' But perhaps this is simply because his purpose in that chapter is to criticize Hume and so he can confine himself to those aspects of justice discussed by Hume. Earlier references to justice *en passant* in chapter 3 suggest the wider, though vaguer, view that justice is 'abstaining from injury'.

Suppose that Hume had not purported to be giving an account of the virtue of justice, but had simply argued that the concept of property and the rules for assigning rights of property were a product of human convention and in that sense artificial. Would anyone have been much disturbed? I would have thought not, despite Locke's inclusion of property among his natural rights; but evidently I would have been mistaken. Kames accepts without comment Hume's virtual identification of justice with the rights of property and directs

---

[1] *Essays on the Principles of Morality and Natural Religion* (Edinburgh, 1751; 2nd edn., rev., 1758); much of the 2nd edn. version of Essay II is reproduced in L. A. Selby-Bigge (ed.), *British Moralists* (Oxford: Clarendon Press, 1897), ii. §§910–57.

his objection purely to the idea that property is artificial. His argument in the first edition of 1751 follows Locke, but in the second edition of 1758 there is a substantial revision with a quite different main argument.

The argument of 1751 is that the desire for self-preservation leads men to labour in order to convert the scarcity of natural products into convenience and even luxury; but they would labour to no purpose if they did not treat the fruits of labour as belonging to the labourer. Although Kames does not repeat Locke's phrase of 'mixing' the labour of one's body with a part of nature, he echoes Locke's doctrine when he says that we conceive the products of our labour 'to be our own, just as much as we conceive our hands, our feet, and our other members to be our own'. At the same time he also echoes Hume in allowing that, if all the conveniences of life were, 'like air and water', available without labour, or if we were disposed to labour for the public good with no selfish inclinations, 'there would be no sense of property, at least such a sense would be superfluous and unnecessary'.

The second edition of 1758 abandons the Lockean argument and relies instead on an instinct to hoard, a term that was barely mentioned in the first version. Kames had evidently come to think that the case made in that version was inadequate. He may have realized that, while his argument explained why the concept of property was necessary, it failed to justify property that was not the fruit of one's labour or to explain the practice of storing up property beyond necessity. He had said that, so far as we know, the history of mankind has always included private property: 'even before agriculture was invented . . . individuals had their own cattle, and enjoyed the produce of their cattle separately.' In the second edition, however, Kames refers to a stage of society preceding that of herding cattle and sheep, an age of fishing and hunting, in which man 'resembled beasts of prey, who devour instantly what they seize'. In the subsequent age of shepherds, animals are kept 'ready at hand for the sustenance of man'. Then 'this contrivance was succeeded by another', the division of land for cultivation, with the product being stored.

Kames is here making use of the theory that human society has developed through four stages, hunting, shepherding, agriculture, and commerce. He deploys this theory (with especial prominence when discussing the history of property) in his *Historical Law Tracts*, also published in 1758 and no doubt composed in the period intervening between the first and second editions of the *Principles of Morality*.[2] The theory has a major role in Adam Smith's lectures on

---

[2] See Ronald L. Meek, 'Smith, Turgot, and the "Four Stages" Theory', *History of Political Economy*, 3 (1971), 15. Meek then gives reasons for thinking that Adam Smith probably propounded the theory at Edinburgh in or before 1750–1. The revision of Kames's discussion of property in the second edition of *Principles of Morality and Natural Religion* is clearly connected with his having recently written *Historical Law Tracts*; it begins by repeating words used in the third essay, on the history of property, in the *Law Tracts*.

jurisprudence, and Kames may have learned of it from Smith. A feature of the theory is that the institution of property first appeared in the age of shepherds, which implies that it did not exist in the most primitive stage of human society. Furthermore, Kames's description of herding and of the division of land as 'contrivances' appears to concede Hume's thesis that property is an artificial invention.

Nevertheless Kames still wants to maintain that property is natural and he now defends the view by distinguishing between the operations of reason and instinct. He says that the 'improvements' of shepherding and of agriculture were prompted by 'reason and reflection', but nature, as in much else, has not left our preservation entirely to the care of reason, which may be put at risk by neglect or indolence. Nature has endowed man, like some other animals, with a hoarding instinct; but in view of human selfishness, the hoarding instinct in man would fail to achieve its aim of preservation if it were not accompanied by a sense of property.

Kames thinks the existence of a hoarding instinct is so obvious that no one will deny it, though the only evidence he adduces is that everyone is concerned to have a 'competency' and that most people are anxious to increase it 'beyond all bounds', in which case it is known as avarice. This argument lacks any cogency. The common concern to save for a rainy day is surely a product of reasoning from experience rather than a non-rational instinct. Hoarding by human beings is neither. It is an instinct in some animals, but the clearest human example of it is the behaviour of a miser, as Kames himself says, and such behaviour, far from being natural, is regarded as an abnormal obsession.

Kames is more perceptive when he criticizes Hume on promises. He points out that the obligation to keep promises is like the obligation to speak the truth. Both concern human intercourse that necessarily presupposes trust on the one side and fidelity on the other. Neither is an artificial convention. Hume's account of a promise goes wrong in thinking of it only in relation to the person who makes the promise. A promise is an act that involves two persons, an act in which one person intentionally produces reliance upon him by the second person. 'The reliance upon us, produced by our own act, constitutes the obligation'.

Thomas Reid was a close friend of Lord Kames and it is not surprising that the general framework of his criticism of Hume on justice is similar to that of Kames. Reid is far superior to Kames in philosophical ability, but on promises at least he seems to have followed Kames's lead, though indicating a wider philosophical context. His discussion of justice and promises is given in *Essays on the Active Powers of Man* (Essay V, chs. 5 and 6).[3] This work was first pub-

---

[3] Thomas Reid, *Essays on the Active Powers of Man* (Edinburgh, 1788); repr. in *Essays on the Powers of the Human Mind* (Edinburgh, 1808), iii. A modern critical edition is in course of prepa-

lished in 1788, long after Adam Smith's *Theory of Moral Sentiments* (1759), but I shall discuss it before Smith's work because, like Kames's critique, it fastens on Hume's concept of justice as an artificial virtue. Smith's contribution to our subject is in fact not so much concerned with criticism of Hume and is more notable for its positive treatment of criminal justice, a topic strangely neglected by Hume and Reid alike. It therefore merits separate and more extensive treatment later.

Reid at first describes justice in terms of a distinction between a favour and an injury. A favour is a benefit while an injury is a hurt, done intentionally to some other person or persons. A favour naturally produces gratitude, and an injury naturally produces resentment. Justice occupies the space between favour and injury; it is conduct that refrains from doing injury but does not do any favour; it provides what is due, while a favour goes beyond what is due.

This image suggests that justice stands in a similar relation to injury as to favour; it does not do injury or favour but resides passively between the two. In fact, however, that cannot be correct, for Reid goes on to say that justice is 'directly opposed' to injury; he would certainly not have said that justice is *opposed* to doing a favour. When he comes to define justice and injustice, Reid does so in terms of rights and the violation of rights (that is to say, injury): 'injustice is the violation of right, and justice is, to yield to every man what is his right.' So justice is not simply a passive abstention from injury but a positive respect for the rights of others. In one place Reid goes so far as to say that 'justice, I think, as well as charity, requires' that those who cannot fend for themselves should have their necessities supplied from the superfluity of the rich. This gives justice a very positive role and allies it with charity or favour. It is worth noting that Reid does not say explicitly in this sentence that the helpless have a *right* to be helped by the rich. In general, however, his view is that justice is identical with respecting rights, and injustice identical with injury. He says that there are six types of injury corresponding to six classes of rights or 'branches of justice'.

While this account is more satisfactory than the initial description of justice as filling the space between injury and favour, it is still rather loose. The concepts of justice and injustice are not identical or even coextensive with the concepts of rights and injury. An essential element of justice is the notion of fairness and that does not necessarily go along with the idea of a right. For example, many people would say that redistributive taxation to help the poor is fair but would not treat this as meaning that the poor have a right to it; the statement of a right

---

ration as part of *The Edinburgh Edition of Thomas Reid* (Edinburgh University Press), series editor Knud Haakonssen. The most common edition available at present is in Sir William Hamilton (ed.), *The Works of Thomas Reid* (1846 and later reprints), but it is often inaccurate.

seems to go further than fairness. (The wording of Reid's sentence about justice and charity, quoted in the preceding paragraph, suggests that he too might have thought this.) Then again there are some rights, as we shall see shortly, whose moral force is quite independent of the claim of fairness or justice.

Reid's own explanation of justice, therefore, is not particularly clear or helpful. But his classification of rights (or, as he sees it, of the branches of justice) enables him to pinpoint some of the deficiencies of Hume's account. He calls on his knowledge of jurisprudence to list the six respects in which a man may be injured, indicating six branches of justice or rights: safety of one's person, safety of one's family, liberty, reputation, property, fidelity to engagements. The first four rights in his list, he says, are traditionally called natural rights. The last two are different in that they come into being as the result of a preceding act (occupation or labour or transfer in the case of property, promise in the case of engagements) and therefore they are called acquired rights. Reid then notes that, although Hume says all justice is artificial, not natural, his arguments refer only to the last two rights in the list, namely the acquired rights of property and of fidelity to engagements. Reid also proceeds to argue that these acquired rights depend on natural rights and so are not wholly artificial or conventional.

On property Reid accepts Locke's view that the earth was given by God to men for their common use and so every man has a natural right to take for himself, to appropriate, what has not already been appropriated. When a man has appropriated a part of the earth or its products, he has an acquired right to it. Although distinguishable from the original natural right to partake of the common stock, the acquired right depends on the natural one, since the natural right was a right not only to use but also to appropriate for future use a part of the common stock. Property is of two kinds, that which must be consumed soon to maintain life and that which may be stored for future use. As to the first, the natural right to life implies a natural right to the necessary means for life. As to the second, the natural right to liberty implies a right to the fruits of one's labour. However, the right to store up wealth is subordinate to the primary right to life and the necessary means for life. In a family, justice requires that the children and the sick, who cannot fend for themselves, should have necessities supplied from the common stock. By analogy we may infer that in mankind as a whole, the great family of God, justice, as well as charity, requires the poor and the disabled to be supplied with necessities from the superfluity of the rich. The argument implies that the poor and the disabled have a natural right to the necessities, but, as I have noted above, Reid does not say explicitly that they have a right to be helped by the rich; he says only that they 'should' have their necessities supplied.

Reid has shown sound grounds for regarding Hume's account of justice as misleadingly limited: Hume writes as if the whole of justice were artificial, while giving an argument that applies only to a segment, commonly distinguished as acquired rather than natural rights. But Reid's own attempt to link the acquired right of property with natural right begs some questions. It assumes acceptance of a fairly detailed theological dogma, that the natural right to appropriate arises from a divine intention (*a*) to bequeath the earth and its products to all human beings for their sustenance, and (*b*) to allow them untrammelled liberty in what they do with the bequest. The notion of appropriation, that is to say, of acquiring an exclusive right of property or ownership, is what needs to be explained. Hume tried to explain it in terms of human experience. Reid's account in terms of theology leaves it obscure. If God's intention is that all human beings equally should have the means of sustenance, why should he give them the right to pile up for the future more than they need; and if that is because liberty is a great good, how are we to know at what point this good is less valuable in God's sight than the sustenance of life for all? What quality of life is it that has priority over the right to liberty: bare existence, or a tolerable life, or a reasonably happy one? Why should God's parental love for all members of the human family not extend equality of care beyond mere sustenance?

Not that Hume gives us a more satisfactory answer to questions about a conflict of rights, but then he does not aim to do so. His aim is to explain our notion of property rights by reference to normal human experience, and his suggestion does clarify the conditions that surround property rights. Reid thinks that our moral intuitions can be clarified by theological interpretation, but then the theology itself has to be explained by analogy with human experience in a family. This does not add clarity, since the *special* obligations and affections that apply to a family stand in marked contrast to the general obligations owed to mankind as a whole. Reid cannot suppose that God, having implanted that contrast in the human mind, nevertheless intends men to ignore it and to act as if they were just like God himself. The analogy with a family can express an ideal but it cannot serve as an explanation.

It is typical of Reid to think of human experience as a key to natural theology; in this respect his method of philosophizing is bound to seem outdated. It is, however, also typical of Reid to have a keen eye for the nuances of language as indicators of important distinctions of thought; and in this respect his philosophy is remarkably close to present-day methods. The trait is prominent both in his theory of knowledge and in his moral philosophy. An example is provided by his criticism of Hume on promises and contracts. As with property, he wishes to show that the relevant right, though acquired, is not a human invention but depends on divine endowment, and so he invokes natural theology again. But he also makes use of a perceptive observation about language.

Kames had noted the affinity between promise keeping and speaking the truth, and had charged Hume with neglecting the interpersonal character of the obligation in both instances: promising and giving information both presuppose trust. In the case of promising, the crucial factor is reliance: a promise creates an obligation by intentionally causing another person to rely on one's doing what is promised.

Reid makes much the same point but within the context of a more general thesis distinguishing between solitary and social operations of the mind. Solitary operations, such as perceiving, reasoning, willing, do not necessarily imply intercourse with another intelligent being. Social operations, such as asking a question, issuing a command, making a promise, do necessarily imply the participation of another intelligent being. For the former, the use of language (or other signs) is accidental; for the latter, it is essential. Reid notes that philosophers have tended to suppose mistakenly that the social operations of the mind are compounded out of the solitary and can be resolved into them, but in fact the social operations are *sui generis* and as much basic or natural as are the solitary operations.

The next step in his argument is weak. He says that if the social operations were artificial inventions, they would have to be invented by each person for himself since the alternative of teaching them presupposes what we are trying to explain, the existence of social intercourse and some means of communication such as language or natural signs. He overlooks the fact that some practices can be learned by observation and imitation, without being taught; it seems reasonable to suppose that many animals learn useful practices in this way.

Reid does recognize that non-human animals exhibit some forms of social intercourse (including operations of the mind) both with other animals and with human beings. He then adds that such intercourse differs from that of human beings because it does not involve communication by language or other signs. In particular, it cannot include testimony or contractual engagement. A fox is said to use stratagem but cannot lie; a dog is said to show fidelity but (Reid mistakenly argues) this is no more than affection since fidelity is adherence to an engagement. Testimony and engagement both require the use of language: without language there can be neither truth telling nor lying, neither promise keeping nor promise breaking. Both testimony and engagement imply trust or reliance on the one side and fidelity on the other. Communication by language need not be explicitly verbal; it can include the use of natural signs such as the body language that even an infant quickly understands and displays. It is, however, according to Reid, confined to human beings, and this is evidence that it is a special endowment designed by God to serve the good of mankind. We may therefore conclude that the socially useful practices of testimony and engagement, depending as they do on linguistic communication, are part of the divine intention and so natural; they are not artificial inventions devised by men.

Reid's theological assumptions are no more convincing in this piece of argumentation than in his treatment of property. If one is ready to attribute to divine intention all endowments, human or animal, that can serve a useful end, the distinction between natural inheritance and artificial invention disappears. The ability, of men or of chimpanzees, to invent tools can be called God-given and the invented product can be called natural. As Hume said in the *Enquiry*, a dispute about distinguishing the natural and the artificial may become purely verbal.

On the other hand, Reid's distinction between social and solitary operations of the mind, and his remarks about the implications of testimony and engagement, strengthen Kames's criticism of Hume by joining it to Reid's more general criticism of philosophic analysis that starts with the isolated individual.

There is one feature of the discussion of promises by Kames and Reid which they fail to see. If the similarity of promise keeping to speaking the truth shows that promising is not an artificial invention, it also throws doubt on the inclusion of promise keeping within justice. We would not say that lying is unjust; we would say it is wrong or a breach of obligation. And that goes for promise breaking too. Likewise these two classes of wrongdoing show that justice is not coexistensive with rights. It is normal and natural to say that the recipient of a promise has a right that it be kept, and that one who asks a question has a right to be given a truthful answer. Yet we would not say that breaches of these rights are 'unjust'. The moral force of some rights is independent of the concept of justice; and, as I have said earlier, the moral force of the fairness element of justice does not always carry with it the idea of a right.

Kames and Reid overlook these distinctions because their thoughts on justice are affected by their special interest in jurisprudence. Their chief concern, of course, is to refute Hume's view that justice (meaning property rights) is artificial, and since Hume gives a similar account of promises they quite properly extend their refutation to cover promises, though Hume did not say, in the *Treatise*, that the obligations and rights of promises are actually a part of justice. Kames, however, defines justice as covering both property and covenants because he knows that civil lawsuits are largely concerned with the rights of property and contract. Although he compares the keeping of covenants with speaking the truth, he does not treat the latter as an obligation of justice, because it is not a requirement of law; law confines itself to what can be enforced.

Reid was not a practitioner of the law like Kames, but he was well versed in the details of jurisprudence, and the manuscript notes of his lectures on the subject show that he gave much more thought to specific rights than to the concept of justice. In those lectures (which he himself chose not to publish), his account of the concept of justice occupies no more than one printed page. He first defines justice as abstaining from injury and then distinguishes between commutative and distributive justice. The first is described in terms of rights, specified rather more widely than in *Active Powers* since Reid allows justice to be synonymous with 'fair dealing, honesty, integrity'. (We must, however, take the published text of *Active Powers*, composed well after his retirement, to be his most considered opinion.) Having set out his view of commutative justice in a sizeable paragraph, Reid disposes of distributive justice in a single sentence as 'the Justice of a Judge in executing the Laws and distributing Rewards and Punishments'.[4] The brevity of the description, and its apparent suggestion that judges allot rewards as frequently as punishments, add to the impression that Reid had not, at this stage, thought deeply about the concept of justice itself. The two chapters in *Active Powers* are more carefully considered, but even there Reid's preoccupation with rights impedes his analysis of justice.

[4] Thomas Reid, *Practical Ethics*, ed. Knud Haakonssen (Princeton: Princeton University Press, 1990), 139.

Chapter 11

ADAM SMITH

Adam Smith's thoughts on the actual concept of justice are given in his book on moral philosophy, *The Theory of Moral Sentiments*, first published in 1759. The main discussion comes in Part II, which is concerned with the notions of merit and demerit, reward and punishment. Smith relates justice to desert and pays special attention to criminal justice. There is also a brief review of the different senses of the term 'justice' in the last part of the book (VI in editions 1–5, VII in edition 6). The sixth edition, published in 1790, contains a substantial new Part VI on the character of virtue. There Smith specifies four cardinal virtues, one of them being justice, on which he adds just a little to what he had written before.

Smith's more famous book on economics, *The Wealth of Nations* (1776), has a chapter on the expense of justice, meaning the cost of administering the law. There are occasional references elsewhere to justice in the abstract, coupling it with natural liberty but without any detail. A more specific reference to justice occurs in Smith's discussion of taxes, which begins with four general maxims 'of evident justice and utility'. The term 'justice' relates to the first maxim, that the obligation of subjects to pay taxes should be in proportion to their 'abilities', that is, 'the revenue which they respectively enjoy under the protection of the state'. This, says Smith, is what is called 'equality of taxation', meaning equality of sacrifice.[1] There are also occasional references to equity, in connection with wages and with the payment of tolls. On wages Smith says that improvement of the condition of workers is welcome both for serving the general interest and because 'it is but equity' that those who feed, clothe, and house the people as a whole 'should have such a share of the produce of their own labour' as to be tolerably fed, clothed, and housed themselves.[2] On tolls to pay for the upkeep of roads, bridges, and canals, Smith says it is plainly equitable to grade the charges

---

[1] Adam Smith, *An Inquiry into the Nature and Causes of the Wealth of Nations*, ed. R. H. Campbell, A. S. Skinner, and W. B. Todd (Oxford: Clarendon Press, 1976), V.ii.b.3, 7; pp. 825, 827.
[2] Ibid. I.viii.36; p. 96.

according to the weight of vehicles or vessels so as to be proportionate to 'wear and tear'; in these circumstances (but not in others) that method makes for 'a very equal tax'.[3] All these references treat justice or equity as proportionate 'equality', the matching of burdens or benefits to a relevant factor. The relevant factor is not the same for all examples: for taxes it is means, for wages it is merit, for tolls it is the eroding use of resources. There is, however, a common element in all of them, recompense, though there is no mention of this in Smith's words. The taxation of income is a recompense for 'the protection of the state'; the reward of productive labour is a recompense for its benefit to society; the charging of tolls is a recompense for 'wear and tear'.

It is worth noting that the relevant factors do not include need. Istvan Hont and Michael Ignatieff have claimed, in their editorial introduction to an influential book, that 'the *Wealth of Nations* was centrally concerned with the issue of justice, with finding a market mechanism capable of reconciling inequality of property with adequate provision for the excluded'. They take 'the issue of justice' to be an 'antinomy between the needs of the poor and the rights of the rich', a problem of 'reconciling property claims against need claims'.[4] Whatever may be thought of the substance of this interpretation of *The Wealth of Nations*, it is certainly mistaken in supposing that Smith regards the needs of the poor as a claim of justice. As we shall see, he does recognize in the *Moral Sentiments* that the term 'justice' can be used in a wide sense to include a suitable exercise of charity or generosity, but justice in that sense 'comprehends all the social virtues' and ceases to be specific. In his lectures on jurisprudence Smith explicitly repudiates the propriety of saying that the beneficiaries of charity have a right, a claim of justice, to be benefited; he says such a use of the term 'right' is metaphorical.[5]

Adam Smith always intended to write a separate book on jurisprudence. At the end of the original version of the *Moral Sentiments* he describes the project as 'an account of the general principles of law and government' and of their history, taking in not only 'justice' but also 'police [meaning economic policy], revenue, and arms'. In the preface to the sixth edition of the *Moral Sentiments* Smith recalls that passage, saying that he has dealt with police, revenue, and arms in *The Wealth of Nations* and that he still has the desire, though no great expectation, of completing what remains, 'the theory of jurisprudence'.[6] He had

---

[3] Smith, *Wealth of Nations*, V.i.d.4–5, 13; pp. 724–5, 728.

[4] 'Needs and justice in the *Wealth of Nations*: an introductory essay', in Istvan Hont and Michael Ignatieff (eds.), *Wealth and Virtue* (Cambridge: Cambridge University Press, 1983), 2, 42.

[5] See Ch. 6 n. 16 above.

[6] Adam Smith, *The Theory of Moral Sentiments*, ed. D. D. Raphael and A. L. Macfie (Oxford: Clarendon Press, 1976; corrected reprint, 1991; hereafter cited as TMS), VII.iv.37, advertisement 2; pp. 342, 3.

been working on it for some years but it remained uncompleted at the time of his death later in 1790, when the manuscript, along with others, was burned at his request.

We have two reports of Smith's lectures on jurisprudence, as delivered at Glasgow in 1762–3 and 1763–4. Both of them are quite cursory in their definition of justice. The first says that the end of justice is to maintain perfect rights; the second amends the words but not the sense in saying that the end of justice is to secure from injury. Smith then goes on to classify rights, the breach of which constitutes injury, and to discuss the principles of law in detail. The draft of his book on jurisprudence probably had more to say about the actual concept of justice. *The Wealth of Nations* too grew out of the lectures on jurisprudence but is vastly superior to its source in theoretical content and much else. It is likely that the same would have been true of the book on 'the theory of jurisprudence', and the new Part VI added to the *Moral Sentiments* in 1790 seems to imply that the jurisprudence book included a substantial discussion of the concept of justice. One may speculate, drawing on the reports of the lectures, that it might have reflected on relations between justice and liberty, and would have made some use of Smith's notion of the impartial spectator, but there is no warrant for anything definite. Smith's insistence that his manuscript be destroyed suggests that he himself was not satisfied with the result of his efforts.

We must therefore content ourselves with what he wrote in the *Moral Sentiments*. I take first the brief remarks, in the final part of the book, about the different senses of the term 'justice'. The first sense, Smith says, is what had come to be called commutative justice. It consists in abstaining from harm to other people in person, estate, or reputation. This, he adds, is what he has discussed in Part II, where he has said that the observance of justice may be enforced and its violation may be punished. The second sense is called distributive justice by some—though, Smith notes, it is not what Aristotle meant by that term. It consists in 'proper beneficence', doing positive good to those connected with us, in accordance with their merit, or using what is our own for the most suitable purposes of charity or generosity. 'In this sense justice comprehends all the social virtues.' A third, still wider, sense is valuing or pursuing an object with that degree of esteem or ardour that the impartial spectator would think it deserves, as when we speak of doing or failing to do justice to a work of art, or indeed to ourselves in a matter of self-interest. In this sense justice has the same meaning as perfect propriety and comprehends all the virtues, including the two species of justice already described.[7] It is clear that Smith regards commutative justice as the most significant sense of the term.

The new Part VI, added in 1790, discourses at length on three of Smith's car-

---

[7] Ibid. VII.ii.1.10; pp. 269–70.

dinal virtues, prudence, beneficence, and self-command. The fourth, justice, is coupled with beneficence as the two virtues directly concerned with our relationship to other people, but Smith says little about justice in particular. This may be because he had already said quite a lot about justice and less about beneficence in the original version of his book. He excuses himself from saying more about justice in the new part for two reasons. First, the principles of justice 'are the subject of a particular science, of all sciences by far the most important . . . that of natural jurisprudence', and so are not apposite for detailed discussion in 'our present subject'. Secondly, the character of a just man, 'a sacred and religious regard not to hurt or disturb in any respect the happiness of our neighbour . . . is a character sufficiently understood, and requires no further explanation'.[8] The first of these reasons suggests that Smith had dealt with the matter comprehensively in his own projected book on natural jurisprudence. The second confirms the impression that refraining from injury, the topic discussed in Part II, was for Smith the kernel of the concept of justice. I turn now to that.

Adam Smith's ethical theory is outstanding for its treatment of the psychology of morals and especially of moral judgement. Part I of the *Moral Sentiments* gives a psychological account of judgements of right and wrong (Smith uses the terms 'propriety' and 'impropriety'). Part II builds upon this in giving an account of judgements of merit and demerit.

According to Smith, the basic form of a moral judgement is one made by a spectator. The judgement that an action of another person is right reflects the spectator's sympathy with the agent's motive. Smith uses the term 'sympathy' in a wide sense. He notes in the first place that, although 'sympathy' is often confined to pity, it can mean fellow feeling of any kind. He explains judgements of right and wrong as the effect of imagining yourself in the situation of the agent. If you find that you would be motivated to act as the real agent does, you may be said to sympathize with his motive and you express this by approval of his action. If you find that you would be motivated differently, you may be said to feel antipathy and you express this by disapproval of the action. Smith goes on later, in Part III, to say that moral judgements about one's own actions are the result of imagining oneself as a spectator of those actions and realizing, from the experience of judging the actions of others, what an impartial spectator would think.

Meanwhile, however, in Part II, he proceeds from the initial sense of propriety to the sense of merit and demerit, still taking the basic moral judgement to be that made by a spectator on the actions of other people. A judgement of merit or demerit reflects a double feeling of sympathy or antipathy, one for the motive

---

[8] Smith, *The Theory of Moral Sentiments*, VI.ii.intro. 2; p. 218.

and one for the consequences of an action. If Bob Cratchit from the kindness of his heart takes a poor waif home to dinner, the waif feels gratitude for the benefit. A normal spectator, imagining himself in Bob's shoes, sympathizes with Bob's motive and so approves of the action as right. He can also imagine himself in the shoes of the waif and sympathizes with the waif's gratitude. The effect of adding the second form of sympathy is a judgement that the action has merit or deserves reward. This judgement is not a reflection of the second form alone, sympathy with the gratitude of the beneficiary: the spectator must also think the action right, that is, he must sympathize with the motive of the agent. If the waif were Oliver Twist and were taken home for dinner by Fagin in order to make a thief of him, a spectator would not judge the action to have merit, even though Oliver would feel grateful for the dinner and the spectator might well sympathize with that. A judgement of merit is the effect of sympathy with gratitude for an action that is also right. A judgement of demerit has for its object an action that is wrong and that has harmful consequences inducing resentment. If the waif had appealed to Scrooge instead of Cratchit, Scrooge would have said 'Bah, humbug!' and might have slapped the waif for impudence, making the waif feel resentment. A spectator would feel antipathy to Scrooge's callousness and sympathy with the waif's resentment. The double reaction would evoke a judgement that Scrooge's action had demerit, that is, was worthy of punishment.

Having devoted the first section of Part II to 'the sense of merit and demerit', Smith spends most of the second section on the related topic of justice, beginning with a contrast between justice and beneficence. Since he ends with a sustained criticism of a utilitarian view of justice, undoubtedly having Hume in mind, one might have expected his contrast between justice and beneficence to include some comment on Hume's contrast between justice and benevolence. It will be recalled that in the *Treatise* Hume held that justice is an artificial and benevolence a natural virtue, while in the *Enquiry* he held that benevolence is partly and justice is wholly dependent on utility. Smith in fact says nothing about these two distinctions. Instead he contrasts justice as enforceable with beneficence as 'free', that is, not liable to being imposed by force. This is because he wants to concentrate on criminal justice and punishment. He is influenced here by Kames rather than Hume. Kames had criticized Hutcheson for neglecting the concepts of justice and duty and the related notions of punishment and remorse. He had gone on to say that justice, being a matter of strict duty, 'is considered as less free than generosity'.[9]

Smith's emphasis on criminal justice is welcome after the neglect of this topic by both Hutcheson and Hume, but he can be criticized in his turn for neglecting

---

[9] *Essays on the Principles of Morality and Natural Religion*, I.ii.4 (1st edn., p. 71).

to take thought of equity or fairness in his account of justice. At the start of his discussion he relates both justice and beneficence to the preceding topic of merit and demerit by noting that merit, the deserving of reward, applies to actions of a beneficent tendency and motive, while demerit, the deserving of punishment, applies to actions of a harmful tendency and motive. He should have acknowledged, as he does in *The Wealth of Nations*, that the rewarding of merit is deemed to be equitable, so that this, as well as the punishing of demerit, is an aspect of justice.

However, the account of justice that he does give has its own typical merit of perceptive psychological explanation. According to Smith, the psychological basis of the impulse to reward is gratitude and the spectator's sympathy with gratitude; the psychological basis of the impulse to punish is resentment and the spectator's sympathy with that. A failure to be beneficent may evoke dislike and disapprobation, but since it does no positive harm it does not normally cause resentment.

Resentment seems to have been given us by nature for defence, and for defence only. It is the safeguard of justice and the security of innocence. It prompts us to beat off the mischief which is attempted to be done to us, and to retaliate that which is already done; that the offender may be made to repent of his injustice, and that others, through fear of the like punishment, may be terrified from being guilty of the like offence.[10]

This psychological reaction is the foundation of the retributive character of punishment. Interestingly enough, Smith's statement of a natural *lex talionis* recognizes that it applies to merit as much as demerit, despite his failure to note earlier that equity, and therefore justice, covers the merit of beneficence as well as the demerit of injury.

As every man doth, so shall it be done to him, and retaliation seems to be the great law which is dictated to us by Nature. Beneficence and generosity we think due to the generous and beneficent. . . . The violator of the laws of justice ought to be made to feel himself that evil which he has done to another.[11]

Few philosophers have stated explicitly that the notion of retributive justice applies to reward as well as punishment.[12] We think of retaliation as striking back and forget that the involved principle of *justice* is the neutral concept of requital, paying back in kind, whether good or ill. The etymological meaning of the Latin word *talio*, derived from *talis*, is simply 'like for like', but the term was

---

[10] TMS II.ii.1.4; p. 79.   [11] Ibid. II.ii.1.10; p. 82.

[12] Two who have are Henry Sidgwick, *The Methods of Ethics*, 7th edn. (London: Macmillan, 1907), 282, and E. F. Carritt, *Ethical and Political Thinking* (Oxford: Clarendon Press, 1947), 99–100.

commandeered for use in the law with the more specific meaning of like punishment for like harm. This is because, as Smith says, the enforcement of law is used for the restraint of harm and not for the promotion of benefit. And the difference in our practice follows the example of nature (as Smith would put it) in that resentment tends to be more forceful than gratitude, no doubt because the preservation of life is more threatened by harm than enhanced by benefit.

Smith goes on to attribute the sense of fair play to our consciousness of the reaction of spectators. Nature implants in everyone an initial preference for himself and his own interests, but because he can see the behaviour of others and, with the capacity of imagination, can see himself as others see him, he knows that to a spectator he is no better than anyone else. Hence he understands that, in 'the race' for the good things of life, he must keep to the rules if he wants to have the good will of spectators, as we all do. They will sympathize with his natural self-love if he simply exerts himself to win by running faster than competitors.

But if he should justle, or throw down any of them, the indulgence of the spectators is entirely at an end. It is a violation of fair play, which they cannot admit of. This man is to them, in every respect, as good as he: they do not enter into that self-love by which he prefers himself so much to this other, and cannot go along with the motive from which he hurt him. They readily, therefore, sympathize with the natural resentment of the injured, and the offender becomes the object of their hatred and indignation. He is sensible that he becomes so, and feels that those sentiments are ready to burst out from all sides against him.[13]

The idea of fair play or impartiality is an element of the concept of justice, and Smith sees this, on less than the idea of just retribution, as an aspect of the sense of merit and demerit founded upon the reaction of spectators. He explains in the same way the claim of retributive justice that the degree of punishment should match the degree of injury: it is because the sympathy of spectators matches the degree of resentment felt by the victim (or by his kin if the victim has been killed or is an infant). The reaction of spectators is also the initial stimulus to shame and remorse on the part of the offender. He fears their hostility and the punishment that it calls for. In reflecting on the reason for it, he too exercises his imagination, puts himself in their shoes, and finds that he 'sympathizes' with their attitude. He shares, in a sense of shame, their judgement that his action was wrong, their grief for its effects, and their pity for its victims. The combination of shame with the fear of hostility and punishment constitutes the sense of remorse.

Having given his psychological explanation of the justice of punishment,

[13] TMS II.ii.2.1; p. 83.

Smith turns to the alternative view that it arises from the thought of utility. He accepts that both justice and beneficence are in fact socially useful, and he adds that justice is indeed quite essential to the maintenance of society while beneficence is not. A society could carry on, as the community of merchants does, from a dispassionate awareness of its utility and without any feelings of mutual love or affection; but no society could subsist without justice, that is, a general abstention from injury. That is why nature has given us especially strong feelings about ill desert and merited punishment to enforce conformity to justice.

Smith suggests that a utilitarian explanation of punishment is an example of a common mistake, the supposition that useful consequences of human actions must have been intended and that this intention was the cause of bringing them about. He considers the distinction between efficient and final causes. Throughout biological phenomena we see means adjusted to ends 'with the nicest artifice' and we 'admire how every thing is contrived for advancing the two great purposes of nature, the support of the individual, and the propagation of the species'.[14] But we do not suppose that the processes which lead to the beneficial consequences have the purpose or intention of producing those consequences. We do not, for example, suppose that blood circulates of its own volition with the purpose or intention of keeping the organism alive. To do so would be like supposing that the spring and wheels of a watch, in causing its hands to move and show the time, have the desire or intention to do so. We distinguish the efficient cause of a beneficial effect from the final (purposeful) cause. In the case of artefacts like the watch, where we know that the final cause was the intention of a watchmaker, there is no possibility of confusing efficient and final causes. In the case of processes in natural bodies, although we do not have direct knowledge of a purposeful designer, we still do not fail to distinguish efficient and final causes. But in accounting for operations of the mind, we are apt to conflate the two. When we are led by natural feelings to do things which are useful, and which on that account *would* be recommended by 'a refined and enlightened reason', we are apt to suppose that our feelings and actions have had such teleological reasoning as their efficient cause. We 'imagine that to be the wisdom of man, which in reality is the wisdom of God. Upon a superficial view . . . the system of human nature seems to be more simple and agreeable when all its different operations are in this manner derived from a single principle.' Smith presumably has in mind philosophical theories that explain all human behaviour in terms of beneficial consequences, either for oneself alone (Epicureanism) or for society at large (utilitarianism).

His criticism of a utilitarian theory of punishment is that the thought of harmful consequences is neither the original nor the common ground of our

---

[14] TMS II.ii.3.5; p. 87.

sense of criminal justice. 'All men, even the most stupid and unthinking, abhor fraud, perfidy, and injustice, and delight to see them punished. But few men have reflected upon the necessity of justice to the existence of society, how obvious soever that necessity may appear to be.'[15] Smith agrees that thoughts of utility may be used to reinforce the original sentiment. When a criminal comes to face his punishment, humane people may find pity replacing resentment, and then consideration of the general interest can help them to balance this partial humanity against a more comprehensive humanity. Or if 'the young and the licentious' ridicule the rules of morality, their questioning implies a rejection of the normal and natural grounds for conformity, so we cast around for other arguments and find the most obvious one in the social disorder that would result if everyone followed what these rebels profess.

A modern utilitarian would not be convinced by these arguments. He would say that the common feelings of 'all men', including 'the most stupid and unthinking', do not afford a rational ground for accepting a practice that manifestly needs justification because in itself it is evil, inflicting pain or deprivation of freedom. Since punishment, and other aspects of common morality, can be questioned, by the young or anyone else who is not blinded by convention, and since the most obvious answer to the challenge is to show the utility of the system, then utility is a more satisfactory ground than natural feelings.

However, Smith follows up his general argument with two specific considerations that cannot be so easily put aside. The first is the concern of justice for the individual, which does not depend on a concern for the happiness of society as a whole. Smith compares concern for the injury done to an individual with concern for the loss of a single guinea. Neither of these concerns depends on the fact that the individual person or coin is part of a larger whole. If we sue for having been cheated of a small sum, our concern is for that sum, not for our whole fortune; and if we demand the punishment of a wrongdoer for injury to an individual, our concern is for that individual, not for society.

Smith writes of what is owed to the individual as a victim of crime, but his argument is not wholly convincing, because crime is prosecuted as an offence against the state, not as an injury to the victim; if the latter is to be dealt with by law, it has to be in a civil action for damages, not a criminal action for punishment. Smith seeks to explain the 'origin' of justice and punishment, and by that term he means both the originating cause and the justifying ground. On originating cause he makes a thoroughly convincing case against utilitarianism. But when he writes about our concern for the individual, he has in mind justifying grounds, and on that score he leaves a loophole for disagreement. His argument refers to the practice and concepts of a developed system of criminal law, and his

---

[15] Ibid. II.ii.3.9; p. 89.

appeal to what 'we', ordinary members of the public, demand of punishment overlooks the formal stance of the law.

His point about the concern of justice for the individual can be made about civil lawsuits. When someone is sued for fraud, the concern of the plaintiff is for the particular sum of money, as Smith says; but he could also have said that the aim of justice is to vindicate the claim of the individual, not the interest or stability of society. The point can also be made about the criminal law if we think, not of the injury to a victim, but of the rights of the person accused in a criminal trial. There are circumstances in which social utility would permit or even require the conviction and punishment of an accused person who appears, from circumstantial evidence, to be guilty but who is in fact innocent; the punishment can act as a deterrent to potential perpetrators of like crimes if they, like others, are persuaded by the circumstantial evidence. But no one would say that utility makes the conviction and punishment just. Justice stands out for the rights of the innocent individual despite the claim of social utility. Jurisdictions that sincerely pursue justice take great pains to protect the rights of an accused person irrespective of social utility. Hence the maxim: 'It is better that ten guilty persons escape than one innocent suffer.'[16]

The second specific consideration that Smith brings up is even more telling, though Smith does not give (in the *Moral Sentiments*) the full force of it. He notes that there are some exceptional instances where the infliction and the approval of punishment do depend purely on social utility, and he argues that the exceptions prove the rule because our attitude is clearly different in the exceptional and in the normal instance. As an example of the exceptions he cites the case of a sentinel in the army who was put to death for falling asleep at his post. It was a real-life case, which evidently impressed Smith by the conflicting feelings that it aroused in him as a typical spectator. He refers to it not only in the *Moral Sentiments* but also in an earlier manuscript of a lecture on justice that happens to have been preserved, and again in the lectures on jurisprudence that he delivered after the publication of the *Moral Sentiments*. A crime like that of the sentinel, Smith said, does not directly harm any individual, but it is thought to be actually or potentially harmful to the whole society (in this case, the army). The severity of the punishment may 'appear necessary, and, for that reason, just and proper. When the preservation of an individual is inconsistent with the safety of a multitude, nothing can be more just than that the many should be preferred to the one.' Yet, despite the necessity, the punishment 'always appears to be excessively severe'. 'The natural atrocity of the crime seems to be so little, and the punishment so great, that it is with great difficulty that our heart can reconcile itself to it.' The punishment does not fit the crime in

---

[16] Sir William Blackstone, *Commentaries on the Laws of England*, 1.7.

terms of desert. 'A man of humanity' has to make an effort to approve of it. Not so when he hears of a similar punishment for 'an ungrateful murderer or parricide'. Then he readily applauds the 'just retaliation'.

The very different sentiments with which the spectator views those different punishments, is a proof that his approbation of the one is far from being founded upon the same principles with that of the other. He looks upon the centinel as an unfortunate victim, who, indeed, must, and ought to be, devoted to the safety of numbers, but whom still, in his heart, he would be glad to save; and he is only sorry, that the interest of the many should oppose it. But if the murderer should escape from punishment, it would excite his highest indignation, and he would call upon God to avenge, in another world, that crime which the injustice of mankind had neglected to chastise upon earth.[17]

Smith has conceded too much to the utilitarian in saying that 'nothing can be more just' than preferring the many to the one in sacrificing the life of the one to secure the safety of the many. The military law is deemed to be *justified*, to be right, on the ground of its utility for the safety of the many; but that does not mean it is *just*, except in the wide sense of justice, which, Smith tells us in Part VII, covers all the virtues and so is more or less synonymous with what is right. That is not the essential sense of justice as a particular virtue discussed in Part II.

The ambiguity of Smith's position is exposed in the earlier manuscript lecture on justice. There too he makes the concession to utilitarianism: 'Nothing can be more just, than that one man should be sacrificed to the security of thousands.' But towards the end of the lecture he adds something which is inconsistent with that: 'Improper punishment, punishment which is either not due at all or which exceeds the demerit of the Crime, is an injury to the Criminal . . .'.[18] Now since, as the *Moral Sentiments* puts it, the punishment of the sentinel 'appears to be excessively severe' because 'the natural atrocity of the crime seems to be so little, and the punishment so great', it is punishment 'which exceeds the demerit of the crime' and is therefore 'an injury to the criminal'. An injury is a breach of justice. So it cannot be true to say that 'nothing can be more just' than the death penalty for the erring sentinel. The conviction is just, since the sentinel's negligence is a breach of military law; but the penalty is unjust, since its severity exceeds the demerit of the crime. One can still claim that the severe penalty is necessary if it is to be effective as a deterrent, and that the requirements of utility are great enough to override the injustice, but *unjust* it remains. The sentinel is an 'unfortunate victim' who must be 'devoted to the safety of numbers'.

---

[17] TMS II.ii.3.11; pp. 90–1.   [18] Ibid. appendix ii, pp. 389, 394.

When Smith worked up his lectures into the book, published in 1759, he omitted the sentence about improper punishment, no doubt having seen the inconsistency. Did he decide that the sentence was untrue, or was he unsure how to resolve the inconsistency? In the student report of his subsequent lectures on jurisprudence, as delivered in 1762–3, Smith seems to evince some doubt about the propriety, let alone the justice, of the death penalty for the sentinel:

> the military laws punish a centinell who falls asleep upon guard with death. This is intirely founded on the consideration of the publick good; and tho we may perhaps approve of the sacrificing one person for the safety of a few, yet such a punishment when it is inflicted affects us in a very different manner from that of a cruel murtherer or other atrocious criminall.

The substitution of 'a few' for 'a multitude' probably goes along with the doubt of 'we may perhaps approve'. The report of the lectures given in 1763–4 reverts to the earlier view, but also (if it is not a reporter's error) substitutes a graver offence, so that the penalty is less shocking: 'if a centinel be put to death for leaving his post, tho' the punishment be just and the injury that might have ensued be very great, yet mankind can never enter into this punishment as if he had been a thief or a robber.'[19]

In both reports of the lectures on jurisprudence, Smith precedes the example of the sentinel with another, which furnishes a more obvious difficulty for the utilitarian case. Because wool was considered the main source of national wealth in England, a statute in the reign of Charles II prohibited the export of wool on pain of death.

That which Grotius and other writers commonly alledge as the originall measure of punishments, viz the consideration of the publick good, will not sufficiently account for the constitution of punishments. So far, say they, as publick utility requires, so far we consent to the punishment of the criminall, and that this is the naturall intention of all punishments. But we will find the case to be otherwise. . . . in those crimes which are punished chiefly from a view to the publick good the punishment enacted by law and that which we can readily enter into is very different. Thus some years ago the British nation took a fancy (a very whimsicall one indeed) that the wealth and strength of the nation depended entirely on the flourishing of their woolen trade, and that this could not prosper if the exportation of wool was permitted. To prevent this it was enacted that the exportation of wool should be punished with death. This exportation was no crime at all, in naturall equity, and was very far from deserving so high a punishment in the eyes of the people; they therefore found that while this was

---

[19] Adam Smith, *Lectures on Jurisprudence*, ed. R. L. Meek, D. D. Raphael, and P. G. Stein (Oxford: Clarendon Press, 1978; hereafter cited as LJ), LJ(A), ii.92, LJ(B), 182; pp. 105, 475–6. Cf. TMS, appendix ii. pp. 394–5.

the punishment they could get neither jury nor informers. No one would consent to the punishment of a thing in itself so innocent by so high a penalty.[20]

In this instance the thought of social utility was clearly overridden by the idea of justice or 'natural equity'. All in all, Smith shows himself an acute critic of utilitarianism.

[20] LJ(A), ii.90–2; pp. 104–5. Cf. LJ(B), 182, p. 475.

Chapter 12

J. S. MILL

Adam Smith perceived that the concept of justice raises a difficulty for a utilitarian theory of ethics. The difficulty was recognized and tackled by leading utilitarians of the nineteenth century, but not by the initial standard-bearer of the doctrine, Jeremy Bentham. His various accounts of utilitarianism as a theory say little about the concept of justice. *An Introduction to the Principles of Morals and Legislation* (1789) refers briefly to justice in a footnote about the notion of 'the votaries of religion' that the dictates of justice 'modify' (meaning 'oppose', says Bentham) the dictates of benevolence. He dismisses this notion as a fiction and simply declares that the dictates of justice are a part of the dictates of benevolence, 'which, on certain occasions, are applied to certain subjects'.[1] *Deontology* (composed 1814–19) is more explicit. Its first reference to justice recalls the note in the *Principles* with similar brevity but less vagueness: 'Considered as exercised under particular circumstances, beneficence assumes the name of "justice". . . . "Justice" is the name given to beneficence, in so far as the exercise of it is regarded as matter of obligation.'[2] This statement is taken up in a subsequent short section that is specifically about justice but does not add much of substance. There Bentham distinguishes the legal and the moral senses of the term and then repeats his view that justice is 'but a modification of benevolence' connected with obligation: 'the dictates of justice may have place in respect of any act in so far as it is considered as being the subject of obligation.'[3]

In two versions of an 'Article on Utilitarianism' (composed in 1829) Bentham quotes with approval a line of Horace which says that utility is virtually the mother of justice and equity. Bentham apparently assumes that its truth is evident without argument. The longer of the two versions does include, in a

---

[1] Jeremy Bentham, *An Introduction to the Principles of Morals and Legislation*, ch. 10, §40, note b2; ed. J. H. Burns and H. L. A. Hart (London: Athlone Press, 1970), 120.
[2] Bentham, *Deontology*, I.2; ed. Amnon Goldworth (Oxford: Clarendon Press, 1983), 127.
[3] I.19; p. 221.

different context, a convoluted passage[4] saying that, if the rules or maxims of justice coincide with precepts emanating from the principle of utility, they may be regarded as conforming, and being subordinate, to that principle. It does not mention the possibility that a maxim of justice may fail to coincide with the precepts of utility.

Such brief and cloudy remarks seem to suggest that Bentham did not pay close attention to the concept of justice, but Dr P. J. Kelly has claimed in a recent book[5] that the conclusion is mistaken. He agrees that Bentham has nothing of substance to say about justice in works that expound the theory of utilitarianism, but he goes on to show that Bentham's writings on civil law (much of them in unpublished manuscripts) operate with a detailed conception of distributive justice, summed up in two principles, the 'security-providing principle' protecting settled rights, and the 'disappointment-preventing principle' guiding reform by balancing the claim of established rights against the claim of subsistence and equality for the underdog. For my own part, however, I have not been able to discern, in the maze of detail, any clear concept of justice as a whole, and the fact remains that Bentham did not face up to the difficulty that justice poses for utilitarianism. I must therefore pass him by and turn to the more accessible work of his champion, John Stuart Mill.

Mill's essay *Utilitarianism* (first published in 1861) gives a firm exposition of the doctrine, supports it with such 'proof' as is possible, and defends it against objections. The principal objection is considered in the final chapter 5, entitled 'On the Connexion between Justice and Utility'. The chapter begins and ends with words showing the crucial importance that Mill rightly attached to this topic. The first sentence says that the idea of justice has always been 'one of the strongest obstacles' to the view that utility is the criterion of right and wrong. The last paragraph goes further; it claims that Mill's discussion has resolved 'the only real difficulty in the utilitarian theory of morals'.

The discussion begins with the common contrast between justice and expediency. According to Mill, this is a matter of 'subjective feeling' and goes along with a recognition that 'objectively' the dictates of justice contribute to general utility. In order to explain the special feeling that attends the idea of justice, he sets out to analyse it. He considers whether all the classes of action and situation called just and unjust have a common attribute or set of attributes. He lists six classes of things that fall under the concept of justice.

First, there are *legal rights*; it is just to respect them and unjust to violate them. Secondly, there are *moral rights*; certain laws may be considered unjust,

---

[4] 'Article on Utilitarianism: Long Version', §50; in *Deontology*, ed. Goldworth, 308.
[5] *Utilitarianism and Distributive Justice: Jeremy Bentham and the Civil Law* (Oxford: Clarendon Press, 1990).

on the ground that they infringe somebody's right, and since this right is not a legal right it is called a moral right. The third species of justice is the requital of *desert*, returning good for good and evil for evil. The fourth concerns *keeping faith*, that is to say, the fulfilment of engagements, 'either express or implied'. Mill adds 'or implied' so as to include not only promises and debts but also any act of deliberately raising expectations of benefits. The fifth species is *impartiality* in situations where showing favour or preference would be improper, as in the exercise of a public office; Mill says it comes down to 'being exclusively influenced by the considerations which it is supposed ought to influence the particular case in hand'. Allied to this notion is *equality*, the sixth species, which often enters into the concept and practice of justice, 'and, in the eyes of many persons, constitutes its essence', though there are marked differences of opinion about the scope and kind of equality that justice requires.

I have already said, in Chapter 7, that Mill is mistaken in supposing that the idea of justice is commonly applied to keeping promises (or, more generally, keeping faith). In normal parlance we speak of promises and other engagements as giving rise to an obligation and a right, but not as a requirement of justice; failure to perform is described as wrong and a breach of obligation, but not as unjust. As we have seen, Mill is not the only philosopher to include promise keeping within the concept of justice: apart from Hobbes, who identified the two, Kames and Reid treated the keeping of promises as a matter of justice because it involves a right. Mill too may have thought that anything which involves a right is thereby a constituent of justice, but that is not true, as I noted at the end of my discussion of Kames and Reid.[6]

This one questionable feature of Mill's lists does not greatly affect the later course of his argument. He says that, although the elements of justice, set out in his list, are diverse, the concept of justice is not regarded as ambiguous, from which it would seem that the different elements have some common character or link, but it is difficult to see what that is. His survey of the six classes of things has brought out a couple of limited affinities: the first two classes share the idea of a right; the last two are akin to each other in barring discrimination. But there is no clearly apparent feature that is shared by all six.

Mill turns for help to etymology, a reasonable move since the history of words is likely to reflect something of the history of their meaning. Unfortunately, however, his attempt to learn from etymology is far from persuasive. The first version of his account was excessively simplistic, and it seems that he was criticized on this score, since the second edition of the essay (1864) introduced some qualifications, but they hardly mend matters. One gets the impression that Mill had made up his mind with the simplistic reasoning of the

---

[6] Ch. 10 above.

J. S. MILL

original version and did not take in the full force of the criticisms. In the version given below I have placed angle brackets around passages that were added in the second edition, and square brackets around words and passages that were deleted in that edition.

In most, if not in all, languages, the etymology of the word which corresponds to Just, points [distinctly] to an origin connected [with the ordinances of law] <either with positive law, or with that which was in most cases the primitive form of law—authoritative custom>. *Justum* is a form of *jussum*, that which has been ordered. <*Jus* is of the same origin.> Δίκαιον comes [directly] from δίκη, <of which the principal meaning, at least in the historical ages of Greece, was> a suit at law. <Originally, indeed, it meant only the mode or *manner* of doing things, but it early came to mean the *prescribed* manner; that which the recognised authorities, patriarchal, judicial, or political, would enforce.> *Recht*, from which came *right* and *righteous*, is synonymous with law. <The original meaning indeed of *recht* did not point to law, but to physical straightness; as *wrong* and its Latin equivalents meant twisted or *tortuous*; and from this it is argued that right did not originally mean law, but on the contrary law meant right. But however this may be, the fact that *recht* and *droit* became restricted in their meaning to positive law, although much which is not required by law is equally necessary to moral straightness or rectitude, is as significant of the original character of moral ideas as if the derivation had been the reverse way.> The courts of justice, the administration of justice, are the courts and the administration of law. *La justice*, in French, is the established term for judicature. [I am not committing the fallacy imputed with some show of truth to Horne Tooke, of assuming that a word must still continue to mean what it originally meant. Etymology is slight evidence of what the idea now signified is, but the very best evidence of how it sprang up.] There can, I think, be no doubt that the *idée mère*, the primitive element, in the formation of the notion of justice, was conformity to law. It constituted the entire idea among the Hebrews, up to the birth of Christianity.[7]

Mill's initial statement about Latin, that *justum* is a form of *jussum*, must have been challenged by a critic who pointed out that *justum* is derived from *jus*; and so Mill tried to defend himself by adding in the second edition that *jus* had the same origin. But he is mistaken. *Justum* and *jus* have nothing to do with the verb *jubeo* ('I command'), to which *jussum* belongs as a past participle passive. Philologists tell us that *jus* comes from a Sanskrit root meaning 'join' or 'bind', illustrated also in the verb *jungo* ('I join'), so that the idea originally signified was that of a bond. (So far as *jubeo* is concerned, philologists have suggested the virtual converse of what Mill says, namely that it is derived from *jus habeo*, 'I have the right', but they do not pretend to any confidence on that matter.) Mill

---

[7] J. S. Mill, *Utilitarianism*, ch. 5; in *Essays on Ethics, Religion and Society, Collected Works of John Stuart Mill*, ed. F. E. L. Priestley and J. M. Robson, x (Toronto: University of Toronto Press; London: Routledge & Kegan Paul, 1969) 244–5.

is better informed in his expanded remarks on the Greek word δίκη (*dike*), but of course they go against his initial assumption, and his general argument, that the original meaning had to do with law.

His statements about German usage are off the mark since the noun *Recht* and the adjective *recht* are not commonly used for 'justice' and 'just'. As he observes, the German term is related to the English 'right' and the Latin *rectus*, all of which had the original meaning of 'straight', leading his critics to say that the use of *Recht* for 'law' depended on an earlier meaning of 'right'. Mill's reply fails to achieve anything. It is simply not true to say, as he does, that *recht*, and likewise the French term *droit*, 'became restricted in their meaning to positive law'; and even if it were true, that would not be 'significant of the *original* character of moral ideas'. The subsequent sentences about the use of the term 'justice' in English and French to refer to the legal system simply indicate one sense of the word but do nothing to clarify etymology.

The final sentence in my quotation asserts that conformity to law 'constituted the entire idea' of justice in the Old Testament. In this instance Mill says nothing, and presumably knew nothing, about the relevant language. He is merely repeating a popular idea about the general character of Old Testament ethics. In Chapter 2 of this book I have discussed in detail the conception of justice in the Old Testament. It will suffice to recall here that the most prominent word for justice, *tzedek*, is essentially ethical and serves as a criterion for assessing the moral validity of legal decisions no less than of personal conduct. A second word that is often used for justice, *mishpat*, does have the original meaning of judgement by a court but it, too, is used normatively to mean a morally sound judgement. I said in Chapter 2 that the word no doubt began with a purely descriptive meaning, but there is little trace of this in the actual usage of even early parts of the Bible. One could almost reverse Mill's assertion and say that the idea of judge-made law in the Old Testament requires conformity to the moral notion of justice. That would not apply to statute-law (*hok* or *hukkah*, 'inscribed' law) which is not represented either as determining or as being determined by the concept of justice. (I should perhaps add that the word *torah*, the comprehensive title of the Five Books of Moses, commonly translated as 'the Law', means a pointing-out, and so instruction or doctrine, not law in any literal sense.) While one cannot expect Mill to have known these linguistic facts about the Hebrew text, a reasonable acquaintance with the Bible in translation should have led him to query, if not to discard, his sweeping generalization.

Mill knew more about Greece and Rome than about the Bible. Despite the supposed conclusion of his etymological inquiry, he goes on to say that nations other than the Hebrews, and particularly the Greeks and the Romans, knew that laws were man-made and could be bad; so they 'were not afraid to admit' that the men who made bad laws might do 'by law' actions which, 'if done by individuals without the sanction of law, would be called unjust'. He apparently does not realize that people who 'admitted' this could not *mean* by 'unjust' that which is contrary to law. He says that in consequence 'the sentiment of justice' came to be restricted to breaches of only 'such laws as *ought* to exist, including such as ought to exist but do not; and to laws themselves, if supposed to be contrary to what ought to be law'. That frame of mind surely suggests that 'the sentiment of justice' does not depend on law. Mill, however, fails to see it, blinded by his dogged preconception of the *idée mère* of justice. 'In this manner the idea of law and of its injunctions was still predominant in the notion of justice, even when the laws actually in force ceased to be accepted as the standard of it.'

He goes on to allow that the concept of justice is applied to many things which are not, and which nobody wants to be, regulated by law. Yet he insists that even then an association with law remains. How so? 'It would always give us pleasure, and chime in with our feelings of fitness, that acts which we deem unjust should be punished, though we do not always think it expedient that this should be done by the tribunals.' That does not seem to me a universal accompaniment of the concept of justice. Quite apart from the gratuitous suggestion that punishment would 'always give us pleasure' (all of us?), the 'fitness' of punishment applies only to some unjust acts. Even in the sphere of law, punishment is not thought apt for injustice in civil suits, such as breaches of the rights of an individual; the fitting response there is restitution or the reparation of damage. Punishment is reserved for criminal acts of wrongdoing, not all of which may be characterized by the notion of injustice anyway. In connecting justice with law. Mill has evidently fixed his attention on the criminal law and has forgotten the civil law. Why should we suppose that a central feature of the criminal law is the source or a key element of the concept of justice in matters that are not regulated by any form of law?

Mill's slipshod train of thought soon leads him into a blind alley for a different reason. His connection of justice with punishment applies only to unjust acts, and so he widens the thought to enforcement, in order to cover positively just acts as well. 'We should be glad to see just conduct enforced and injustice repressed. . . . When we think that a person is bound in justice to do a thing, it is an ordinary form of language to say, that he ought to be compelled to do it.' If that is a natural form of language to use, is it because the person is bound *in justice* or simply because he is *bound*? So far as Mill's own utilitarian theory is concerned, the answer is the second alternative.

Mill's theory is to be gleaned from the preceding chapters of *Utilitarianism* taken together with the final chapter of an earlier work, *A System of Logic*. That chapter gives Mill's view of the place of morality among the practical 'arts'. (It also shows, more clearly than *Utilitarianism*, that he regarded the language of ethics as being cast in the imperative mood.) For Mill, the criterion of moral action is not utility alone. The sphere of morality is the sphere of duty or right and wrong, and should be distinguished from the wider sphere of the good or desirable, of which it is one species among others. The good or desirable is always happiness, and the doctrine of utilitarianism, which commends happiness as the sole ultimate end, embraces more than morality. It covers 'the Art of Life, in its three departments, Morality, Prudence or Policy, and Æsthetics; the Right, the Expedient, and the Beautiful or Noble, in human conduct and works'.[8] Virtues that go beyond the requirements of strict duty are assigned by Mill to the category of aesthetics ('the beautiful or noble') and not to the category of morality.

Morality, then, is a species of the good or desirable, and justice is a subspecies of morality. Throughout the category of morality we speak of duties or obligations, of right and wrong, of what ought and ought not to be done. These words are all more forceful than the value terms that we are ready to use in the categories of prudence and aesthetics. They are more forceful, not simply in expressing our wishes and feelings with greater emphasis, but in expressing a desire that force might be applied, if necessary, to produce compliant conduct. In short, morality for Mill is that class of actions which we should wish to see enforced by the sanction of punishment for breaches.

But then that is precisely what Mill has come to offer as the essence of justice after discussing the origin and development of that concept. He realizes this himself and observes that he has not yet distinguished justice from moral obligation in general. The idea of desiring enforcement and the sanction of punishment attends the notions of duty, obligation, and wrong action. It is indeed 'the characteristic difference which marks off, not only justice, but morality in general, from the remaining provinces of Expediency and Worthiness'. He must still find the character that differentiates justice from the rest of morality.

He thinks it can be found by attending to the distinction drawn by philosophers and jurists between duties of perfect obligation and duties of imperfect obligation. The former are strictly specified in respect of time and of individuals affected by the action; the latter leave the agent free to choose the occasions of performance and the particular persons who are to be the object of his action. When there is a duty of perfect obligation there is also a correlative right for the person or persons to whom the duty is owed. With a duty of imperfect obligation there is no correlative right. Mill does not like the 'ill-chosen expressions,

---

[8] *A System of Logic*, VI.12.6; in *Collected Works*, viii (1974), 949. This section of the chapter was rewritten for the 3rd edn. of the work (1851). The 1st and 2nd edns. (1843 and 1846) do not contain the passage I have quoted. They do, however, contain, in the opening section of the chapter, an explicit statement that moral judgements are expressed 'in the imperative mood, or in periphrases equivalent to it'. The 1851 version of §6 says that the propositions of Art, as contrasted with those of Science, 'enjoin or recommend that something should be'.

duties of perfect and of imperfect obligation'; he thinks that the presence or absence of a correlative right is a clearer mark of distinction, and so he concludes that 'this feature in the case—a right in some person, correlative to the moral obligation—constitutes the specific difference between justice and generosity or beneficence'. He calls the right a moral right, and so he makes justice coextensive with moral rights, despite his earlier classification of moral rights as only one of six categories to which the term 'justice' is applied. He now claims that in the earlier survey 'the term appeared generally to involve the idea of a personal right' similar to the proprietary rights conferred by law, and he indicates briefly how this applies to the other five categories. If you deprive someone of a possession (breach of *legal right*), or *break faith* with him, or treat him worse than he *deserves*, or worse than other people with no better claim (breach of *impartiality* or *equality*), you do 'a wrong' to 'some assignable person', which Mill takes to mean that you breach a moral right.

It seems to me that the most significant feature of Mill's conception of a moral right and of his distinction between justice and the rest of morality is his emphasis on *individual persons*. Justice, he says, involves 'the idea of a personal right—a claim on the part of one or more individuals'; injustice implies 'a wrong done, and some assignable person who is wronged'; justice implies something that 'some individual person can claim from us as his moral right'; by contrast, there is no moral right to generosity or beneficence, because 'we are not morally bound to practise those virtues towards any given individual'. Mill states the conclusion of his analysis as a recognition that 'the two essential ingredients in the sentiment of justice are, the desire to punish a person who has done harm, and the knowledge or belief that there is some definite individual or individuals to whom harm has been done'. In what follows, however, Mill neglects or forgets this emphasis on the individual; instead he thinks of the second ingredient simply as a constituent of the idea of a right.

Having completed his analysis of justice, Mill proceeds to explain the origin of the two ingredients and their relation to utility. He tells us that the desire to punish arises out of the natural impulse 'to resent, and to repel or retaliate' harm that is done to us or to those near and dear to us. This natural sentiment is moralized when it is directed by social sympathy towards the interest of society instead of being confined to our own narrow interest. As for the second ingredient, Mill does not explain why justice highlights the claim of the individual; he simply concentrates on the notion of a right and says that it is an especially important element of utility, the vital interest of security. Because it is vital, its defence is regarded as a special obligation of society as a whole and as having a 'character of absoluteness', making it feel different from 'ordinary expediency'.

When he comes to apply this account to the various manifestations of justice, Mill runs into some difficulties because one cannot assimilate the whole of justice to the right of protection from harm. Mill has to say that the injustice of breaking a promise, and of ingratitude or failing to reward good desert, consists in disappointing a reasonable expectation, that such disappointing is a form of harming, and that it stirs resentment comparable with the resentment caused by direct injury. When he had listed keeping faith as a category of justice, he had said that this included 'implied' engagements, in which expectations are raised 'knowingly and voluntarily'; but that does not cover the justice of rewarding good desert or the obligation to show gratitude and to return good for good. If someone has found a wallet and restores it to the owner, he deserves reward and may perhaps expect it (though he is more likely to hope rather than expect), but there is no question of the owner having knowingly and voluntarily raised such an expectation—unless the owner has advertised a reward, in which case there is the obligation of a promise, not one of simply recognizing merit. A utilitarian would do better to say that the justice of rewarding merit depends on the social utility of encouraging virtuous (themselves especially useful) actions; it strains credibility to say that the justice depends on avoiding the harm of disappointed expectation. Likewise an expectation of gratitude is not something that has been raised by any deliberate action of the person who has been benefited and is expected to be grateful and reciprocate the benefit. The benefactor may think that his *own* action entitles him to expect gratitude and perhaps reciprocal benefit some time, though we would not normally think of this as an instance of justice and might hesitate even to speak of a right.

In all these situations the difficulty for a utilitarian theory of ethics is that the obligation depends on the past, not the future. A utilitarian may reply that the general practice has arisen and is commended because of its utility for the general interest. The pain of disappointed expectation is of course a part of the total sum of pleasures and pains that make up the general interest, but it is a very minor part. I suppose Mill fastens upon it in order to show a connection with the rights of the individuals who are affected by the actions concerned. We should, however, recall his contention that rights are connected with utility by being vital interests of security. It is ridiculous to suggest that the expectation of reward or gratitude for doing good is a vital interest of security.

When Mill comes to the last pair of his six categories of justice, impartiality and equality, he faces a different sort of difficulty. The obligation here arises, not from some particular past action, but from a timeless general principle. Mill's explanation is complex. In the first place he says, fairly enough, that impartiality is required of judges as a necessary condition for fulfilling the other obligations of justice; in other words, judicial impartiality is enjoined because of its utility. But Mill recognizes that the general obligation of impartiality and equality is of much wider application than that, and so he suggests, secondly, that it is a special case of requiting desert, equal treatment for equal desert. The suggestion presupposes that, if we do not know of any differences in desert, we should assume that there are none. That is a curious assumption, since it runs counter to common experience. We may indeed think that it is *unfair* to treat people as if being of different desert when we do not know what their deserts are; but then that implies that equal treatment, in the absence of known reasons for discrimination, is fair on its own account, not on account of a pretence which we know to be false. Be that as it may, Mill does not rest satisfied with this suggestion and proceeds to a third ground, 'a still deeper foundation', namely that the principle of equality is 'a direct emanation from the first principle of morals'.

It is involved in the very meaning of Utility, or the Greatest-Happiness Principle. That principle is a mere form of words without rational signification, unless one person's happiness, supposed equal in degree (with the proper allowance made for kind), is counted for exactly as much as another's. Those conditions being supplied, Bentham's dictum, 'everybody to count for one, nobody for more than one,' might be written under the principle of utility as an explanatory commentary.

At this point Mill adds a note about a criticism voiced by Herbert Spencer that 'the principle of utility presupposes the anterior principle, that everybody has an equal right to happiness'. Mill replies that the second proposition is more correctly stated as 'supposing that equal amounts of happiness are equally desirable' and that it is not a presupposition of the principle of utility 'but the very principle itself', since the principle of utility treats 'happiness' and 'desirable' as synonymous terms.

In chapter 2 of his essay Mill says that 'Utility, or the Greatest Happiness Principle, holds that actions are right in proportion as they tend to promote happiness, wrong as they tend to produce the reverse of happiness.' This refers purely to the production of happiness, not to its distribution. We may assume, however, that Mill intends to support Bentham's view that actions are right if and because they produce the greatest (possible) happiness for the greatest (possible) number. That criterion includes two principles, one 'aggregative',[9] referring to the total amount of happiness produced, the other 'distributive', referring to the way in which that happiness is shared among different people. When Bentham said 'everybody to count for one, nobody for more than one', he was interpreting the distributive principle: if an action is to be right, the maximum happiness it produces should be shared in equal amounts by as many people as possible. That is a principle of justice (as understood by egalitarians). When Bentham incorporates it into his criterion of right action, he is adding a principle of distribution to one of aggregation.

---

[9] The term 'aggregative', in correlation with 'distributive', to express this distinction, was first suggested by Brian Barry, *Political Argument* (London: Routledge & Kegan Paul, 1965), ch. 3.

Herbert Spencer's formulation in terms of everyone having an equal *right* brings out the character of the distributive principle as one of justice. We need not follow Spencer in saying it is a presupposed anterior principle, but we cannot follow Mill in saying that it is the same as (or a part of?) the principle of maximizing happiness. It certainly is not, as Mill contends, the tautologous statement that 'equal amounts of happiness are equally desirable' (tautologous because, according to Mill, it treats 'happiness' and 'desirable' as synonymous). It does not make sense to question a tautologous statement, and nobody would in fact wish to question this particular statement even if regarding it as a truism rather than a tautology. On the other hand, it does make sense to ask whether everybody has an equal right to happiness, and some people would deny it or at least ask for reasons to accept it.

Mill himself appears not to be an egalitarian. He says that one person's happiness counts for as much as another's *if* it is 'supposed equal in degree (with the proper allowance made for kind)'. Mill has told us in chapter 2 what he means by a difference of kind. Some pleasures are of higher quality than others, and some people are more capable than others of experiencing the higher pleasures; the happiness of which Socrates is capable is superior in kind to the happiness of an easily satisfied fool. In our present passage, the qualifying phrase, 'with the proper allowance made for kind', implies that the fool's right to happiness is not equal to that of Socrates.

If the distributive principle is understood in its natural sense of egalitarian justice, which is surely what Bentham meant by 'everybody to count for one, nobody for more than one', it presents a difficulty for utilitarianism because it can conflict with the aggregative principle. Such a conflict is common in social and political affairs. I gave a real-life example in Chapter 9 of this book, where I recalled the administration of conscription and demobilization in Britain during the Second World War. Discrimination in favour of men with useful skills was thought desirable on grounds of the general interest but repugnant on grounds of egalitarian fairness. Utility was held to be undoubtedly paramount for the call-up, but for demobilization egalitarian fairness was thought to have a preponderant (though not an absolute) claim. This example is helpful here because the claim of justice was clearly one of equal treatment for everyone concerned. In other circumstances the claim of justice may depend rather on desert or on need (I think that the claim of need is at root egalitarian but that is not obvious).

Such conflicts present a practical problem irrespective of ethical theory; and every theory that aims to elucidate the standard of right action has to consider whether it can offer guidance for dealing with the conflicts. The theory of utilitarianism claims to be superior to its rivals in providing a single basic criterion of right action, a principle which underlies all the rules of common-sense morality and which can therefore be used to decide conflicts that may arise between two or more of those rules. If, however, utilitarianism has two basic principles, not one, and if those two basic principles can at times conflict with each other, the theory has not lived up to its pretensions. Conflicts between utility and justice are among the most striking of moral dilemmas, and that is why the concept of justice has been 'one of the strongest obstacles' to the acceptance of the theory of utilitarianism.

In differentiating justice from the rest of morality in terms of rights, Mill pointedly described those rights as claims of particular or 'assignable' individuals. Adam Smith, as we saw in Chapter 11, observed that a claim of justice may be especially concerned with an individual as contrasted with a concern for the general interest. This feature of the concept of justice has been neglected by most theorists, and Mill is to be commended for fastening upon it. Unfortunately, however, he does not grasp its full significance, as we may see from his ensuing explanation of the two 'ingredients' of justice.

Quite early in his explanation, having stated that the desire to punish arises from the desire for vengeance and is then moralized by sympathy with the interest of society as a whole, Mill considers and rebuts an objection: 'It is no objection against this doctrine to say, that when we feel our sentiment of justice outraged, we are not thinking of society at large, or of any collective interest, but only of the individual case.' The objection is precisely the one put by Adam Smith and it is possible that Mill had that in mind. But his reply fails to see the point. He supposes that 'the individual case' must be the objector's *own* individual case. 'It is common enough', he says, to feel resentment for oneself, but a person who has that feeling does not have a concern for justice 'if he is regarding the act solely as it affects him individually'; he must 'feel that he is asserting a rule which is for the benefit of others as well as for his own'.

This is thoroughly perverse. The force of the objection does not lie in thinking of 'the individual case' as one's own case; that would cut little ice. The moral force lies in thinking of our neighbour, or of someone in the news, or of a character in history such as Socrates, Jeanne d'Arc, or Captain Dreyfus, individual victims of injustice for the sake of social or national expediency. In speaking of injustice we are affirming the claims of an innocent individual against the general interest of the society. Of course we are appealing to a rule 'which is for the benefit of others' as well as for our own. The point of the objection is that the rule insists on the benefit of those others as *individuals*, in contrast to the general benefit of society at large.

This does not mean that there is a total opposition between justice and utility. As Mill claims at the beginning of his chapter, most people will allow that in general justice coincides with 'a part of the field of General Expediency'. Yet it remains true that justice and utility can and do conflict at times. When they do, the principles of justice proclaim the rights of the individual. Mill's analysis of the concept of justice led him to see this, but the heritage of utilitarianism blinkered his perception and caused him to miss the significance of his own insight.

Chapter 13

HENRY SIDGWICK

Sidgwick's book, *The Methods of Ethics*, first published in 1874, is the most comprehensive and the best-argued version of classical utilitarianism. Its discussion of justice is a little disappointing because it does not face the special difficulty that justice poses for utilitarianism. Nevertheless its admirable analysis of the concept marks a clear advance on earlier treatments.

Before proceeding to details of Sidgwick's account of justice, I shall say something of the general plan of the book. What does Sidgwick mean by the *methods* of ethics? He writes of three methods, egoist, intuitionist, and utilitarian. You could say that they are three theories of ethics, three different accounts of moral judgement. Egoism says that actions are properly judged to be right for their contribution to the interest of the agent. Intuitionism says that the judgement of an action as right does not depend on some other consideration; it stands on its own ground as a direct awareness. Utilitarianism says that a proper judgement depends on the contribution of the action to the general interest. Why does Sidgwick not write of them as theories? Because they have a practical as well as a theoretical purpose. They are not simply positive explanations, under a unifying formula, of what moral judgements have in common; they are also normative justifications that serve to recommend the formula as a guide to resolve practical dilemmas. Each of the theories describes a method of thinking that tends to take place without deliberate design, and also prescribes it for deliberate use when we are uncertain.

Sidgwick believes that all three methods are rational but not to the same degree. He presents an argument to persuade the Egoist that a rational regard for one's own happiness (Egoistic Hedonism) implies that one should have the same regard for the happiness of all (Universalistic Hedonism, that is, Utilitarianism). As for Intuitionism, he distinguishes three forms of it, Perceptional, Dogmatic, and Philosophical Intuitionism. They are given in ascending order of rationality, and the limitations of the first two should lead to acceptance of the third. According to Sidgwick, Philosophical Intuitionism is identical with his version of Utilitarianism.

The argument addressed to the Egoist runs like this. The Egoist regards his own happiness as a good and can understand from this that everyone else is in the same boat. Hence we must allow that, 'from the point of view of the Universe', the good of any one individual is no more important than that of any other;[1] if the happiness of one person is a good, the happiness of every person is a good. Egoistic Hedonism can thus lead to Universalistic Hedonism. However, as C. D. Broad observed,[2] the argument is unlikely to cut much ice with the Egoist, who can reply that he is not the Universe and sees no reason why he should adopt the Universe's point of view (whatever that might mean) instead of the natural point of view of an individual.

The argument addressed to the Intuitionist is more worthy of attention. Perceptional Intuitionism, the most primitive form, holds that we just 'perceive' what is right in each individual instance. This is hardly a theory at all, since it does not bring the plurality of the data under any unifying principle or principles. Yet some indications of the view can be found in reputable philosophers: Aristotle, for example, says more than once that, for ascertaining what is right in particular cases, 'the judgement is in the perception'.[3] Bishop Butler says that, while 'men of leisure' may seek a general rule for distinguishing good actions from bad, 'any plain honest man' simply has to ask himself, before he acts, whether his proposed action is right or wrong, good or evil, and he can give a true answer 'in almost any circumstance'.[4] We cannot, however, rest satisfied with that. Even in a trite particular situation we can always give a reason for judging that an action is right or wrong: it is right because it is helping someone in need; it is wrong because it breaks a promise. So Perceptional Intuitionism has to be abandoned in favour of Dogmatic Intuitionism, the view that actions are right in virtue of exemplifying one of several self-evident principles.

The term 'dogmatic' seems tendentious, especially since Sidgwick thinks that this view gives an accurate account of the morality of common sense. He calls it dogmatic because it is too easily satisfied with its several principles. Their boundaries are not clear and they can conflict with each other. We should therefore question their alleged self-evidence. Truly self-evident principles are perfectly clear and are consistent with each other. Examining the various principles of the morality of common sense, Sidgwick finds that some are not self-evident and that others owe their self-evidence to simple tautology and so lack substance. He also finds, like others before him, that much of the force of common principles depends on utility. He ends up with just three very general principles

---

[1] Henry Sidgwick, *The Methods of Ethics*, 7th edn. (London: Macmillan, 1907), 382.
[2] C. D. Broad, *Five Types of Ethical Theory* (London: Kegan Paul, 1930), 244–5.
[3] Aristotle, *Nicomachean Ethics*, 1109^{b}23, 1126^{b}4.
[4] Joseph Butler, *Fifteen Sermons*, III (D. D. Raphael, *British Moralists 1650–1800*, §405).

that he thinks are really self-evident, the principles of prudence, benevolence, and equity. They prescribe the pursuit of maximum happiness for oneself, the pursuit of maximum happiness for others, and an equal regard for every person. This is his version of Utilitarianism or Philosophical Intuitionism.

It is philosophical because it accepts principles as self-evident only after critical examination. It is intuitionist because the principles are substantial truths about right and good that are directly apprehended by reason. Sidgwick thinks that a viable ethical theory must rest on intuited truths; ultimate principles about value cannot be derived, as J. S. Mill supposed, from empirically observed facts such as the fact that everyone desires his own happiness.

A further notable feature of Sidgwick's theory concerns the utility of the less general principles to which common-sense morality appeals. Again differing from Mill, Sidgwick does not think that these principles have been reached from a conscious recognition of their utility. He knows very well that common-sense thinking treats the different virtues and their principles of action as having a moral force independent of the social utility that may or may not attend them. Sidgwick proposes a hypothesis of 'unconscious utilitarianism': the principles and virtues have come to be followed and praised because they are in fact generally useful, but this has not been deliberately worked out, like a process of legislation; it has been an unconscious process of evolution, the character of which can now be discerned by critical thought. In this respect too, Sidgwick's version of utilitarianism is philosophical. It also conforms to his view that a worthy theory of ethics should have a practical as well as an explanatory function: the recognition that morality has been unconsciously utilitarian enables us to recommend utilitarian criteria for further development.

In his critical examination of Dogmatic Intuitionism, Sidgwick analyses the virtues that make up the morality of common sense, one of them being justice. His analysis of common-sense thinking about justice (Book III, ch. 5) is patient and scrupulously unprejudiced. He notes first that justice in the law has a wider and a narrower sense. The wider sense identifies justice with the system of law as a whole, while the narrower sense refers to the objective that law aims to protect and promote. This narrower or specific meaning is fairly close to the ethical concept of justice.

Proceeding to describe the specific concept, Sidgwick highlights its concern with individuals: justice in the law deals with the distribution to individuals of benefits and burdens (including the burdens of reparation for harm and punishment for crime). And what are the features that go to make such distribution just? First, equality. Justice requires laws to be administered impartially, showing no 'respect for persons', no discrimination for or against particular persons because of wealth, status, or any other 'arbitrary' reason.

This is not as clear as one would wish. Sidgwick himself observes that, in the private conduct of individuals, arbitrary discrimination is not necessarily considered unjust even though it could be called 'unreasonable and capricious'.[5] He tries to clarify the idea by specifying claims that justify departures from equality. They are the claims of contract and similar 'binding engagements'. Sidgwick then considers how far the latter phrase extends. He is inclined to say it includes 'all such expectations (of services, etc.) as arise naturally and normally out of the relations, voluntary or involuntary, in which we stand towards other human beings'.[6] Sidgwick recognizes that this account is disturbingly indefinite for a virtue that is supposed to be firm and exact, but adds that it is a fact of life. There are undoubtedly some situations in which the rejection of a person's natural expectations is considered unjust, and others in which it seems harsh to require the maintenance of a custom from someone who has given no pledge to follow it. Sidgwick illustrates the uncertainty of common-sense attitudes with an example: 'if a poor man were to leave one tradesman and deal with another because the first had turned Quaker, we should hardly call it an act of injustice, however unreasonable we might think it: but if a rich country gentleman were to act similarly towards a poor neighbour, many persons would say that it was unjust persecution.'[7]

Reflecting further on the notion of natural expectations, Sidgwick observes that its ambiguity is worse than its indefiniteness. The term 'natural' can mean what is common or what is primitive or what is ideal. The last two senses are often coalesced in the belief that the ideal is what God established originally. If we dismiss that belief as myth, we see more clearly the distinction and the contrast between two prominent features of the notion of justice: we think of the customary distribution of benefits and burdens as just, but we also think of a different pattern of distribution as ideally just. Hence we expect the law to protect customary rights and to reinstate them if breached, and yet we also seek reform of the existing system in the name of justice. Sidgwick describes the two conceptions as Conservative and Ideal Justice. Conservative Justice protects the claims of contract and (imprecisely) of normal expectations. The latter include the expectation that laws will be upheld, and therefore Conservative Justice serves to maintain the whole of existing law, even though some parts of it may be considered unjust in terms of Ideal Justice. 'It is the reconciliation between these two views which is the chief problem of political Justice.'[8]

Sidgwick's distinction between conservative and ideal justice is a very helpful contribution towards understanding the complexity of our notions of justice. Although I do not consciously remember having done so, I must have derived from him the distinction that I myself drew between conservative and prosthetic

---

[5] Sidgwick, *Methods*, 268 n.   [6] Ibid. 269.   [7] Ibid. 270.   [8] Ibid. 273.

(or reformative) justice.[9] Sidgwick's account of conservative justice is particularly enlightening on the functions of the law. His analysis of ideal justice is somewhat limited.

He notes that there have been different views of an ideal distribution of benefits and burdens. One widely held view has been that the law should grant and protect Natural Rights for all. There is little agreement about the precise content or the foundation of natural rights, but, so he says, there has been strong support for the view that all natural rights may be summed up in the right to freedom from interference. Ideal justice, then, would be equality of freedom for all.

Sidgwick finds several difficulties in this suggestion. First, it implies that no one should be coerced simply for his own good, but we must surely except children and insane persons from such a rule; and since in their case we give their own good priority over their freedom, should we perhaps do the same for sane adults who are not well equipped to judge or pursue their own good? Hence some thinkers have said that the rule does not apply to peoples that are not highly civilized. So it seems, after all, that the rule is not truly self-evident and basic but is subordinate to the wider principle of promoting the happiness of mankind.

Second, freedom from interference is ambiguous. If interference is restricted to action, the rule will not cover annoyance, which can at times be intolerable. Yet to include all forms of annoyance would restrict the freedom of others beyond measure. To find a reasonable balance we must weigh up pleasures and pains, again subordinating the rule of freedom to a more general utilitarian principle.

Third, a right to freedom must include a right to limit one's own freedom by contract, and since contracts are legally enforceable we get the paradoxical consequence of freedom leading to unfreedom, even allowing a person to contract himself out of freedom into slavery.

Fourth, the right to freedom is commonly thought to include a right to property, but how? A right to freedom from interference clearly forbids interference with the present active use of material things. Does it forbid interference with the possibility of future use, that is, does it protect property as such? If so, does that not limit the freedom of another potential user? If you say that he has the right to appropriate a similar thing for his own use, he may not be able to find something else that suits his purpose.

So the right to equal freedom from interference is unclear and cannot cover

---

[9] 'Conservative and Prosthetic Justice', *Political Studies*, 12 (1964); *Problems of Political Philosophy* (London: Pall Mall, 1970), ch. 7 (ch. 5 in 2nd rev. edn., London: Macmillan, 1990); *Moral Philosophy* (Oxford: Oxford University Press, 1981; 2nd enlarged edn., 1994), ch. 7.

all natural rights. Furthermore, it does not exhaust the common notion of ideal justice, which affects the distribution of other benefits and of burdens too. Nor is it self-evident and fundamental: it admits of exceptions and can lead to self-contradiction; and when we try to account for some of these weaknesses, we find that we have to appeal to utility as a more basic principle. Sidgwick therefore concludes that this first suggestion for the content of ideal justice must be rejected.

It is surprising that he should have taken this suggestion seriously in the first place. One can understand that some people may think ideal justice is constituted by natural rights, but why should they suppose it is constituted simply by freedom from interference? Common-sense thought treats the ideas of justice and liberty as distinct from each other and at times liable to conflict. Sidgwick says that the unification of natural rights under freedom from interference has been held by 'influential thinkers' and, 'though now perhaps somewhat antiquated, is still sufficiently current to deserve careful examination'.[10]

I suppose he has in mind an interpretation of Locke's idea of natural rights. Locke lists three: life, liberty, and estate. The right to life is primarily a right not to be killed. I suggested at the end of Chapter 6 that Locke might have taken it to include the right to be given positive help if one were threatened with starvation; but certainly the main, if not the sole, thought in Locke's mind was the negative notion of not being killed. One can reasonably regard this as a form of freedom from interference. Locke's natural right to 'estate' is intended to justify the acquisition of property, and the rights of property cover more than freedom from interference with possession and use, but that is undoubtedly a cardinal feature of it. The natural right that replaces 'estate' in the American Declaration of Independence, the pursuit of happiness, is more obviously a right to non-interference. So it is not unreasonable to say that Locke's natural rights of life, liberty, and estate, and Jefferson's addition of the pursuit of happiness, are all rights to liberty, freedom from interference by other people. Even so, that is a slipshod way of reaching the conclusion that equal freedom from interference constitutes justice; Locke himself would have been surprised to hear it.

A little later in his chapter, Sidgwick reverts to freedom as a candidate for the substance of ideal justice, though it is a different aspect of liberty, as we shall see. Meanwhile, however, he has rejected the first suggestion that ideal justice is the right to non-interference.

He proposes instead that the basic principle of ideal justice is the requital of desert, a universalization of the feelings of gratitude for benefit and resentment of harm. He distinguishes this from two concepts that are sometimes incor-

---

[10] Sidgwick, *Methods*, 274.

rectly associated with desert. The first is the reparation of harm, which Sidgwick seems to think is required simply by the duty of benevolence. (I would say it is required by conservative justice, repairing unwarranted damage to the existing order of things.) The second is something which Sidgwick calls fitness and which he illustrates by the Aristotelian precept of distributing instruments to those who can best use them, and, more generally, of distributing functions to those who are most fitted to perform them. This apparent element of justice is more usually described in terms of talent. The distribution of benefits and responsibilities in accordance with talent is indeed different from distribution according to desert, but Sidgwick does not explain why they are often treated as similar. I have given the reason in discussing Aristotle, who writes of distribution according to 'worth', a term that can cover both desert and talent. One does not in fact often find talent equated with *desert* but it is often subsumed under 'merit', which can cover both earned and unearned worth. Sidgwick does note, quite rightly, that the value of talent is given recognition for reasons of utility.

He then proceeds to review the various uncertainties and perplexities that arise in practice for the requital of desert. The concept of desert, both good and ill, presupposes freedom of choice; but part of our knowledge and experience, and for that matter some aspects of our moral thought, induce doubt about the existence of free will. Then, accepting the presumption of free will, is the degree of desert to be estimated from effort or results? If results, it is not actual results that count but what the agent had in mind; and on that score, does merit depend simply on intention (what results he aimed to achieve) or does it depend also, or instead, on motive (what feeling, desire, or thought prompted him)?

Then, assuming we have managed to estimate the degree of desert, what is the criterion for determining a 'fair' requital? So far as a fair price for services is concerned, in practice we often follow custom or analogy from custom; but if we take custom to be the test of fairness, Sidgwick says, we are reverting to conservative justice, while what we are after just now is the character of ideal justice. A less wooden but still practical criterion is the 'market value', the price that is acceptable to both the supplier and the receiver of the service. It is at this point that Sidgwick introduces again the idea of freedom. Market value is determined by the free choice of participants in conditions of competition. A society that aimed at maximum liberty would take market value to be the universal criterion for the remuneration of services; so that even if freedom is not the first principle of ideal justice, it is the best means to achieve justice understood as the requital of desert. Free choice in conditions of competition is not quite the same as freedom from interference in doing what you choose to do, but they are connected: both are called freedom because there is an absence of constraint.

Sidgwick goes on to show that the market value method of valuing work has its difficulties. Most people know little of the nature and effects of important services, so their judgement distorts market value away from true value. In individual instances the ignorance of one party about 'the real utility' of what he buys or sells places him at an unfair disadvantage, even though we would not stigmatize the other party as unjust for profiting from his superior knowledge. Common sense finds itself in a quandary about the equity or justice of such a situation, and Sidgwick concludes that economic considerations afford no help in the analysis of justice. It is to be noted that here, as elsewhere, 'true' answers, as Sidgwick conceives of them, have reference to utility,

The alternative to using market value is to try to determine the 'intrinsic value' of work by 'enlightened and competent judges',[11] but this, Sidgwick recognizes, is easier said than done. Is the value of a service to be matched with the amount of happiness it produces? If so, apart from the general difficulty of calculating the amount of happiness, how are we to compare the enjoyment of necessities with that of luxuries? We are more conscious of the enjoyment that luxuries afford but we could not have them if we did not have the necessities. Then again, when an enterprise depends on the co-operation of different kinds of labour, how are we to compare the value of the various skills, design with production, general supervision with execution of detail, discovery with application?

Having outlined these problems and uncertainties about requiting desert, Sidgwick concludes that analysis of the common-sense concept of justice is of no help towards solving them. The pursuit of ideal justice is impossible. All we can do in practice is to look to utility, asking what reward will procure a service and whether the social benefit of the service outweighs the cost of the reward.

Sidgwick calls the free market interpretation of ideal justice the 'Individualistic Ideal' and the alternative view the 'Socialistic Ideal'. The point of the adjective 'individualistic' is clear enough: free market choices are made by individuals. It is not so clear why the alternative view should be called socialistic. The determination of the degree of merit and of its reward is to be made by 'enlightened and competent judges' on behalf of the society as a whole, but that in itself is not socialist. After all, in dealing with socially harmful behaviour in the form of crime, the degree of demerit and of its punishment is determined in all but primitive societies by judges, but we do not call the system socialist on that account. It is possible that Sidgwick is thinking of the socialist dictum of distributive justice, 'to each according to his work', which no doubt assumes that the work is to be valued for its contribution to the general interest and not for meeting the needs of the individual.

It is unfortunate that Sidgwick did not pay more attention to the penal sys-

---

[11] Sidgwick, *Methods*, 289.

tem, for he might then have seen that the concept of desert in the notion of justice does have a realistic role in practice and cannot be wholly replaced by utility. He discusses crime and punishment after reaching the conclusion that the problems of rewarding merit cannot be solved in terms of the common idea of justice, but he confines himself to rehearsing difficulties analogous to those of rewarding merit. In an earlier part of the work, when writing about free will and determinism, Sidgwick refers very briefly to the retributive element of punishment. He says that if the retributive view is taken alone, 'abstracting completely from the preventive view—it brings our conception of Justice into conflict with Benevolence, as punishment presents itself as a purely useless evil'.[12] He nowhere asks himself what happens to punishment if the utilitarian elements are taken alone, 'abstracting completely from desert'.

Even in Sidgwick's time it was exceptional for a thinker to hold the retributive view of punishment quite alone. I doubt if any serious theorist takes that position today. And while most supporters of retributivism give it a positive role along with the utilitarian factors of prevention, deterrence, and reform, I for my part think that the strength of retributivism lies in its negative function of protecting innocence by insisting that desert in the form of guilt is a necessary condition of the possibility of punishment. There must be ill desert before the infliction of punishment can be considered. I think, with utilitarians, that a positive decision to inflict punishment and to determine its amount can be justified only by considerations of utility; but if utility is taken to be sufficient to permit punishment in the first place, the concept of justice protests loud and clear. I am not alone in taking this view. It is essentially the view of that hard-headed thinker Hobbes, as we saw in Chapter 7. Sidgwick, who was exceptionally knowledgeable about the history of ethical theory, must have been aware of this and ought to have taken account of it in his own theory.

Like other utilitarians, Sidgwick argues that although the moral thinking of ordinary life appeals to a number of different principles and virtues, it nevertheless accepts utility as the criterion for decision when those principles lead to conflict or uncertainty. Unlike others, however, Sidgwick does not claim that the principles of common-sense morality have been adopted because they are known to be generally useful. So far as justice is concerned, he thinks it originates from the natural feelings of gratitude for benefit and resentment of harm, not from the thought that reward for the one and punishment for the other are useful. He no doubt acquired his psychological explanation from earlier thinkers and especially perhaps from Adam Smith. It is certainly more credible than the sophisticated hypothesis that the principles of justice are generalizations of experienced utility. Sidgwick's own addition is also sophisticated but

---

[12] Ibid. 72.

more interesting, a 'hypothesis of Unconscious Utilitarianism'. The idea is that the key importance of general utility is borne in upon moral thought as the result of having to deal with uncertainties and conflicts. 'It is therefore not as the mode of regulating conduct with which mankind began, but rather as that to which we can now see that human development has always been tending, as the adult and not the germinal form of Morality, that Utilitarianism may most reasonably claim the acceptance of Common Sense.'[13]

But does general utility replace the whole of the principles of 'dogmatic intuitionism'? Sidgwick agrees that it does not, for his version of utilitarianism, otherwise called philosophical intuitionism, includes a principle of equity, retained from the concept of justice, as well as two principles of maximizing happiness. That principle of equity is a simple one, virtually a repetition of Bentham's 'Everyone to count for one' but couched in more precise language. So it is not a material addition to Benthamite utilitarianism, but it is given in a more clear-sighted perspective. Sidgwick recognizes that it is a principle of distribution independent of the aggregative principles of producing as much happiness as possible. Now since it is an independent principle, it may not necessarily harmonize with the aggregative principles. In other words, there can be a conflict between utility properly speaking (seeking a maximum of general happiness) and justice. And on this matter, as on the question of merit, Sidgwick does not appreciate the force of the difficulty.

His theory contains three basic principles which he takes to be self-evident: rational self-love or prudence, rational benevolence, and equity. Sidgwick acknowledges that the first two may conflict and he goes so far as to say that he regards the relation between them 'as the profoundest problem of Ethics' and that a harmony between them 'must be somehow demonstrated if morality is to be made completely rational'.[14] He deals with the problem in the last chapter of his book and is prepared to countenance (though not to claim proof of) the theological hypothesis that God will ensure the congruity of altruistic virtue with one's own interest.

Yet Sidgwick evidently sees no problem of a conflict between the objective of these two principles and that of equity. He notes that the principle of equity should be the determining factor when we cannot decide which of two alternative actions would produce the greater amount of happiness. It is of course most unlikely that the sum of happiness resulting from their consequences would in fact be equal, but our limited knowledge often prevents us from discerning the difference. If, so far as we can see, their utility appears to be much the same in total amount, we should follow the principle of equity and choose

---

[13] Sidgwick, *Methods*, 454, 456–7.
[14] Ibid. 386 *n*. 4, 498.

the alternative that comes nearer to equality in its distribution of happiness. But suppose we are faced with alternative actions or policies, one of which would add more to the sum of happiness but in an unequal fashion, while the other would yield a lesser total of added happiness but would distribute it in a way that promotes equality. What then?

Sidgwick seems to think that, whenever one alternative yields a greater total of happiness, that factor must be the criterion for choice. There are two pointers to this conclusion. One is that he brings in equity as the deciding principle only when we cannot determine which alternative will add more to the sum of happiness. The other is that, in the same place (Book IV, ch. 1), he discusses the relevance of utilitarianism to population policy. Assuming that human life on average brings a balance of pleasure over pain, he says, we ought to encourage an increase in human population so long as the total of that balance remains a positive sum of happiness, instead of following Malthusian economists in making a maximum of average individual happiness our target. It seems clear that Sidgwick's notion of utilitarianism always gives priority to a maximum total of happiness over a concern for individuals, a concern which Sidgwick himself has noted as the mark of justice.

In Sidgwick's day the prospect of a government following socialist policies had not yet appeared, so we cannot complain of his failure to consider the dilemma of a conflict between utility and the egalitarian element of justice. When he writes of the 'socialistic' ideal of justice he thinks of desert, not equality. A Socialist government today treats equality as one, or even the chief, of its ideals. And while modern Conservatives may argue that their free enterprise policy will bring more benefit to the poor as well as to society as a whole, they do agree that some value should be attached to equality. Both sides of the political divide accept utility and equality as worthy aims but they differ in the relative weight to be given to each. Philosophical analysis cannot resolve their difference of opinion but should certainly take note of it in thinking about the nature of justice.

Chapter 14

HASTINGS RASHDALL

In the history of utilitarianism Sidgwick's elaboration of the classical theory was followed by a version which held that happiness is not the sole intrinsic good. The exponents of this view were G. E. Moore in *Principia Ethica* (1903) and *Ethics* (1912), and Hastings Rashdall in *The Theory of Good and Evil* (1907). Both acknowledged the influence of Sidgwick on their thought. Rashdall gave his theory the name of Ideal Utilitarianism and this term has been used by later scholars to describe the theory of Moore too, though Moore himself did not use it.

Ideal utilitarianism agrees with classical hedonistic utilitarianism in holding that an action is right if and because it makes the greatest possible contribution to the increase of good or decrease of evil. But whereas hedonistic utilitarianism maintains that the only intrinsic good is pleasure, ideal utilitarianism says that there are other intrinsic goods which, even if associated with pleasure or happiness, do not owe their goodness to that pleasure but have an independent value of their own. Moore and Rashdall differ in the rating that they attribute to these other goods. For Moore there are many intrinsic goods, the greatest being personal affection and the enjoyment of beauty, an outlook reminiscent of Plato. For Rashdall the great intrinsic goods are virtue (meaning, for the most part, rational benevolence), happiness, and knowledge (together with true belief and culture generally) in that order of priority.

Moore's *Principia Ethica* was a landmark in the development of British analytic philosophy and as such is a far more important book than Rashdall's *Theory of Good and Evil*. Its importance affects ethical theory in its exploration of the nature of value judgements. But its treatment of problems about the content of ethical thought is less satisfactory, and on our subject of justice it says nothing at all. Moore's later book *Ethics* has in one place a brief critical comment on the adage that justice should be done though the heavens may fall, but does not consider what is meant by justice.

Rashdall, on the other hand, devotes a long chapter (vol. i, ch. 8) to the actual concept of justice and has additional relevant discussion in the two adjoining chapters, first about the necessity of regulating benevolence with justice and then about the justice of punishment. His treatment recognizes the difficulty that some aspects of justice raise for a purely utilitarian theory of ethics and he faces that difficulty with an admirable absence of the sophistry that tries to reduce the whole of justice to utility. Although his own method of solving the problem is unconvincing, later utilitarians could learn from his honesty.

Justice, according to Rashdall, concerns the distribution of good and consists of two principles or ideals, a claim of equality and a claim of recompense or reward. They are, at first appearance, inconsistent with each other, for the distribution of good as reward for good works or other forms of merit will usually be an unequal distribution. Rashdall thinks the inconsistency is only apparent because he concludes that the equality claimed by justice is equality of consideration, which allows unequal distribution of actual good or well-being. This conclusion is not designed as a stratagem to avoid the inconsistency between the claims of equality and reward. Rashdall reaches it from an examination of two other issues. First, he shows in some detail the practical impossibility of realizing more substantial forms of equality, equality of desirable things such as wealth or power, and likewise equality of opportunity to seek desirable things. Secondly, he is troubled by a conflict between the claim of equality and the value of high culture that is inevitably restricted to a few. As one might expect from an intellectual in an elite university (Oxford), he rates very highly the value of scholarly inquiry and enjoyment, while recognizing that it is costly and often wasteful. But he is also a man with a social conscience who appreciates the moral force of socialist ideals, and he is therefore not prepared to say that high culture for the few should be accommodated at the cost of a miserable life for the many. Provided, however, that the many can lead a tolerably happy life, Rashdall does not think it right to let high culture disappear for the sake of greater equality.

Does this train of thought give any real scope to a principle of equality? Rashdall certainly believes that, if the general utilitarian principle of maximizing good comes into conflict with the principle of equality, the maximizing of good is usually paramount. In his examination of the possible conflict between high culture for a few and an imperfect, though tolerable, life for the many, he suggests, more in a spirit of hope than from assured evidence, that the value of the high culture brings a wider benefit in the long run. He does recognize, however, that the inequality for the existing generation is morally disturbing and he does not just dismiss it as obviously outweighed by (supposed) utility in the long run. Accepting the dilemma, Rashdall candidly decides to give a preference to the value of culture as such, irrespective of its possible wider effects in the future. To a degree he is prepared to give up the claim of justice. He himself, however, does not think he is giving up justice, for he genuinely believes that the principle of equality must be understood as a claim to equality of consideration, which can be satisfied by his decision in favour of the few.

I find a difficulty with his idea of equality of consideration. He begins his discussion by describing the first of the two elements of justice as 'the principle that every human being is of equal intrinsic value, and is therefore entitled to equal respect'.[1] To move from equal respect to equal consideration is not a big step, but does Rashdall hold on to the equal intrinsic value of every human being? There is an indication in the preceding chapter that he does not. In a brief anticipation of his view of justice he says: 'It is self-evident to me . . . that I ought to regard the good of one man as of equal intrinsic value with the like good of any one else'; and then he adds that 'the ultimate meaning of absolute Justice is to be sought in this equal distribution of good'.[2] The first statement *could* mean that the good of each person is in fact like the good of every other; but it becomes plain from the later discussion that Rashdall means that there is equal value *if* the good of one person is like the good of another, and that often it is not. The view that the good of a person is of equal intrinsic value to that of another if they are like goods, which they may not be, is not the same as the view that 'every human being is of equal intrinsic value'; nor is acting upon the former view 'an equal distribution of good'.

Let us consider first what is meant by equality of consideration. It certainly means that everyone concerned must be considered, with no exceptions. But if that were all, the term 'equality *of* consideration' would be pointless. The expression implies that everyone should be given the same amount of consideration, and how is one to understand that? It might mean that one should spend the same amount of time in considering the claim of each person; but that is surely trivial and silly. Or it might be suggested that equal consideration means giving equally serious attention to each claim, but that is simply a way of saying that the consideration should always be genuine, never perfunctory; the idea of greater and lesser amounts of seriousness, taken literally, hardly makes sense. Of course one does not expect greater and less consideration to be measurable, but if equality of consideration is a real alternative to equality of happiness (or means to happiness) and to equality of opportunity, one would expect rough comparisons of greater and less to be possible. We cannot judge that Tom is twice as happy (or has twice the means to happiness) as Dick, but we can often say with some confidence that he has a happier life. And although we cannot even go that far with the general idea of opportunity, we can say of important types of opportunity, such as the availability of education or satisfying employment, that Mary has more opportunity than Martha. Furthermore, having

---

[1] Hastings Rashdall, *The Theory of Good and Evil* (Oxford: Clarendon Press, 1907), i. 223.
[2] Ibid. 185.

made such judgements, we can often pinpoint practical measures to reduce (I do not say remove) the gap. Can the notion of equal consideration be likewise understood realistically? We do not get much help from Rashdall.

After introducing the equality element of justice as 'the principle that every human being is of equal intrinsic value', Rashdall goes on to say that Bentham's maxim 'Every one to count for one and nobody for more than one' does not assert that 'every one ought to receive an equal share of wealth, or of political power, or of social consideration, but simply equal consideration in the distribution of ultimate good'.[3] A little later he is more specific. He thinks that animals cannot be excluded from ethical consideration but the lives of human beings are more valuable than those of animals. The criterion is potentiality: we must admit that 'the life of one sentient being may be more valuable than the life of another, on account of its greater potentialities'.[4] Consequently the life of some human beings is more valuable than that of others, though the difference in value is far less than that between the life of any human being and the life of a non-human animal. This conclusion, Rashdall says, calls for a modification of Bentham's principle.

We may still say that every one is to count for one so long as all we know about him is that he is one. We may still say, '*Caeteris paribus*, every one is to count for one.' But then, this will only amount to the assertion, 'Every one is to count equally, so long as he is equal; but the capacity for a higher life may be a ground for treating men unequally.' Or more simply we may say 'Every man's good to count as equal to the *like good* of every other man.'[5]

Plainly this represents a departure from egalitarianism; it is the Aristotelian doctrine of 'proportionate equality', in which the so-called equality is a matching of the distributed good to the 'worth' of the beneficiaries. It is allied to the principle of distribution in accordance with merit and cannot, without equivocation, claim to exemplify the egalitarian principle with which Rashdall began, namely that 'every human being is of equal intrinsic value'. Although Rashdall's interpretation of the equality principle of justice is not designed to assimilate it to the merit principle, that is the effect of his conclusion.

When Rashdall turns to the second principle of justice, he considers two alternative forms of it: 'to every man according to his merit' and 'to every man according to his work'. He notes that, while the term 'merit' can be applied to both, this does not remove the difference between them, for 'merit' is then used in two different senses, the one moral, the other economic. Rashdall examines each of them and comes to the conclusion that neither can satisfy in practice our idea of what would be just.

[3] Ibid. 224.   [4] Ibid. 239.   [5] Ibid. 240.

He deals first with the socialist doctrine, 'to each according to his work'. It understands 'work' to mean service to the community and it intends to reward that. In the practice of existing capitalist society, work is valued by what people are prepared to exchange for it, and that depends on competition, which has nothing to do with a sense of justice: wages, like prices, go up and down in accordance with supply and demand, so that there is no absolute standard for deciding what a particular piece or species of work should have in the way of reward. A socialist may wish to think of an ideal situation where society is managed by a regard to justice and not left to the unplanned effects of competition. He might try to determine the value of work in terms of its amount; but how is that to be done? If you judge simply by the length of time spent on the work, you ignore the difference between hard and easy work; and if you try to use that distinction, you come up against the objection that some easy work, work that requires little effort, can be disagreeable if it is monotonous, while some hard work, requiring great effort, can be enjoyable for people who are good at it. So you have to take as your criterion the degree to which the work is disagreeable or pleasant.

That might be judged by the amount of different kinds of work that an average man would be prepared to do for the same compensation. The resulting evaluation would be vastly different from that which we find in practice; for example, a doctor would be paid less than a ploughman. Although many people would think it ridiculous to rate the ploughman's simple labour as more valuable to society than the complex skill of the doctor, acquired by a long training, Rashdall points out that, while some of us would die prematurely or suffer in the absence of doctors, we should all die in the absence of ploughmen or other producers of food. Even so, the hypothesis of paying the doctor less than the ploughman in a managed socialist society would not achieve justice, for the doctor could reasonably complain of having been allocated to a poorly paid occupation instead of being told of the consequences and given a choice.

Is there an alternative method of evaluating work, one that would be just? Some advocates of reward in accordance with work, Rashdall says, 'assume that what is commonly considered the higher work, that which employs the highest faculties, intellectual work, artistic work, spiritual work, &c., should be remunerated more highly than the lower, more mechanical, more animal work'.[6] This view could be based on either of two grounds, first that the 'higher work' is a higher service to society, or second that the 'higher faculties' should receive higher remuneration simply because they are higher.

The first ground, Rashdall shrewdly argues, is not a claim of justice. 'The man who prints Bibles no doubt renders a higher service to the community than

---

[6] Rashdall, *The Theory of Good and Evil*, i. 249.

the man who prints "penny dreadfuls" '; but if both perform a legitimate service, the higher and lower consequences of what they print do not justify unequal rewards for the same kind of work. If it be said that the work itself is different, Rashdall replies that there cannot be a difference in kind, relevant to valuation, between one work and another if abstracted from social consequences or the faculties employed. He has already dealt with social consequences and he now turns to faculties, the second of the two possible grounds for the view being discussed.

Why should there be higher remuneration for intellectual, aesthetic, or spiritual activities? It cannot be treated as compensation for disagreeable work, since such activity is in fact much pleasanter than more mundane occupations—for the people who are able to do it. Nor can it be justified on grounds of merit, since the ability to engage in such work comes mainly from education and natural talent, for neither of which can the fortunate beneficiary claim credit. It is expedient to foster high intellectual ability by education and then, for especially useful occupations, by high pay, but these provisions are not a requirement of justice. The person who has such gifts often needs special facilities—books, leisure, space, and so forth—and it is right that he should have the money to afford them. This is not, however, a reward for the talent with which he happens to be blessed; it is required as a necessary means for the realization of an intrinsic good.

So the ground for unequal distribution 'according to work' turns out to be the same as the ground for it after 'equality of consideration', namely the unequal possession of intrinsic good. Distribution according to work, it will be recalled, was one of two possible interpretations of a reward or merit principle of justice, the other being distribution in accordance with merit understood in a moral sense. Rashdall's subsequent consideration of the moral alternative comes to a similar conclusion.

Ought virtue to be rewarded? The first obvious answer, says Rashdall, is that it should, for the purely practical reason of utility: virtue is a great good, which we should try to maximize, and common experience tells us that reward helps to foster it. Rashdall does not suggest that this is a claim of justice and he goes on to ask whether virtue merits reward quite apart from utility. His answer is idiosyncratic.

If the matter be treated as an abstract question of merit and reward, I can see no reason at all why superior moral goodness should be assigned a superior quantity of external goods, that is to say, the means of indulging desires which have no connexion with this superior goodness. So far as the word 'merit' means anything more than 'intrinsic worth' or 'value', it must be treated as one possessing no intelligible meaning. Goodness does not merit material reward, as though goodness were a loss to the possessor which can only be rationalized if he be paid for it.[7]

[7] Ibid. 257.

There is point in asking why moral goodness should be associated with the satisfaction of desires that have no connection with it. But could Rashdall really find no intelligible meaning in 'merit' apart from the more general idea of intrinsic worth or value? His next sentence shows that he does attach a more specific meaning to the word, for he takes it to be a claim of compensation for loss, as he has done in his earlier discussion of the socialist maxim 'to each according to his work'. Surprisingly he makes no use of the synonym 'desert' either here or in his later discussion of punishment. To offer a synonym as the meaning of a word is not to explain, but at least it shows up the oddity of saying that 'merit' has no intelligible meaning apart from value.

Rashdall goes on to substitute the more general question whether a good man ought to be made happy, and answers that he certainly should, the reason being that a good man is capable of enjoying a kind of happiness that is of greater intrinsic value than the happiness of a less virtuous man. So Rashdall ends up again with an interpretation of justice that makes it depend on intrinsic value.

Nevertheless he remains uneasy about the appearance of 'reducing our two maxims of Justice and Benevolence to one and the same all-embracing precept—that of promoting a maximum of good on the whole'. There can still be a conflict between utility and equality. 'What are we to do when we can only satisfy equal claims to good by diminishing the total amount of good to be enjoyed?' Treating the equality principle of justice as equality of consideration, with due preference given to higher good, should usually result in a maximum of good, but one cannot be sure that it will always be so. 'What if a very slight increase of good on the whole could be secured by a very gross inequality in its distribution? Ought we never to sacrifice something in the total amount of good that there may be a greater amount of fairness . . . in its enjoyment?' A rigid insistence on preference for maximum good would in practice 'lead to a sacrifice of unfortunate minorities—the weak in mind or body, the sick, the halt, the maimed—such as common humanity would condemn'. As before, Rashdall's social conscience obstructs his utilitarianism. Yet he is equally racked by his yearning for a unified theory: 'it is a matter of life and death to our position' to find a common denominator for justice and benevolence. His solution is to include justice among intrinsic goods, so that the problem of weighing up the competing claims becomes 'an ordinary case of comparison of values', still difficult in practice 'but offering no particular difficulty in theory'.[8]

A theory that tried to solve a 'life and death' problem by a mere change of words would not carry any conviction. But Rashdall's solution does not rest simply on calling justice a good. He considers seriously how this move can be

---

[8] The quotations in this paragraph come from pp. 264–6.

warranted. He thinks that, if the proposed candidate for goodness were a just distribution, it would be reasonable to object that distribution in itself is too 'abstract' a thing to be a good. He appears to follow Sidgwick's view that intrinsic good must be related to states of consciousness, and his suggestion about justice is that the disposition and will to distribute justly is an intrinsic good.

This may satisfy his desire to subsume the competing claims under the one rubric of intrinsic good, but the suggestion about justice directs attention to the wrong place. When one is weighing up the claim of a fair distribution of happiness against the competing claim of producing a maximum of good, what matters for the first claim is not the mental state of those responsible for distribution but the effect of the distribution on those who get a poor deal.

The suggestion does, however, bring Rashdall to see a vital aspect of justice that he has not mentioned before. Reflecting on the state of mind concerned with justice, he writes of 'sympathy and mercy to individuals', 'kindness and goodwill for individuals', and 'solicitude for individual interests', as contrasted with care for the interest of 'society at large'. The summary of his conclusion includes the following sentences:

> Benevolence asserts the value of good. Justice asserts the value of persons. There is no real and final collision between these aspects of the ideal end, for good is ultimately the good of definite individuals. Justice and Benevolence are thus the correlatives of one another. . . . Too great a sacrifice of the individuals does present itself to us as unjust even when it might be prescribed by the principle of maximum good. But when this is the case, it is because consideration for the claims of individuals no less than consideration for the whole forms part of that ideal character which is itself the highest element of the good.[9]

Rashdall's trite unification of justice and benevolence as elements of an ideal character is of no help, theoretical or practical, for dealing with the problem of conflict between them; but his perception that justice pleads the cause of 'individuals' and 'asserts the value of persons'[10] helps to show why justice is a problem for utilitarianism, which gives undue prominence to the total amount of good to be realized.

Rashdall supplements his chapter on the concept of justice with one on the ethics of punishment. His discussion of that topic is notable for severe criticism of the view that retribution is the essence of punishment and for replacing it with the idea of punishment as educative. He does not mean by this that punishment should educate the offender; he agrees with retributivists such as F. H. Bradley that reform is a desirable adjunct of punishment but not its essence. What he means is that one aspect of retribution, expressing public indignation

---

[9] Ibid. 268–9.   [10] Ibid. 186, 268.

at crime, serves also to educate the public about the function and importance of the criminal law. That is a useful contribution to thought on the subject. Rashdall's criticism of retributive theory, however, is flawed by failure to meet its main point: he says nothing about desert.

The retributive theory maintains that a criminal is to be punished because of what he has done, not for the sake of future consequences. Most of its supporters acknowledge that once punishment is justified it should aim at deterrence and reform, but consideration of these utilitarian objectives has no place unless the person concerned has committed an offence and thereby rendered himself liable to be punished; in short, he must deserve punishment. The two thinkers whom Rashdall picks out for criticism as arch defenders of the retributive theory are Kant and F. H. Bradley. He quotes a substantial passage from each of them. (It must be said that his quotation from Kant gives a misleading picture, since, by omitting parts in the interests of brevity, it makes Kant appear primitive and bloodthirsty when the full text belies that impression.) In both passages the concept of deserving punishment is treated as crucial; without desert punishment would be a blatant injustice. Rashdall says not a word in reply to this.

I have noted earlier that in his discussion of the principle of rewarding merit he says that the term 'merit' has no intelligible meaning apart from intrinsic worth or value. He knows very well, and mentions in that place, that reward and punishment are correlative concepts. Well, if merit, the deserving of reward, means no more than having intrinsic worth or value, would Rashdall say that demerit, the deserving of punishment, means no more than having intrinsic unworth or disvalue? The nouns 'merit' and 'desert' arise from the verbs 'merit' and 'deserve', and those verbs refer to a relation between past action and a response to it that is felt to be appropriate. To suggest that the concept involved has no specific meaning shows a lack of thought if not a blind spot in moral consciousness.

I must add, however, that in his discussion of reward Rashdall seems to be more clear-sighted than the many utilitarians who think they can easily account for the concept of merit as a form of utility. They argue that socially useful courses of conduct are rewarded as a socially useful incentive to keep up the good work and to serve as an example for others to do likewise; the approval, both of the conduct and of the reward, given originally for their utility, becomes ingrained as a matter of principle and so is thought to be a special feature of ethics in its own right. Rashdall has a detailed account of the 'economic' sense of merit in his discussion of distribution of reward according to work. When he turns to the 'moral' sense of merit he is well aware that there, too, utility plays a part, but he recognizes that there is a residual element in our idea of justice which is not utilitarian. If he had attended more carefully to the notion of desert in thought about punishment, he might have seen that a function of justice is to protect the innocent against being subjected to penal measures for the sake of social utility.

One can perhaps say something similar about his statement that an untrammelled preference for maximum good as against equality would 'lead to a sacrifice of unfortunate minorities—the weak in mind or body, the sick, the halt, the maimed—such as common humanity would condemn'. It is noteworthy that Rashdall should associate such humane feelings with the equality principle of justice. As we have seen, he has some sympathy with the socialist thesis that justice should distribute the means to well-being in accordance with work. He does not mention the analogous thesis, called communist by Marx, that the distribution should be according to need. Many thinkers say that the claim of need is a matter for charity, benevolence, humanity, not for justice, and it is reasonable to suppose that Rashdall would share that view. Yet here is a place where he associates humane concern for the weak, the sick, and the maimed with a principle of justice.

Chapter 15

PETER KROPOTKIN

'From each according to his ability, to each according to his needs.' This maxim of social responsibility was first enunciated by Louis Blanc in 1839 and was taken up by Karl Marx in 1875.[1] Neither of them thought it necessary to provide a theoretical ground for the principle of distribution according to need. They were concerned with the practical polemics of social reformers, not with abstract philosophy. Louis Blanc's formulation arose from his criticism of Saint-Simon, who advocated, as socialist doctrine, the desert principle that the pay of workers should match the value of their contribution. Blanc thought that justice required instead 'the law written by God' in the human constitution: '*à chacun selon ses besoins, de chacun selon ses facultés*'; but he did not explain why the following of needs rather than desert is the God-given law of human nature. Karl Marx's repetition of the maxim occurs, again as if obvious, in a passage where he distinguishes between a first and an eventual 'higher' phase of communism. If and when the latter is attained, 'only then can the narrow horizon of bourgeois right be crossed in its entirety and society inscribe on its banners: "From each according to his ability, to each according to his needs!" '

The succour of need requires no specific justification as a general principle of morality. What is new in these thoughts of the nineteenth century is the idea that need rather than desert is a requirement of justice. Theoretical backing for this view had to wait for the writings of Peter Kropotkin—though, as we shall see, it is doubtful whether he brought it under the category of justice.

Kropotkin was born in 1842 and died in 1921. He was a Russian aristocrat who, after a period of military service and then achieving distinction as a geographer, became an active advocate of revolutionary anarchism, for which he was imprisoned in 1874. He escaped in 1876 and spent most of his subsequent years in France and England, writing profusely on anarchist communism, economics, evolution, and ethics, being content to eke out a rather meagre existence

[1] Louis Blanc, *L'Organisation du travail*; Karl Marx, *Critique of the Gotha Programme*, 1.3.

from those works. He returned to his native Russia after the Revolution of 1917 and was offered the post of Minister of Education, but, being by now old and infirm, he declined and in fact became disillusioned by the character of the Bolshevik regime. His political thought is not purely idealistic; he believed and said frankly that revolution and expropriation were necessary to bring about the kind of society that he espoused. Nevertheless his writings give the impression of a man of noble character, and his life bears that out, as does the testimony of countless people who knew him.

Kropotkin was not a philosopher in the professional sense of that word. Expounding the theory of anarchism was certainly one of his aims, but it was done as part of the wider task of furthering the cause and showing in some detail how anarchism would work out in practice. So he does not trouble to connect the theory systematically with an account of human nature and of ethics in general. He did in his last years write a history of ethics (*Ethics: Origin and Development*, published posthumously in 1924) and had intended to follow it up with a systematic treatment of his own view of ethics, but he did not live to fulfil the latter half of his project. It would undoubtedly have been distinctive in linking ethics with natural science; Kropotkin bases ethics on 'mutual aid', a disposition that is manifested in non-human animals as well as man and, he believes, is a major factor in evolution.

He seems to think of mutual aid as instinctive at root, though he does also write of it as a set of 'moral habits of mutual support' that 'grow' in both human and animal society.[2] The concept of justice is more specific. Kropotkin refers to it in a number of places, notably when discussing the views of earlier thinkers in his history of ethics, but he shows little inclination to pin down a consistent view of his own. He approves of identifying justice with equity and he thinks that the essence of equity lies in the Golden Rule, which he expresses in the form, '*Treat others as you would like them to treat you under similar circumstances*'. He frequently refers to the Golden Rule as 'the principle of equality' and is ready to declare flatly that equality is 'the synonym of equity'.[3] His argument for distribution according to need implicitly recognizes that the alternative idea of distribution according to work thinks of equity in terms of desert; he rejects the latter principle because he thinks it is impracticable, not because it has misunderstood the meaning of equity. We do not normally think of equity as synonymous with equality, though most people would agree that there are some circumstances in which an equal distribution seems to be the fairest, the most equitable, thing to do.

[2] Peter Kropotkin, 'Anarchist Communism: its basis and principles' (first published in 1887), II; included in *Kropotkin's Revolutionary Pamphlets*, ed. Roger N. Baldwin (New York: Dover Publications, 1970), 74.
[3] Peter Kropotkin, 'Anarchist Morality' (1909), VI–VIII; Baldwin, 97, 98–106, 99.

Quite apart from that issue, however, in what way is the Golden Rule the principle of equality? Dr David Miller, who has a comprehensive discussion of Kropotkin in his book *Social Justice*, refers us to a passage of *Modern Science and Anarchism* in which Kropotkin writes of the need to 'analyze to what extent the idea of *Justice* implies that of *Equality*'.

The question is an important one, because only those who regard *others* as their *equals* can obey the rule: 'Do not do to *others* what you do not wish them to do to you.' A serf-owner and a slave merchant can evidently not recognize the 'universal law' or the 'categorical imperative' as regards serfs and negroes, because they do not look upon them as equals. And if our remark be correct, let us see whether it is possible to inculcate morality while inculcating ideas of inequality.[4]

Is it true that the Golden Rule can be followed only by those who regard others as their equals? It is certainly true that serf-owners and slave traders breach the rule and reject equality between themselves and their serfs or slaves. What they reject is a basic equality of all mankind, the sharing of a right to exercise the power of choice in one's way of life, the right to be treated by others as a person and not as a chattel. That basic right is, of course, of the greatest importance and it is fair to say that those who do not respect it cannot conform to the moral law. But as examples of inegalitarianism they are extreme. Lots of people who would never dream of denying the basic right of autonomy for any sane human being, nevertheless do not regard all others as their equals. The typical local squire does not regard peasants as his equals; yet in his dealings with them he is likely to follow the Golden Rule, at least in the negative form quoted above. And if we look back at the positive form quoted earlier from 'Anarchist Morality' and deliberately emphasized with italics, we may note that it enjoins doing as we would be done by '*under similar circumstances*', which could naturally be taken to mean 'if your positions were reversed'. The squire might sincerely think that, if he were a peasant, he would wish his squire to treat him in the way that he now, as a squire, treats his peasants. No sensible person regards everyone as equals in respect of abilities, and if a talented person is given responsibilities that require him to be relieved of chores, he will not think he is obliged to do for his servants what he wishes them to do for him. So what kind of equality does Kropotkin have in mind? If it is no more than the right of all human beings to be treated as persons, that has little to do with the equality associated with justice.

It seems to me that in the *Modern Science and Anarchism* passage Kropotkin is thinking of morality generally rather than of justice in particular.

---

[4] Peter Kropotkin, *Modern Science and Anarchism*, 2nd edn. (London, 1923), 74; quoted (apart from the initial words given here) by David Miller, *Social Justice* (Oxford: Clarendon Press, 1976), 220 n. Essential parts of the earlier version of *Modern Science and Anarchism* are reproduced in Baldwin's volume; the relevant passage is on p. 176.

This suggestion is supported by the fact that in the revised version, quoted above, Kropotkin added the words 'or the categorical imperative' to explain the term 'the universal law'. The categorical imperative is, of course, Kant's name for the basic principle of morality as a whole. Why, then, does Kropotkin retain the word 'justice' when introducing the passage? I think it is because he was inclined to give 'justice' a broad meaning, maybe influenced by his anarchist predecessors, Godwin and Proudhon, both of whom used the term in a wide sense.

When discussing the Golden Rule in 'Anarchist Morality', Kropotkin refers to a different application of the principle of equality. 'And yet if societies knew only this principle of equality; if each man practised merely the equity of a trader, taking care all day long not to give others anything more than he was receiving from them, society would die of it.'[5] Here, where the equality is between what you receive and what you give in return, Kropotkin is clearly thinking of equity or justice in a more specific way. He goes on to say that 'something grander . . . than mere equity . . . greater than justice' is required, namely 'service of the human race without asking anything in return', which he then calls 'true morality', contrasted with what is 'merely equality in relations'.[6] The principle of equality in this passage has a narrower scope and is less admirable than it is made to appear in the extract from *Modern Science and Anarchism*.

'From each according to his ability, to each according to his needs', surely belongs to the 'true morality' of service rather than to justice, 'the equity of a trader'. The alternative principle of distribution according to work fits the equity of a trader, equalizing the benefit received with that which is bestowed in return. When Kropotkin sets out his argument for distribution according to need, he does not speak of it as a principle of justice. His argument is concerned with service to society as a whole and with the seamless bond that ties up the contribution of individuals. He therefore calls the formula a principle of communism, to be contrasted with individualism. He does note in the course of his argument that the prescription of distribution according to work claims to be a principle of justice, and he argues that in fact it gives effect to injustice because it allots unequal rewards for different jobs which are all equally essential in a joint enterprise. But he does not seem to imply that justice requires instead a distribution according to need. The obvious implication would be that justice requires an equal distribution, but Kropotkin knows very well the practical difficulties of trying to achieve that result. He is also severely critical of the idea that needs will be met by charity, 'Christian charity, organized by the State this time'.[7] One would suppose that the alternative is to assign the function to jus-

---

[5] 'Anarchist Morality', VIII; Baldwin, 106.   [6] Ibid. 107–8.

[7] Peter Kropotkin, *The Conquest of Bread*, ch. 13.4; ed. Paul Avrich (London: Allen Lane, The Penguin Press, 1972), 188.

tice, but Kropotkin gives no hint of that. Justice, it seems, simply does not come into the picture. This conclusion is not altogether surprising if we recall that the most perceptive theorists of justice have seized on its championship of the individual. Kropotkin's argument is truly communist and dismissive of individualism.

The argument is first given in an early pamphlet, 'Anarchist Communism: its basis and principles', originally published as a pair of articles in 1887. It reappears in a book, *The Conquest of Bread* (1906), with some elaboration but essentially retaining the same reasoning and much of the same supportive evidence. It rests both on moral grounds and on an inference from the natural course of development. Kropotkin recognizes a distinction between the two elements of his argument but he makes no effort to separate the force of each element. This is probably because he thinks they are connected, even perhaps two sides of the same coin, since he believes that morality is a product of natural evolution.

The moral case is stated most clearly in *The Conquest of Bread*:

> the means of production being the collective work of humanity, the product should be the collective property of the race. Individual appropriation is neither just nor serviceable. All belongs to all. All things are for all men, since all men have need of them, since all men have worked in the measure of their strength to produce them, and since it is not possible to evaluate every one's part in the production of the world's wealth.[8]

Apart from one short phrase, the argument of this passage rests on the claim of desert (and is therefore an appeal to justice, though Kropotkin does not say so). The benefit of what is produced by work 'belongs to', should go to, those who have produced it, and since their individual contributions are linked so that it is impossible to evaluate them separately, entitlement to the benefit is a joint possession. All men are entitled to participate in the possession, and therefore in the use, of the product because they have worked for it; it is a merited recompense for their work.

But in justifying the conclusion that 'all things are for all men', Kropotkin does not confine himself to the premiss 'since all men have worked . . . to produce them'; he first adds the premiss 'since all men have need of them'. This could be part of the same argument: one could say that, while work merits possession, and therefore eligibility to use the product, actual use (which diminishes the stock) requires the further claim of need; it would not be justifiable for any individual to use up wastefully part of a possession that belongs to all. But judging from Kropotkin's remarks about need elsewhere, it seems unlikely that this is what he had in mind. It is more probable that he regards need as an independent justification for receiving benefit. He would not say that the entitlement of

---

[8] Kropotkin, *The Conquest of Bread*, ch. 1.3; Avrich, 49.

children or the elderly or the chronically sick to have their needs met from the common stock depends on the contribution that they will make in the future or have made in the past. In his examples of the actual operation of the needs principle, Kropotkin says that questions of desert are irrelevant when needs are met, say in the use of a public library or in rescue from shipwreck or in aid for released prisoners. 'Here are men in need of a service; they are *fellow* men, and no further rights are required'.[9]

The main thrust of the passage in *The Conquest of Bread* is to attack individual appropriation and to advocate communism, the view that 'all belongs to all'. The rightness of distributing benefit in accordance with need comes in by the way and is taken to be self-evident.

Kropotkin spells out more fully the second element of his argument, the thesis that historical development shows an increasing tendency towards communism, including the principle of need.

We hold further that Communism is not only desirable, but that existing societies, founded on Individualism, *are inevitably impelled in the direction of Communism.* . . . new organizations, based on the same principle—*to every man according to his needs*—spring up under a thousand different forms . . . The bridges, for which a toll was levied in the old days, have become public property and are free to all; so are the high roads . . . Museums, free libraries, free schools, free meals for children; parks and gardens open to all; streets paved and lighted, free to all; water supplied to every house without measure or stint—all such arrangements are founded on the principle: 'Take what you need.'

Kropotkin elaborates several other examples and ends by noting that in a situation of calamity a normally egotistic society would give priority to the needs of the most vulnerable, such as children and the aged, 'without asking what services they had rendered, or were likely to render'.[10]

'Take what you need.' How does one decide what is need and what goes beyond need? Kropotkin is evidently not bothered by this question. Chapter 9 of *The Conquest of Bread* is entitled 'The need for luxury' and is ready to include all leisure pursuits, especially the arts, in the category of need. In existing society they are regarded as luxuries, available only to the rich, who can afford them, while the poor are expected to spend all their time working for a pittance to pay for needs—bread, rough clothes, and a simple dwelling. The society of anarchist communism, however, will understand that 'while it produces all that is necessary to material life, it must also strive to satisfy all manifestations of the human mind'.[11]

---

[9] 'Anarchist Communism', II; Baldwin, 60–1. Cf. *The Conquest of Bread*, 64–5.
[10] *The Conquest of Bread*, ch. 3.1; Avrich, 62–3, 65. Cf. 'Anarchist Communism', II; Baldwin, 59–61. [11] *The Conquest of Bread*, ch. 9.1; Avrich, 126.

What about the cost of this idyll? Kropotkin sees no problem. He is severely critical of orthodox economics, which, he says, fixes its attention on consumption instead of production, which could be greatly improved so as to support the world's population with ease. He disapproves of the division of labour with its specialization, which condemns manual workers to tedious repetitive tasks that could be done by machines. (Consequently he takes a poor view of Adam Smith's *Wealth of Nations*, while praising *The Theory of Moral Sentiments*; he is the only person, so far as I know, to share Smith's own opinion that the *Moral Sentiments* was the better book.) He deplores reliance upon foreign trade instead of going for self-sufficiency and giving priority to agriculture. He believes that his programme for economics would reduce the working day of the manual labourer to four or five hours, leaving him plenty of time for leisure activities.

This of course assumes that the labourers will put forth their best endeavours to serve society during their working hours. Can one expect everyone, or nearly everyone, to acquire the character of a Kropotkin and subordinate natural self-interest to the common good? Kropotkin believes that the egotism which is now so pervasive is fostered by individualism and that communist society would as a matter of course change our moral habits. What about inveterate idlers? Most of them, Kropotkin reasonably contends, are square pegs in round holes; if society made some effort to discover and cater for their natural bent, they would make a fair contribution. He allows, however, that this may not be true of all and he thinks that the fellow workers of an idler can deal with him, saying: 'Friend, we should like to work with you; but as you are often absent from your post, and you do your work negligently, we must part. Go and find other comrades who will put up with your indifference!'[12]

Much of Kropotkin's theorizing is unrealistic but we can learn something from his defence of the principle. 'To each according to his needs'. Although he wants to make it take the place of the desert maxim, 'To each according to his work', Kropotkin does not explicitly call it a principle of justice, and, as I have noted, his argument implies acceptance of the usual view that the requital of desert is just. Most people think that the requital of desert and the succour of need are both valid moral claims. Kropotkin's examples of increasing recourse to the principle of need in actual practice do not imply that it will or should replace the claim of desert entirely. When it does apply, is it, like desert, a claim of justice? A number of thinkers would say no: the requital of desert is a claim of justice, but the succour of need is not; it should be assigned to the virtue, the higher virtue, of charity. Kropotkin's examples cast serious doubt on this thesis. Who would think of rescue from shipwreck by lifeboatmen, or aid for released

---

[12] *The Conquest of Bread*, ch. 12.3; Avrich, 168.

prisoners, as acts of charity—or, for that matter, of *caritas* (love)? To regard them simply as acts of benevolence is not good enough; they are strict obligations of humanity, which is more or less what Kropotkin said ('Here are men in need of a service; they are *fellow* men'). Whether they should be assigned to the category of justice is uncertain. The scope of the concepts of justice and rights has expanded and seems likely to expand further.

Chapter 16

CHAÏM PERELMAN

The most substantial and the most important of Chaïm Perelman's writings on justice is a long essay, *De la justice*, first published in 1945. It is a powerful piece of work which has had a wide influence, and for these reasons it calls for critical examination even though Perelman himself might have thought that some aspects of it were superseded by his later publications. For example, the English translation that appeared in 1963 under the title 'Concerning Justice'[1] includes a footnote implying that Perelman had modified his view that values are 'logically arbitrary'. The footnote says that, since writing those remarks about values in the essay on justice, 'the author has tried to present, through his theory of argumentation, a way of reasoning about values', indicating that his later theory of argumentation (developed particularly in a book called *Traité de l'argumentation: La Nouvelle Rhétorique*[2]) qualifies the earlier bare statement that values are arbitrary. I shall take account of this in what I have to say. Even in the original form of the essay on justice there is a clear link with Perelman's views on logic and rhetoric, for his distinction between formal and concrete justice illustrates the difference that he saw between the reasoning of formal logic and the kind of debate that goes on in the area of rhetoric. He uses the term 'rhetoric' in the wide sense given to it by Aristotle, meaning not just the devices of persuasive language but the general character of reasoning, other than that of formal logic, which is used to support a case.

It is notorious that differences of opinion about justice, both among philosophers and among practising politicians, are sharper than such differences on most

---

[1] In Ch. Perelman, *The Idea of Justice and the Problem of Argument* (London: Routledge & Kegan Paul, 1963). My references are to this version of the essay. The footnote modifying the statement that values are logically arbitrary is on p. 57.

[2] Ch. Perelman and L. Olbrechts-Tyteca, *Traité de l'argumentation. La Nouvelle Rhétorique* (Paris: Presses Universitaires de France, 1958); English trans., *The New Rhetoric: A Treatise on Argumentation* (Notre Dame, Ind.: University of Notre Dame Press, 1969). My references are to the English translation.

other values. Perelman's essay does not aim at ending controversy; on the contrary, it insists on recognizing that there must always be controversy about basic social values. Its intention is rather to clarify the character of the controversy and to narrow its scope by distinguishing what is necessarily incontrovertible from what is necessarily controvertible. Having first listed a number of different suggested principles of justice, each of which appears to have some solidity, Perelman argues that all of them conform to what he calls the principle of formal justice. This is the principle that 'beings of the same essential category must be treated in the same way'. The differences arise over what is to constitute 'the essential category', and the various principles offered for that purpose are alternative views of concrete justice.

The notion of a principle of formal justice, common to all the conflicting conceptions of justice, is undoubtedly a helpful contribution to philosophical understanding and it has been adopted (if not always precisely in Perelman's terms) in various later treatments of the subject. Perelman points out that there can be no controversy about formal justice simply because it is purely formal and abstract. So long as you leave aside the question of what counts as the essential category to qualify for identical treatment, nobody can query the precept that all members of this one category should be treated alike: if they all belong to the same category, and if that category is essential for the purpose in hand, there cannot be any reason to differentiate between them; it is obviously rational to treat them alike.

The acceptance of such rationality, according to Perelman, is a consequence of our tendency to inertia,[3] a prime example being the juridical practice of conforming to precedent. Formal rationality, on this account, depends on the universality (or near-universality) of a psychological trait analogous to the universal law of inertia that governs the behaviour of all physical bodies. Such a universal causal agency is to be contrasted with the particular causes constituted by social conditions in different milieux, which will lead to different conceptions of concrete justice. One cannot expect to find universal acceptance of the rationality of any such conception, since the rationality in this case does not depend on a psychological trait common to all mankind. Individual history and experience of specific social conditions are the causal influences on judgements about the principle of concrete justice, on whether moral merit, or hard work, or rank, or need, is the proper criterion for a 'just' distribution. So any argument in favour of one of these conceptions must take account of the different susceptibilities of different audiences; it must conform to the principles of rhetoric, not to those of formal logic.

This is an interesting thesis, with a good deal of persuasiveness about it. The

---

[3] *The New Rhetoric*, 105–7, 218–19; *The Idea of Justice*, 86, 119.

attribution of 'persuasiveness' to Perelman's exposition raises the question whether, on his view, most of philosophy itself, including his own theories, comes into the category of rhetoric. At the beginning of *The New Rhetoric* (§6) he distinguishes between persuading and convincing. Convincing is possible when a piece of argumentation can appeal to a universal audience, as in formal logic. Perelman notes (§7) that philosophers always claim to address themselves to a universal audience and that the validity of this claim does not depend on any hope of actually gaining the assent of all men.[4] He says, with italics for emphasis, that '*The agreement of a universal audience is thus a matter, not of fact, but of right*'. He then proceeds, however, to cast doubt on the idea that philosophy can rely on any genuine objective facts or truths which would be acceptable at all times to a universal audience. So it seems that the argumentation of philosophy, and even of natural science,[5] must be regarded, in the last resort, as having the character of rhetoric. If this is correct, I cannot hope that any comment which I make will carry conviction; I can only try to persuade.

However that may be, I do have some questions to raise about Perelman's view of justice. His main distinction between formal and concrete justice is valuable. It is certainly true that his principle of formal justice has a rationality which is incontrovertible, a universality independent of particular feelings engendered by particular conditions. We must likewise acknowledge that the various principles of concrete justice present a wholly different picture. What seems rational to one group is sheer prejudice in the eyes of another. Very often (though not always) a man's predilection for a particular conception depends on his personal history: people who have experienced or seen at close quarters the grinding evil of poverty will generally say that justice should have regard to needs, while people who have seen the beneficial social effects of hard work and the appalling consequences of idleness will at least add that justice should look to merit.

Nevertheless I suggest that Perelman's distinction between formal and concrete justice is too sharp. In the first place, I think that formal justice is not *completely* formal. Secondly, I think that Perelman exaggerates the arbitrary character of the values that lie behind different conceptions of concrete justice. One can show rational connections between them so as to reduce the number of competing principles; and although a genuine conflict remains, there is more rationality to it than Perelman allows. This leads me to a third and final comment about the relation between rational justification and causal explanation.

Perelman's principle of formal justice is not entirely formal, that is to say, it is not a logical truth. Taken simply as it stands, it has a *positive* subject and a *norma-*

---

[4] *The New Rhetoric*, 31.   [5] Cf. *The New Rhetoric*, 34.

tive predicate. When it says that members of the same category 'must be' treated in the same way, the expression 'must be' (*doivent être*) conveys a moral imperative, not a logical necessity. The meaning is more clearly set out in the statement that beings who *are* members of the same category *ought to be* treated in the same way, and this, of course, is not an analytic statement. From the fact that two persons or things are members of the same class it follows logically that they are also members of a wider class which includes the first, but from the *positive fact* of belonging to a class no *norm of action* can be deduced.

This comment might be challenged on the ground that Perelman's principle refers to membership of the same *essential* category and that the word 'essential' has normative import. The reply has point if we think of one popular version of concrete justice, the principle that people should be treated according to their *needs*. The concept of need differs from that of want. A want is a bare psychological fact, but a need is a want which, by general agreement, *ought* to be met. So, if we fill out the principle of formal justice with the specification that all persons who belong to the same category of being in need, ought to receive the same treatment of having their needs met, we can claim to be enunciating a logical truth; for our principle is equivalent to the analytic statement that all persons who have wants which ought to be met, ought to have those wants met. But this analytic principle is not Perelman's general principle of formal justice; it is one version of concrete justice, one (contestable) way of giving particular values (in the mathematical sense of that term) to the variables of the general principle. The proposed defence of Perelman therefore turns out to support a thesis which is the reverse of his: it claims that one version of *concrete* justice is a logical truth, while he claims that principles of concrete justice are never of this character.

But perhaps it is true that a category selected as 'essential' in terms of the principle of formal justice is thereby rendered a normative category. Suppose, for example, that we select merit rather than need as the essential category. Merit means the same as desert, and what a man deserves is what he ought to have. So if we say that everyone who belongs to the same category of merit ought to be treated in the same way, we mean that everyone who deserves (= ought to have) good in return for his own good actions, ought to be treated in the same way, that is, ought to receive good.

Perelman's list of popular principles of distributive justice includes, as one would expect, need and merit as possible criteria. It also cites work, rank, and legal entitlement as alternative criteria. The criterion of work is clearly related to that of merit. If we take work instead of merit as the essential category for filling out the principle of formal justice, do we again find that this necessarily introduces a normative element? Can we say that the concept of having worked, or at any rate of having worked hard, of having shown effort, is itself normative, implying that the person concerned ought to be treated in some way or other? I cannot see that this is true—unless we *add* the concept of merit to that of work. It is reasonable to say that a person who has worked hard is meritorious, but this statement itself is not a logical truth: it is a synthetic normative judgement, that is to say, the predicate adds an idea (a normative idea) which is not contained in the meaning of the subject.

Much the same sort of thing applies to another specification of concrete justice in the list given by Perelman, namely the principle that people ought to be treated according to their rank. We may say that the concept of rank, which involves comparative evaluation of superior and inferior, implies the normative requirement that those of inferior rank should show signs of respect to those of superior rank. The idea of rank includes (if it is not simply equivalent to) that of status, and the idea of status is normative in requiring respect. But that is all. Superior rank or status does not in itself imply any other requirement or entitlement, for instance concerning the receipt of material goods or the appointment to lucrative or responsible posts. So if the principle of concrete justice in terms of rank is taken to mean, not simply that people should be *respected* according to their rank, but that they should receive material goods or appointments in accordance with their rank, this is not a logical truth—again unless we *add* the concept of merit to that of rank. No doubt most people who adopt a principle of concrete justice in terms of rank do think that people of high rank are more meritorious than others (because, for example, they or their ancestors have benefited the nation), and would defend a differential distribution on that ground; but this means, as with the principle of distribution according to work, that the character of logical truth can be claimed only if we understand the principle of distribution according to rank as a species of the principle of distribution according to merit.

So far we have made a case for saying that the two *concrete* principles of treatment according to need and of treatment according to merit can be interpreted as logical truths. The suggestion I have been considering in the last three paragraphs is that *all* concrete specifications of the principle of formal justice have this character and that it is a consequence of the fact that the principle of formal justice refers to an 'essential' category, meaning by that a category of normative requirement. But this turns out not to be true of two of Perelman's specifications of concrete justice, treatment according to work and treatment according to rank. If the 'essential category' is, in each of these two instances, taken to be merit, then of course it is a normative category. But Perelman himself evidently thought that work alone, or rank alone, without the addition of merit, can serve as an 'essential category' for the purpose of supplying concrete specification for the variables of the principle of formal justice. This being so, my original comment remains valid. The principle of formal justice, as understood by Perelman, is not a logical truth and is therefore not purely formal. It is a synthetic statement in which a normative predicate is attached to a non-normative subject, or at any rate to a subject which may be non-normative.

It is instructive to see how this comment affects a further possible principle of concrete justice in Perelman's list of them. This is the principle that people should be treated according to their legal entitlement. Here the 'essential category', legal entitlement, is obviously normative, and so it seems at first sight that this principle, like the principles of need and merit, could be treated as a logical truth. An entitlement is a right, what is due to its possessor, what he ought to have. So to say that a person ought to be treated in accordance with his entitlement, is to say that he ought to be given what he ought to have: which seems near enough to a logical truth (though there is a bit of a problem in explaining how 'I ought to *have* X' logically implies that someone—who exactly, and why?—ought to *give* me X). But in fact this formulation of concrete justice is not a logical truth. Although its subject and predicate both include a normative concept, the norms come from different universes of discourse and therefore cannot stand to each other in a straightforward logical relation of implication. The suggested principle of concrete justice, 'Everyone ought to be treated according to his legal entitlement', does not, of course, mean merely that everyone *legally* ought to be given what he *legally* ought to have. It means that everyone *morally* ought to be given what he *legally* ought to have. This, needless to say, is far from being a logical truth and does not pretend to be one. It is (as Perelman recognizes) a confessedly contentious synthetic principle. If it did claim to be a logical truth, it would be attempting to deduce a moral 'ought' from a legal 'ought', and from the point of view of logic the fallacy would be the same as trying to deduce an 'ought' from an 'is'.

Someone may protest that I have been reading too much into Perelman's use of the term 'formal'. When he wrote of the principle of formal justice, he did not imply that it was purely formal in the sense of being a logical truth. His intention was simply to show that it is *relatively* formal as compared with the more substantial principles of concrete justice. It is formal in relation to them because it sets out what is common to all of them.

I entirely agree with the point made in this hypothetical protest. My comment about formal justice is not a criticism of Perelman's position. It is rather an elaboration, showing the limited character of the formality attributed to the principle of formal justice. But it is relevant to my critical remark that Perelman's distinction between formal and concrete justice is drawn too sharply; for, as will have been evident from my discussion, the different principles of concrete justice are not all non-formal in the same way. The principles of distribution according to need and of distribution according to merit can each be understood in a manner that makes them formal, indeed even more formal than the principle of formal justice because they, unlike it, can be taken to be logical truths. On the other hand, the principles of distribution according to work and of distribution according to rank are dependent upon the principle of distribution according to merit, and so are not *immediately* subordinate to the principle of formal justice.

Perelman gives a list of six popular principles of justice:[6]

1. To each the same thing.
2. To each according to his merits.
3. To each according to his works.
4. To each according to his needs.
5. To each according to his rank.
6. To each according to his legal entitlement.

Perelman points out[7] that the first of these can be regarded as simply a version of the principle of formal justice, but less clear than his own version because it does not show the principle of formal justice to be a generic one common to all proposed principles of concrete justice. That seems very reasonable. But Perelman then goes on to treat all the other five principles in his list as having much the same sort of logical relationship to the principle of formal justice. That is to say, he regards merit, work, need, rank, and legal entitlement as being each an independent value (in the mathematical sense — but also in the ethical sense) for the variable 'the same essential category'. According to the doctrine of the essay 'Concerning Justice', each of these values is chosen arbitrarily by those who make it the essential category for justice. As I observed at the beginning of this chapter, Perelman notes in the English version of his essay that his early view of the arbitrary character of values is qualified by his later theory of argumentation. I shall comment on his original view in the present section and on the later view in my final section.

It seems to me that principles 2–6 in Perelman's list are not all simple alternatives to each other, and that the adoption of certain of them is not a matter of arbitrary choice.

First of all, principle 6 is quite different from all the rest. Perelman himself[8] acknowledges a difference in that principle 6 does not leave us free to make our own judgement but ties us down to what the law has decreed. It is, however, also different in the nature of its goal. Principle 6 is concerned with the retention of the status quo of rights, while all the rest contemplate a distribution of new rights or a redistribution of old ones. In Chapter 1 I distinguished between conservative and reforming aspects of the concept of justice. Principle 6 belongs

---

[6] *The Idea of Justice*, 6–10.   [7] Ibid. 18.   [8] Ibid. 24.

to the conservative aspect. Whatever principle or principles of reformative justice people may accept, most of them will *also* accept principle 6 as a necessary principle of conservative justice. Everyone who agrees that a society needs laws will agree that the rights conferred by those laws ought to be maintained. The only people who will reject principle 6 are anarchists, and they will reject it simply because they reject the need for a state and law.

The difference of opinion between anarchists and non-anarchists does not depend on any difference in values; it depends on different judgements of certain facts. The values of the anarchist are the values of the liberal: individual liberty, self-determination, voluntary co-operation. The question at issue between the anarchist and the non-anarchist is the practical possibility of giving effect to liberal values without having a state. It is true that a state and its law imply some limitation on individual liberty, but in a democratic state this is in order to achieve a maximum of liberty for all. The opponent of anarchism believes that without the constraints of law and state there will be less liberty overall because of the deficiencies of human nature. His dispute with the anarchist is about psychological facts, not about values.

Apart from anarchists, then, everyone will accept principle 6 as a necessary principle of (conservative) justice. This does not exclude the acceptance, in addition, of one or more principles of reformative justice. But of course it also does not require the acceptance of any such additional principle. It is possible to hold principle 6 as the *only* principle of justice, as meaning that each person should receive his legal entitlement and nothing more. Such a view might perhaps be taken by arch-conservatives, believing that the idea of justice relates only to the maintenance of the status quo.

At first sight one is inclined to say that the difference of opinion between them and those who think of justice as also a reformative concept is a difference in value judgement. But I am not sure that this is correct. If one wanted to argue with an arch-conservative, it would not be very effective to do so by invoking sympathy for the underprivileged. The arch-conservative could reply: 'Of course I sympathize with these people. Of course I agree that it is a good action, perhaps even a duty, to help them. What I deny is that it is a matter of justice. The value involved is a matter of charity or benevolence, not of justice.' In order to change his opinion, you need to alter his conception of the meaning and implications of justice, rather than to persuade him to accept a value which he does not now accept. You might try to do it by pointing out to him that no system of law is static and no society is altogether static. As society changes, law needs to change. In order to decide what changes should be made in the law, one must have non-legal criteria for judging what new laws should be made and what old laws should be repealed. Thus there must be some principle or principles for reforming the law. Some of these reformative principles, designed to affect law, are commonly called principles of fairness or equity or 'natural justice', and if they are necessary there is no reason to deny them the name of principles of justice. At any rate this seems a possible way of arguing with the arch-conservative and trying to persuade him to widen his concept of justice. As in the dispute between anarchists and non-anarchists, the difference of opinion does not really rest on the holding of different values. The argument points to facts, this time sociological facts.

I turn now to the remaining principles in Perelman's list, distribution according to merit, work, need, or rank. As I have indicated earlier, there is an affinity between distribution according to merit and distribution according to work or rank: if taken as essential categories for distributive justice, work and rank are dependent upon the more general category of merit. This can be seen more easily if we substitute for 'merit' the term 'worth' (*axia*), which Aristotle uses in his formulation of distributive justice.[9] The concept of worth includes not only moral merit but also talent. Aristotle's example is that flutes should be given to those with a talent for flute-playing. Talent is a species of worth. Effort, whether in the form of moral effort or of hard work, is a species of worth. Rank or status is counted as a species of worth. The principle that it is just to distribute benefits or responsibilities according to worth can be interpreted so as to include the recognition of talent, moral merit, work, and rank.

The valuing of all these different species of worth as relevant for just distribution is not an arbitrary matter; it depends largely on the thought of utility. If flutes are in short supply, the most efficient use of them is to give them to people who can make pleasing music with them. If facilities for higher education are limited, society will benefit most by giving those facilities to people who have the talents that can be developed by higher education. The actions that are called morally virtuous are commonly useful to society and this is at least a main reason why they are commended; the rewarding of moral virtue is itself useful because it encourages such virtue. Hard work is likewise commended because of its social utility, and the justice of rewarding such effort depends on the utility of encouraging it. The utilitarian foundation in this instance is especially clear from the fact that nobody would think it proper to reward work that is pointless or socially harmful. As for the valuation of rank, this depends on the idea that rank was originally bestowed as a reward for valuable service to the community (or perhaps, in the case of hereditary monarchy, as the recognition of talent for the office); and in periods when people have thought it just to distribute benefits and responsibilities according to rank, they did so because they supposed that the useful qualities which had earned the rank were transmitted by heredity.

---

[9] Cf. Ch. 5 above.

If the justice of distribution according to worth depends on the thought of utility, then utility can also supply a rational criterion for judging between competing claims of the different kinds of worth. For example, if we have to choose between distribution according to work and distribution according to rank, it is rational to prefer the one which is obviously useful rather than the one which is doubtfully so. It is less easy to decide between work and talent or between either of these and moral merit, but in principle we have a criterion for judgement. While our personal preferences have no doubt been heavily influenced by the psychological effects of individual circumstances, the comparison of these different values is not arbitrary, nor are the values themselves independent of each other.

I should add, however, that the justice of distribution according to worth does not depend *entirely* on the thought of social utility. When we value talent and the provision for its development, we are not thinking *only* of social utility; we are thinking also of the self-realization of the individual concerned. A flute for the flute-player will give pleasure to the public who hear him; but it also gives pleasure to the flute-player himself, and surely this is part of what we have in mind when we decide to spend public money on scholarships for young people with a talent for playing the flute. Public provision for education of all kinds depends in part on the social utility of developing talents and in part on the valuing of self-development for its own sake. There is a similar duality in our valuation of moral merit. The moral virtues are socially useful and are valued largely for that reason; but they are also valued as an essential part of self-realization as a human being. I doubt whether the same thing applies to work as such (though some people would say it does), and I do not believe for a moment that it applies to rank.

The principle of distribution according to need is quite different from all these variations on the theme of distribution according to worth. You cannot regard need as a species of worth in the way that talent, moral merit, work, and rank are all species of worth. We do not commend or value need as we commend or value talent, merit, and work. Need in itself is an evil, not a good; something to be removed, not something to be fostered. Distribution according to needs has nothing to do with deserts; if we regard needs, we must treat deserts as irrelevant. The really serious conflicts in the application of justice are precisely those in which we have to choose between needs and deserts — or, looking at it in a different light, between needs and social utility. A good deal of the differences in social policy between socialists and conservatives depends on the relative emphasis that they give to the conflicting principles of justice, the one regarding needs, the other regarding worth or social utility.

The meeting of needs is not entirely independent of social utility. The slave-owner who valued his slave solely for utility would meet the slave's need for food and health in order that the slave could go on working. Marx's analysis of capitalism assumes that employers generally take the same attitude towards their workers. And certainly it is true that the maintenance of life and health in the working population of a society is necessary for the continuance of their work, and so is socially useful. But what about the non-working section of the population? In the case of the children there is the future to be thought of: children must be kept alive and well now if they are to make their contribution when they are grown up. The same can be said of the curably sick: although they cannot work at present, they will be able to contribute once more to society if they are cared for and helped to recover. There remain the old and the incurably sick. They are no longer able to contribute to the welfare of society. From the point of view of social utility, there is no reason to meet their needs. So the claim of justice in their case cannot be based on the thought of utility.

What is more, although the desirability of meeting needs in other cases *can* be based on utility, this is surely not what we have in mind when we think of the claim of need as a claim of *justice*. So far as the claim of need is concerned, there is no difference between those who can contribute to society and those who cannot. That is why Marx's condemnation of the capitalist attitude is so effective: in his picture of them, the capitalists, like the slave-owners, think only of the use value of the workers and pay no regard to their needs as human beings. The principle of justice that looks to needs depends on the valuation of individual human beings for their own sakes. In Kantian language, it regards them as ends-in-themselves.

Kant uses the term in one of his formulations of the categorical imperative, the basic principle of moral action. Like many readers of Kant, I find this formulation the most enlightening feature of Kant's theory of ethics. It says that we should treat all human beings as ends (ends-in-themselves) and not simply as means to our own ends. To treat a person as an end, Kant explains, is to make that person's ends your own: that is to say, you should act in respect of his ends, his purposes, as you naturally act in respect of your own ends. Your own ends, your purposes or aims, afford motives for action as a matter of course: you try to achieve what you desire. To make another person's ends your own is to treat his purposes as if they were yours: you either try to help him achieve what he desires or, if he does not need positive help, you avoid obstructing him in his pursuit of his aim. So regarding all human beings as ends-in-themselves is a matter of respecting their purposes, recognizing that those purposes have for them the same sort of value as your purposes have for you, and accepting a moral obligation to co-operate with them in their efforts to fulfil their purposes.

The next thing to observe is that the needs principle of justice has an affinity with the egalitarian principle. While Perelman is quite right to point to similarities between some versions of an equality principle and his own principle of formal justice, egalitarians have in practice been concerned with something more substantial. While meritarians pay chief attention to those differences among human beings that are relevant to utility—differences of capacity and effort—egalitarians pay chief attention to the things that all human beings have in common. The principle of distribution according to need has been supported by egalitarians as a principle of levelling up. Different people differ in their needs, and so distribution according to need is a differentiated form of distribution: those in greater need receive more, those in lesser need receive less. At first sight, therefore, the needs principle seems similar to the worth principle, which also gives more to some and less to others. But the end result of a needs distribution is to reduce inequality, while the end result of a worth distribution is to increase inequality. If the man with greater needs is given more than the one with lesser needs, the intended result is that each of them should have, or at least approach, the same level of satisfaction; the inequality of nature is corrected. But if the man of greater talent or greater industry is rewarded more than the man of lesser talent or industry, the pre-existing inequality between them is increased; for the man of greater talent or industry is in any case likely to achieve greater satisfaction for himself by his own efforts, and if he is rewarded in addition he will be better off still.

In my view, therefore, the first five of the popular principles of justice in Perelman's list should be classified into two groups. On the one side, the principles of merit, work, and rank go together; on the other side, the egalitarian principle and the principle of need. The former group depends largely on the valuation of social utility, the latter group depends on the valuation of all human beings as ends-in-themselves. I have noted, however, that some aspects of the first group do not depend entirely on the thought of social utility but also take account of the value of individual self-realization. The latter value is an aspect of the Kantian idea that each human being is an end-in-himself.

The Kantian notion is itself not free from internal conflict, for we often have to weigh up the claims of one individual human being (or of one group of them) against the claims of another. Nevertheless it seems to me that many of the most serious conflicts of values in *social* life, many of the serious differences of value judgement in different ideologies, boil down to a conflict between the claims of the general interest and the claims of the individual—in philosophical terms, between utilitarian ethics and Kantian ethics. I have no formula, of universal acceptability, for resolving this fundamental conflict. But the analysis that I have presented does introduce a greater element of rationality into principles of justice than does Perelman's account.

My final comment is concerned with Perelman's revised view of values in his book *The New Rhetoric*. I have quoted his note, in the English translation of the essay on justice, qualifying his view that choosing values for concrete justice is an arbitrary matter. In *The New Rhetoric* he assigns a limited form of rationality to such choice. He regards the rationality of argumentation as a matter of acceptability to audiences. The full rationality of formal justice lies in its being acceptable to a universal audience and depends upon the universal, or near-universal, character of a psychological trait of inertia. Perelman thinks this is illustrated by the juridical practice of following precedent. In his view, the practice seems rational simply because our habit of inertia leads us naturally to react in the same way to a repetition of the same circumstances. The more limited rationality of rhetorical argumentation is to be understood in terms of sociology: a conclusion can appear rational to a particular audience because it appeals to a value which just happens, as a contingent sociological fact, to be accepted by that particular audience.

The account implies that rational justification is to be understood in terms of causal explanation: it implies that the psychological or sociological origin of a practice or belief is fundamentally identical with the sufficient reason for continuing to follow the practice or belief. It seems to me that this identification of rational justification with causal explanation is not borne out by experience.

Let us take first Perelman's own illustration of the rationality of formal justice, namely the juridical practice of following precedent. It might perhaps owe its origin to a psychological trait of inertia, and, if so, it is also possible that inertia is the cause of our feeling that the practice is 'just' or 'fair'. But when courts and jurists give *reasons* for the legal principle of *stare decisis* (keep to the precedents), they do not refer to this general feeling or to a psychological reluctance to innovate. Their reasons are firmly utilitarian. The practice of following precedent is defended on the ground of 'certainty', that is, of enabling lawyers to predict, in cases without novel features, what a court would decide, and so to advise their clients with confidence. Certainly in the United Kingdom it is taken for granted that this is the rationale of following precedent. Confirmation may be found in two *dicta* of the House of Lords (the final court of appeal). One was a Practice Statement of 1966,[10] announcing that the House of Lords would, in future, not necessarily be bound by its own past decisions; while making this change, it also set out the reasons why the general insistence on precedent is desirable. The other *dictum* was in a judgement of 1978,[11] in which the House of

---

[10] The Practice Statement begins: 'Their Lordships regard the use of precedent as an indispensable foundation upon which to decide what is the law and its application to individual cases. It provides at least some degree of certainty upon which individuals can rely in the conduct of their affairs, as well as a basis for orderly development of legal rules.' Cf. Sir Rupert Cross, *Precedent in English Law*, 3rd edn. (Oxford: Clarendon Press, 1977), 109.

[11] *Davis v. Johnson*, [1979] AC 264. The considered judgement of the House on this point was delivered by Lord Diplock at 326: 'In an appellate court of last resort a balance must be struck

Lords insisted that the Court of Appeal (that is, the court immediately below the House of Lords) should be bound by that court's own past decisions. When a higher court, such as the British House of Lords, finds it necessary to give reasons for the practice of *stare decisis*, it is because, in a particular case, the practice has appeared to *conflict* with sentiments of justice or fairness, and the issue for the higher court has been one of weighing up the general utility of the practice of following precedent against the apparent injustice of applying it in a particular case.

Turning now to particular principles of concrete justice, my earlier discussion of these has shown that the appeal of each of them does not rest on a specific value which is accepted by some particular audience and not by others. If the principle of distribution according to rank were taken to be independent of all the others, it would appear to support Perelman's view. For support of this principle of justice is confined to particular societies over a limited period of time; there is virtually no support for it in modern societies. But once we see that its rationale depends on the wider concept of merit or worth, we can no longer say that rational argumentation about it depends entirely on sociological conditions. We can argue about the respective claims of the principles of rank, merit, work, and talents in terms of their common subordination to the concept of social utility, a value of universal acceptability.

The same sort of thing can be said, with some qualification, about the Kantian value which underlies the egalitarian and the needs concept of justice, and which partly sustains the principles of moral merit and talents. It is, of course, not true to say that all societies have in fact accepted the Kantian idea that all human beings are ends-in-themselves. But, unlike the more restricted principles of value which many societies have in fact followed, the Kantian principle is by its very nature universal in application and in appeal. A principle that gives value to all human beings can be valued by all human beings. At any rate, the rationality of an argument which depends on the Kantian principle cannot be called particularistic.

It remains true that conflicts are apt to arise between the principle of utility and the principle of valuing individuals as ends-in-themselves—and indeed within the latter principle alone, when a choice has to be made between serving the ends of different individuals. The universality of the two principles is no guarantee against having to face moral dilemmas. The process of deliberation which we undertake in such circumstances may well conform more to Perelman's picture of rhetorical argumentation. It is easy to think of conflicts of

---

between the need on the one side for the legal certainty resulting from the binding effect of previous decisions, and, on the other side the avoidance of undue restriction on the proper development of the law.'

values in which different decisions would seem right to an average West European democrat and an average Russian communist (to say nothing of the views of Chinese, or Indians, or West Africans, or whatever). I should not want to claim that there is some form of universally acceptable reasoning which would yield a single right answer, and I am therefore ready to follow Perelman in his view that the rationality of deliberation in such moral dilemmas cannot go beyond sociological factors. Nevertheless it seems to me that, even in the realm of values, there is wider scope for universal rationality than Perelman has allowed.

Chapter 17

DAVID MILLER

David Miller's <u>Social Justice</u> was published in 1976, a few years after John Rawls's *A Theory of Justice*, but I think it is appropriate to discuss Miller first. The main substance of his book was written before Rawls's *Theory* appeared, and while Miller added in the published version an account of Rawls, with critical discussion, he saw no grounds to doubt or modify his own contribution to the subject. Another, more cogent, reason for considering Miller's views first is that they continue the line of tradition that I have traced in the preceding chapters of this book; in particular, they follow on naturally from Perelman's treatment. I do not think that Miller was at all influenced by Perelman, but his account is in fact of the same genre, though much more thorough, and his conclusions turn out to be similar to Perelman's in giving a sociological explanation for the differences in the prominent notions of justice. But whereas Perelman did not explicitly acknowledge, or perhaps recognize, the sociological character of his conclusion, Miller moves into sociology deliberately and with scholarly examination of relevant sociological writings.

In the earlier parts of his book Miller exercises an admirable competence in philosophical analysis of the various concepts associated with justice and in a critical exposition of the views of three thinkers of the past. Although I cannot accept the whole of his conclusions, I think that his book is more helpful than any other for clarifying our understanding of the idea of justice. Rawls's book has attracted far more attention, not so much for its conclusions, or for clarification, as for the originality of its method. Originality of perspective is rightly prized in philosophy, for it awakens us from the risk of dogmatic slumber. Miller's book does not match Rawls's in that respect. All the same, it deserves more attention than it has received. Its subject is social justice, not justice in general, and so it is not strictly comparable with most of the works discussed elsewhere in this book, including Rawls's theory. Indeed its reflections on the more general concept of justice *tout court* suffer a little from its neglect of the idea in legal contexts. Nevertheless Miller's initial analysis of the general concept is both more detailed and more perceptive than most accounts.

Miller's book is divided into three parts. The first is a philosophical analysis of the concept of social justice, its elements and their connections, as found in the language and reflective thought of ordinary life today. He finds three principles or interpretations of the general idea of justice: a distribution of benefits and burdens as called for by rights, or by deserts, or by needs. Then in Part II he examines in detail the views of Hume, Herbert Spencer, and Kropotkin, taken to be leading exponents respectively of the three interpretations of justice. We might then wish to ask, in the light of the initial analysis and the subsequent defences, which of the three interpretations has the strongest case. In Part III Miller tells us that there is no straightforward answer to this question: each of the interpretations has been linked to a particular form of social structure, as we may see from relevant sociological studies.

I shall leave aside Part II, in which Miller claims that, in their accounts of justice, Hume exemplifies the rights principle, Spencer deserts, and Kropotkin needs. I have discussed Hume and Kropotkin in earlier chapters and, rightly or wrongly, I have not been moved to examine Herbert Spencer's views. My account of Kropotkin is more or less in line with Miller's, though I found that Kropotkin does not, strictly speaking, urge that the claim of need is a claim of justice. My treatment of Hume has a different emphasis from Miller's, but I would not dispute the legitimacy or interest of his account. However, his case for a sociological perspective does not depend crucially on his taking these three thinkers as exemplars of the three principles of justice, and his discussions in Parts I and III are more directly relevant to my general purpose in this book.

In Part I, Miller starts off with the general definition of justice adopted in traditional jurisprudence, *suum cuique*, which he translates as 'to each his due'. The definition, he observes, indicates that justice is concerned with distribution, but it is merely formal, lacks substance, in that it does not tell us what sort of thing may be due. Various answers have been given to that question, presenting us with substantial principles of justice, and we need to consider how they are related to each other: are they incompatible alternatives or are they elements of a coherent whole, some perhaps being subsumed under others?

He takes note, in the first place, of the distinction drawn by Sidgwick between conservative and ideal justice, and then revived by me with Sidgwick's 'ideal' justice being renamed 'prosthetic' justice (by analogy with conservative and prosthetic dentistry). Sidgwick described conservative justice as maintaining 'the *customary* distribution of rights, goods, and privileges, as well as burdens and pains', while I wrote that the object of conservative justice is 'to preserve an existing order of rights and possessions, or to restore it when any breaches have been made'. Miller accordingly takes conservative justice to be a principle about *rights*, a principle that would give substance to his initial general definition by means of the requirement 'to each according to his rights', rights being derived from 'publicly acknowledged rules, established practices, or past transactions' (such as promises or contracts).[1]

Existing rights are, however, liable to be criticized and revised in the name of justice, and this, Miller continues, is the aspect of justice that Sidgwick called ideal and I called prosthetic. Sidgwick identified ideal justice with the principle of desert, while I, according to Miller, argued 'that the criterion of need is more central to prosthetic (ideal) justice than the notion of desert'.[2] He is referring to an article, 'Conservative and Prosthetic Justice', in which I in fact coupled the claim of need with that of equality, treating the claim of equality as the more basic of the two.[3] Miller, as we shall see, also couples the two but with need as the more basic.

From his review of the distinction between conservative and ideal justice, he concludes that there are three principles or interpretations of justice: distribution in accordance with rights, with desert, and with need. All three are liable to conflict with each other, but, he notes, the conflict between the claims of desert and need is more radical than that between either of them and the claim of rights. This is because the conflict between rights (conservative justice) and either of the other two (ideal justice) can, in principle at any rate, be resolved, since we may try to reach a social order in which rights have been modified to match the ideal; but desert and need cannot be reconciled, since a distribution according to desert is incompatible with a distribution according to need.

Part I proceeds with a detailed analysis of each of the three principles as found in common usage. The chapters on rights and desert also highlight the fallacies of utilitarian accounts of these concepts. The chapter on need begins by noting that need, unlike rights and desert, is not universally accepted as an element of justice, and Miller spends some time defending the thesis that the claim of need is a valid and independent component of the concept of justice.

Many thinkers insist that the claim of need is one of humanity or benevolence, not of justice. Miller replies that the obligation to relieve need includes a concern for the distribution of the relief: if, in a famine, someone were charged to relieve need from a limited supply of food, *any* distribution that reduced suffering would meet the obligation of humanity, but a distribution that helped some sufferers and disregarded others would be regarded as unfair and as having failed to fulfil the charge of relieving need.

That particular objection is quite common. In earlier chapters of this book

---

[1] David Miller, *Social Justice* (Oxford: Clarendon Press, 1976), 25–6.
[2] Ibid. 27.
[3] D. D. Raphael, 'Conservative and Prosthetic Justice', §vi, in *Political Studies*, 12 (1964), 158; repr. in D. D. Raphael, *Justice and Liberty* (London: Athlone Press, 1980), 85, and in Anthony de Crespigny and Alan Wertheimer (eds.), *Contemporary Political Theory* (New York: Atherton Press, 1970; Sunbury-on-Thames: Thomas Nelson, 1971).

we have seen that the inclusion of need in justice is a relatively late development, and so it is reasonable and natural to wonder whether the concept of justice genuinely contains this element. Some individual philosophers, however, have queried the claim of need with less obvious arguments. One has contended that, when need gives rise to a claim of justice, it is because the need has become a right; another that it is really a claim of desert. Miller disposes of these suggestions without difficulty.

He takes more seriously, however, the view of Brian Barry that need is not an independent idea. According to Barry, to say that someone needs something is to make an incomplete statement: he needs it for a purpose; for example, he needs food in order to keep alive. The need therefore is a means to an end and the justification for meeting the need is the end that it serves; in our example the justification for the claim to be given food is the more basic claim to be kept alive. Barry's discussion[4] is concerned with justification generally and is not tied specifically to claims in the name of justice; but if his view is accepted, it does imply that need is not an independent element of the concept of justice.

Miller rejects this conclusion by distinguishing three types of need. The first is 'instrumental': for example, one needs a key in order to unlock a door; one needs a licence in order to be permitted to drive a car. The second is 'functional': for example, a surgeon needs manual dexterity, a lecturer needs books. The third is 'intrinsic': for example, a person, indeed any animal, needs food; some poor souls need a person to understand them.

The first category conforms to Barry's analysis: the need is for a means to an end. Miller contends that this is not true of the second and third types. The statement that a surgeon needs manual dexterity or that a lecturer needs books is, according to Miller, complete in itself: to add 'in order to do his job' is otiose; to say that a *surgeon* needs the one and a *lecturer* needs the other already implies that the need is for doing the work of a surgeon or a lecturer. One can of course ask why those particular jobs involve those particular needs, and the reply would explain to the ignorant questioner what sort of thing the surgeon or the lecturer has to do; but it would not be referring to any *distinct* ends for which manual dexterity or books were specially required.

Likewise the third category of need is not concerned with means to an end: what is needed, Miller suggests, is a part of the end, not a means to it. When one says of someone that he needs food, it is understood that he needs it to keep alive, but what is understood, Miller thinks, is that eating food is part of the process of keeping alive. The relation between them is not like the relation between the key and the door. When one has opened the door, the key, the means to the end of opening the door, is no longer needed and can be discarded; but keeping alive is

---

[4] Brian Barry, *Political Argument* (London: Routledge & Kegan Paul, 1965), 47–9.

not a one-off action that is completed when one has had a meal; it is an ongoing process that continues to require food as a component part of it. Similarly the poor soul who needs someone to understand him (in order, say, to preserve a state of mental well-being) does not cease to have the requirement once the understanding person has listened and expressed his understanding; the continued presence of such a person is a part of the desired end of mental well-being.

This suggestion that an 'intrinsic' need is *part* of the desired end seems to me dubious. I suppose that the person in need of an understanding companion may well think of their conversations as a part of the mental well-being that he or she seeks. But what about the need for food? It is possible to regard the pleasure of food as part of the pleasure of life, but it strikes me as odd to say that eating food is a part of keeping alive. It is certainly true that, if we think of the need for food as a means to the end of keeping alive, it differs in character from the key as a means to opening the door, but is not this due to a difference in the end? Opening the door is a brief act, while keeping alive is a continuing process, and that is why one cannot think of discarding the eating of food after a meal as one can discard the key when the door has been opened. Consider some other examples of a continuing process. One needs to take exercise to keep healthy. It seems perfectly sensible to say that the exercise is a means to health, but questionable to say that the exercise is a part of keeping healthy. One needs education to make the most of one's abilities. It is sensible to say that education is a means to that end, but only dubiously possible to say that the education is a part of the end. A short-sighted person needs spectacles to see clearly. It is sensible to say that they are a means to clear vision, but odd to say that they are a part of the clear vision. It is perhaps less odd to say that wearing the spectacles is a part of enjoying clear vision, but it would still seem more natural and more accurate to say that wearing the spectacles is a means to enjoying clear vision.

So I am inclined to agree with Barry that the needs which are relevant to the concept of justice are dependent on the ends which they serve, and that therefore the justification for help which they supply comes from those ends, such as keeping alive, enjoying tolerably good health, and being able to benefit from one's natural abilities. If this implies that the concept of needs is not itself, strictly speaking, an element of justice, so be it. We have seen that Kropotkin, the champion of meeting needs, did not explicitly assign the claim of needs to justice. The alternative is to assign it to humanity. Miller rejected this on the ground that, in the relief of distress, *any* distribution would meet the claim of humanity even though a markedly unequal distribution would be thought unfair and so would fail to meet the claim of justice. But what this difficulty shows is that justice calls for *equality* in certain circumstances of distributing benefits. It does not preclude the view that the claim for providing benefit comes from the principle of humanity.

What does Miller offer instead? Having rejected Barry's view as a satisfactory account of all needs. Miller works out his own analysis of 'intrinsic' needs. In the first place he disposes of the possible suggestion that needs are 'wants', by which he means objects of desire. The term 'want' as a noun is in fact normally used to mean a lack of something regarded as essential, and that is not a bad description of a 'need'. But Miller follows Barry's usage in taking the noun 'want' to mean something that is wanted, an object of desire. Needs are usually objects of desire but they form only a segment of that category. So Miller turns to the more promising notion of a lack and suggests that 'A needs X' means 'A will suffer harm if he lacks X', and then explains his understanding of 'harm' in this context by reference to a person's plan of life. Different persons have their own individual plans of life, and harm is anything that interferes with the activities essential to a plan of life.

In making this suggestion Miller wants to avoid two common views: first, that there is a standard concept of what is a sound human nature and of what is harmful to it; and second, that the extent of 'wants' that are counted as needs is a matter of social convention, increasing as the general standard of living increases. The second of these common views is reflected in the benefits associated nowadays with the 'welfare state'. Miller thinks it is a mistaken view of needs because it implies that personal needs would diminish as well as expand in accordance with changes in the general standard of living. He quotes a sentence from a book by Benn and Peters which illustrates this and which he thinks is clearly false: 'Where poor sight is common and spectacles rare, there would be no basic need for spectacles.'[5] Benn and Peters are in fact using the term 'basic need' for one specially defined category of needs, and Miller's objection is to the use of the word 'need' rather than to alleged sociological fact. It is indeed paradoxical to say that the *need* for spectacles depends on the supply, but Miller would presumably not deny that there cannot be an obligation to provide spectacles if none are available: 'ought' implies 'can'. And where there cannot be an obligation, there also cannot be a corresponding claim. So it is reasonable to say that the claim of justice for needs to be met has to be confined within the realm of the possible. In times of extremity, such as war and famine, necessities are rationed and one cannot complain of injustice because some needs are not met. That would be true also of a decline in living standards, and in welfare-state benefits, if for some reason (perhaps overpopulation or climatic change) economic contraction were to replace the economic growth to which we have become accustomed.

I return to the question whether the claim of need should be assigned to the

---

[5] S. I. Benn and R. S. Peters, *Social Principles and the Democratic State* (London: Allan & Unwin, 1959), 146; quoted in *Social Justice*, 138.

concept of justice or that of humanity. Miller goes for justice because humanity would not require that the relief of need be distributed equally, and I have said that this is an argument for regarding equality rather than need itself as the concern of justice. Miller does proceed to consider, in the final section of his chapter on needs, the relationship between need and equality as principles of justice. He concludes that the principle of equality is 'a natural extension of the principle of need',[6] but his reasons are not altogether clear. He says that to see the satisfaction of needs as a matter of justice is to rely on an underlying premiss, 'that every man is as worthy of respect as every other', and he elaborates this statement as follows:

That is to say, although men plainly differ in moral virtue, in merit, in personal success, in usefulness to society, there is an underlying equality which consists in the fact that each man is a unique individual with his own aims, ideals, and outlook on the world, and that consequently he must be treated as such. . . . Unless the premiss is granted, we cannot show why it is *unjust* (and not merely inhumane) to satisfy one man's needs and not the needs of another. But the same premiss can be used to take us beyond the satisfaction of intrinsic needs, for it also shows why each person has an equal claim to benefits which are not needed in the true sense.[7]

If, as Miller rightly says, the underlying premiss carries us beyond the satisfaction of intrinsic needs or indeed beyond any needs 'in the true sense', why does he conclude that the principle of equality is an extension of the principle of need rather than a principle in its own right? I think it is because he has started off with the assumption that rights, desert, and need are the full complement of substantial interpretations of justice, and since he finds that egalitarians emphasize the connection between equality and need, he supposes that the claim to equality must be an offshoot of the claim of need.

After writing the passage quoted above, Miller does ask himself whether one should reverse the relationship between the two, 'whether, in fact, the idea of justice as distribution according to need is more fully expressed in the principle of equality'; and he suggests that equality refers to the end result while 'justice refers to the way in which each man has been treated—namely, according to his peculiar needs and wants'. He says that this conclusion fits the general conception of justice as *suum cuique*. But then on the next page he seems ready to accept an alternative view, that 'the principle of need represents the most urgent part of the principle of equality', which seems to make equality the more basic of the two.[8]

The claim of need must loom large in a book chiefly concerned with *social* justice, and this is why Miller's consideration of equality is focused upon its con-

[6] *Social Justice*, 147. [7] Ibid. 146–7. [8] Ibid. 147–9.

nection with need. If he had given more attention to the concept of justice in general, and especially to its place in the thought and practice of law, he would have seen that the idea of equality has a wider, and a more deeply rooted, role.

So much for Part I of David Miller's book. His examination, in Part II, of Hume, Spencer, and Kropotkin shows that their different conceptions of justice are influenced by their different views of social structure, and this leads him to ask, in Part III, what can be learned in general from the relation between social structure and concepts of justice. He considers three major types of social structure, primitive, 'hierarchical', and market society. He does not regard this classification as exhaustive: its purpose is to throw light on the social thought of modern market society by comparing it with corresponding ideas in markedly different types of society. His evidence is drawn largely from works of social anthropology, sociology, and social history.

In primitive society, he finds, there is hardly any explicit idea of social justice as understood in modern market society. There is a limited notion of rights of ownership. In the nineteenth century observers of tribal societies tended to say that all ownership there was communal, an opinion inherited and popularized by Marx and Engels, but modern anthropologists are clear that this view of tribal society is mistaken. There is private ownership, and consequently a notion of property rights, but these rights are more limited than the exclusive property right that is the norm in market society. The limitation shows a concern for general social need, in sharp contrast to the individualism of market society. There is emphasis on the duty of generosity to those in need, illustrated also in the obligations of hospitality to guests and of presenting or exchanging gifts. This duty of generosity, however, is not purely altruistic; it is part of a network of reciprocity, binding the society together and dealing with social problems (such as helping the destitute or curbing great inequality of wealth) that are dealt with in market society by duties of justice. Both rights and need, then, in primitive society are linked to the idea of generosity in the interests of social well-being rather than to an idea of justice. As for the third element of social justice, desert, meritorious acts are acknowledged as such, and sometimes honoured with a symbolic decoration, but they are not rewarded by any material benefit.

Miller offers two complementary hypotheses to explain the virtual absence of a concept of social justice in primitive society. The first is economic and is taken from Hume's thoughts on justice. Primitive societies, generally speaking, live in conditions of scarcity, so that they have to think continually about avoiding starvation. In such circumstances close attention to individual rights or desert is irrelevant in comparison with measures to ensure simple survival for the whole society. The second hypothesis concerns the character of social relationship. Primitive societies are small and close-knit; their members are well known to each other and feel bound by ties of kinship and close association. Such a society comes near to being a single extended family. In market society, by contrast, social relationship, beyond the circle of family and friends, is a cooler affair, relatively impersonal; and so transactions between individuals (between employer and employee, for example) are divorced from personal feeling and are settled by reference to impersonal rules.

For hierarchical society Miller turns to the feudalism of Western Europe. Not that he regards this example as typical of hierarchical society in general. On the contrary, he notes at the end of his discussion that a caste system is seen by scholars as 'the purest type of hierarchical society',[9] and that a caste system is likely to have a different sense of justice from that of feudalism. He presumably picked on West European feudalism because it is relatively familiar and has been widely studied. We should remember that his aim is not to make an exhaustive survey but to show up contrasts with modern market society.

The social structure of feudalism is one of reciprocal obligations between inferiors and superiors. The vassal or serf owes services to his lord in return for protection and the right to own or to till a piece of land. Inequality is taken for granted as the norm and as right and proper. Feudal law values custom more than enactment, supporting established practice but allowing scope for flexibility. The social ideas of feudalism were derived from the tradition of Christianity, but that tradition adapted itself to the social structure: the natural law notion that all men were free and equal, and that the earth was given to them for common use, was subordinated to the need to preserve the social organism. Justice was conceived to be primarily observance of the law, and since the law emphasized customary practice, justice was first and foremost a protection of established rights. There was, however, a secondary feature of justice retained from the older tradition of Christianity, a concern for the relief of need. Although the doctrines of equality and common ownership had gone by the board, the rights of private property were subject to a distinction between necessities and superfluities: necessities, interpreted as what was necessary to maintain one's status, were entirely at the disposal of the owner; what remained were superfluities and the owner had a duty to use these to relieve the needs of the poor. This duty was conceived by theologians to be a part of the virtue of justice, as we saw in Chapter 6. A distinctive feature of the notion as applied in feudalism was that the duty was owed by a lord specifically to his vassals and serfs, thereby strengthening the force of the individual relationship between superior and inferior.

Miller adds that there is little or no reference to desert in the feudal conception of justice. The just price in buying and selling goods is given some prominence in medieval theology and in feudal law, but it was based simply on traditional or

---

[9] *Social Justice*, 286.

current practice, not on recompense for the effort expended in producing the commodity. There is, Miller concedes, a recognition that the producer's effort *entitles* him to a profit but not that it determines the amount. It seems to me that the recognition of entitlement here *is* a recognition of desert, even though it does not extend to calculating degree. The determination of the amount of the just price by reference to tradition or convention can properly be compared to the customary rights of status, but that does not mean that the whole of the concept of the just price is of the same character.

To explain the differences he has found between primitive and feudal society, Miller notes that feudal society was not beset by scarcity and fear of starvation; its main concern was rather the preservation of order amid the potential rivalry of independent lords. Emphasis upon established rights would contribute to the preservation of the existing structure.

However, the secondary but still emphatic role given to the relief of need is due to traditional Christian doctrine, not to social structure. Social structure determined the form it took, requiring individual lords to succour their individual vassals or serfs, and that of course did strengthen the ties of loyalty in the established order; but the actual duty to relieve need, and the idea of calling it a duty of justice, stem from a religious tradition that pre-dates the social structure of feudalism.

It is in market society, Miller tells us, that the desert element of justice comes into its own. He uses the term 'market society' to refer to dominant features of early capitalism in Western Europe and the USA, but since those dominant features are not the whole story, Miller's picture is an abstraction, what sociologists call an ideal type, rather than an accurate representation of actual societies. It describes the middle class of merchants, shopkeepers, and some other groups of self-employed persons such as farmers and independent artisans; it is not true of aristocratic landowners and is only partially true of the working class (meaning manual workers employed by other people). Nevertheless, Miller would claim, it gives us the general ethos of the society. The social structure is one of free and equal individuals engaged in exchanges and contractual dealings with each other. Their social obligations arise from such engagements, freely undertaken. Unlike the members of primitive or feudal society, their freedom is not limited by obligations of kinship or status. They can conduct their activities just as they please and their customary motivation is the desire to better themselves. These characteristics lead Miller to call market society individualist. Since each party to a transaction enters it because he thinks it will serve his interest, and usually it does, the result is of mutual benefit and the overall practice of market procedure contributes to an ethical end, the greatest happiness of the greatest number. The success or failure of each individual is largely due to his own efforts or skill and is therefore what he deserves; that outcome of desert constitutes justice.

It was appreciated, however, that success or failure is not wholly due to personal effort: the slings and arrows of fortune may overwhelm diligence, just as her capricious bounty may mock effort. So the ethics of market society drew a distinction between the deserving and the undeserving poor. But since personal effort and skill are the chief agent of success, desert was still given priority in dealing with poverty. You might think that the relief of poverty, whether deserving or undeserving, would be grounded on need. But not so, according to Miller. There is evidence, in England at least, that in the relief of poverty need was subordinated to desert, either by confining aid to the deserving poor or by linking it to a workhouse system fostering habits of industry. This does not mean that people denied any obligation to meet need; they would accept it in the private ethics of the family if nowhere else. But it does show that they discounted it in the public sphere of social ethics and did not think of it as an obligation of justice.

The working class, Miller tells us, was in an ambiguous position. It was partly affected by the ethos of the middle class since it, too, performed its work on the basis of contract, even though few of its members had much real choice in practice. But it was also affected by co-operation in trade unions and co-operative societies, a tendency that militated against individualism and favoured a concept of justice focused upon need. This second attitude was strengthened when market society came to be modified into a later form of capitalism which Miller calls organized capitalism.

That change has come about from the growth of various elements: large enterprises; non-market agencies such as government bureaucracy and other bodies of public or semi-public administration; the number of people practising professions; the scope and power of the trade union movement. All these developments have weakened the force of individualism and substituted the idea of service to an organized community as the motive for work. So far as social justice is concerned, Miller says, desert continues to be the main element, though judged differently, and the claim of need has been reinstated.

The difference for desert goes like this. In the individualistic thought of market society, desert was a simple matter: each person was an independent agent producing goods or providing services; the gain that he obtained from the operation of the market constituted his just reward. In organized capitalism goods and services are provided by groups of people working together; the desert of an individual cannot be assessed from the value of a product or service that can be assigned to him alone. Desert is worked out in two stages: first, grading the value of positions in an organization by judging their contribution to what is finally produced, and fixing the remuneration for each position in accordance with its value; then secondly, appointing people to the graded positions by some selection procedure that assesses their capacity to do the job well.

Thus each person is rewarded on the dual basis of meriting the post and receiving as remuneration the value that the post contributes to the goods or services produced.

As for the reinstatement of the claim of need, Miller presents an argument which seems contrived. He has told us that the growth of organization makes service to the community the dominant motive for work. He now explains why. The man who holds a well-paid position is paid more than others because he makes a greater contribution to social well-being.

But social well-being must eventually be broken down into individual benefits, and the chief constituent of individual well-being is the satisfaction of needs. Thus the better-off can show their own rewards to be just by meeting the just claims to their services made by those in need. It is important here that the needy have a claim of *justice* to the benefits created by others, otherwise the notion of 'service' degenerates into paternalistic charity.[10]

Why do the better off have to regard claims of need as *just* claims? Their own rewards are counted as just because they are *deserved* in terms of the two-stage process of evaluation described earlier. True, the social well-being that gives value to their work is made up of benefit to individuals, benefit that includes the satisfaction of needs, which Miller calls the 'chief constituent' of their well-being ('basic constituent' might be more apt). Allowing all that, it is the *value* of well-being (or 'benefit' or 'satisfactions') that forms the ground of desert in the producers; and since desert is unquestionably a principle of justice, the producers do not have to think of the 'just claim' of need in order to show that their rewards are just. As for 'paternalistic charity', the well-rewarded producers do not hand out benefit gratis to the needy. The product is made available at a price, for the needy and the non-needy alike.

It is no doubt true that a concern for need is more prominent or more widespread in organized capitalism than in market society, but Miller has not shown that this is due to the difference of social structure. He has agreed that a concern for need did have a secondary role in thoughts about justice in market society. Such concern was not confined to the working class. Many doctors were ready to reduce their fee when treating the poor and to think of their work as a public service and not simply a source of income. For that matter, an individualistic shopkeeper or artisan might genuinely think of his work as a service to his customers in addition to being a source of livelihood for himself. At the stage of organized capitalism the increased strength of trade unions will certainly have helped to promote the view that justice requires a decent wage for all workers and will in general have aroused some sympathy for a socialist ethic; but it is not

---

[10] *Social Justice*, 309.

at all clear that the other elements in the growth of organization have had a similar effect. Miller himself cites ample evidence that a majority of businessmen think of the interest of the company as their chief objective and accept social responsibility as a secondary aim simply because, they suppose, it contributes to business success.

Whatever the causes, the claim of need is now widely regarded as an element of justice. Recalling his earlier thesis that desert and need conflict with each other, Miller notes that there is an underlying moral conflict about equality. The reward of desert presupposes an acceptance of inequality, inequalities of reward being linked to inequalities of skill and ability; on the other side, to think of the claims of need as a matter of justice presupposes some sense of human equality. Miller turns to planned egalitarian communities that go all out for a needs conception of social justice. He notes that they differ from primitive society despite the common feature of giving priority to need. In primitive society, as he has explained earlier, the care for need is not a principle of justice; in planned egalitarian communities that is its essence. Sociological studies of such communities suggest that their egalitarianism is sustained by a 'solidarist' social structure of close-knit harmony with an attitude of comradeship; if that gives way to a looser kind of co-operation, joint action simply for the sake of mutual advantage, the notion of justice becomes more conventional by including the reward of desert. With this type of society, then, the concept of justice does seem to depend on social structure for its maintenance.

This, of course, does not imply that the egalitarians' original adoption of their concept of justice depends on social structure, and that fact is relevant to the final reflections of Miller's book. He asks whether the results of his sociological treatment leave any room for political theory, and especially for prescriptive political theory. He mainly has in mind Rawls's attempt to reach by theory a specific concept of justice that can be used to evaluate social policy. Miller thinks his own inquiry has shown that political theory can analyse the different concepts of justice that have been held but cannot itself transcend the culture within which it operates. Each of the three principles now ascribed to justice can be associated with a particular form of society, but that does not enable us to argue for the supremacy of one principle over the others. When there is a conflict, different people take different views about assigning priority. Political theory can help them to clarify their thoughts but is in no special position to decide between them.

Chapter 18

JOHN RAWLS

John Rawls's book *A Theory of Justice*[1] has received an enormous amount of attention, probably more than any other twentieth-century work of political philosophy. I have not come upon any knowledgeable scholar who has been ready to accept Rawls's conclusions as a sound view of justice. Yet they all agree that the book is an important one. Why so? Because it uses a novel method and so presents the subject in a new perspective, always a virtue in philosophy.

The novelty does not lie in the basic feature of the method, a hypothetical contract, but in its application. The idea of a social contract is familiar and indeed ancient in political philosophy, having been used to explain and justify political obligation, the citizen's duty to obey the laws of the state. Rawls's innovation lies in transferring the idea to explaining the concept of justice. It is true that the earliest use of the idea in philosophical literature occurs in Plato's *Republic*, whose initial subject is *dikaiosyne*, justice in the wide sense of what is right, and perhaps that suggested to Rawls the possibility of adopting the idea in a new way.[2] Even so, the novelty of his approach is nonetheless striking and stimulating.

That is not the only reason for rating Rawls's book as an important one. It is a long, complex work, covering more than its nominal subject of justice. While

---

[1] John Rawls, *A Theory of Justice* (Cambridge, Mass.: Harvard University Press, 1971; Oxford: Clarendon Press, 1972).

[2] The first version of Rawls's contractual theory of justice was given in an article, 'Justice as Fairness', published in the *Philosophical Review*, 67 (1958). Note 8 of that article reminds the reader that in Plato's *Republic*, Book II, Glaucon suggests that justice is the result of a social contract. Note 8 is omitted from the revised version of 'Justice as Fairness' printed in Peter Laslett and W. C. Runciman (eds.), *Philosophy, Politics and Society*, 2nd ser. (Oxford: Blackwell, 1962), but it is in the reprint of the original version in Louis P. Pojman (ed.), *Classics of Philosophy* (New York: Oxford University Press, 1998), 1252.

Chapter 4 above observes that *dikaiosyne* in the social contract theory put forward by Glaucon has a wide sense: it is a theory about law and morality in general, about justice as meaning the whole system of law.

concentrating on that topic, often in considerable detail, it is also a treatise on moral and social philosophy generally, with special attention given to the relevance of economics and moral psychology. Its theory of justice often spills over into a theory of what is right, and since that requires consideration of the relation between the right and the good Rawls gives us his view of the good also. What he has to say on these more general issues is always of interest, but here I shall confine myself almost entirely to his view of justice. This is not easily isolated because, as I have said, his discussion of justice tends to spill over into a theory of the right and one is sometimes left uncertain which of the two he has in mind.[3]

It seems that Rawls was initially led into examining the concept of justice by his dissatisfaction with utilitarianism as a general theory of ethics. He saw that the chief defect of utilitarianism is a failure to accommodate the claims of justice and he decided that a sounder view of justice was to be found in the idea of social contract. He first set out this conception of justice in an article called 'Justice as Fairness' (1958). Chapter 1 of *A Theory of Justice* (1971) has the same title, and throughout the work Rawls uses that phrase to refer to his distinctive notion of justice. You might think that there is nothing distinctive in the phrase itself: the term 'fairness' is surely just a synonym for justice or, more accurately, for a major part of justice. Rawls is well aware of this, as he makes plain at the beginning of the original article:

It might seem at first sight that the concepts of justice and fairness are the same, and that there is no reason to distinguish them or to say that one is more fundamental than the other. I think that this impression is mistaken. In this paper I wish to show that the fundamental idea in the concept of justice is fairness; and I wish to offer an analysis of the concept of justice from this point of view.... I shall then argue that it is this aspect of justice for which utilitarianism, in its classical form, is unable to account, but which is expressed, even if misleadingly, by the ideas of the social contract.

Rawls applies the term 'fairness' both to the content of his conception and to his method of reaching it. The method is a form of social contract and that is why he says that fairness is expressed by the ideas of the social contract. He imagines people considering together what basic principles they should agree upon for the ordering of social institutions. In 'Justice as Fairness' he simply asks us to suppose that they approach the task from a standpoint of rational self-interest, his purpose being to find an alternative form of judgement to simple intuition, which is unlikely to yield a unanimous view. In *A Theory of Justice* he elaborates the hypothesis: he asks us to think of these persons as being in an 'original position',

---

[3] Cf. Joel Feinberg, 'Rawls and Intuitionism', in Norman Daniels (ed.), *Reading Rawls* (Oxford: Blackwell, 1975), 108–9.

deprived of attributes that would introduce bias into their thought. He calls this a 'veil of ignorance'. The participants have knowledge of the general laws of psychology and the social sciences but are ignorant of particular facts both about themselves and about the society in which they live. They are conceived to be self-interested and rational (that is, disposed to choose the most efficient means to predetermined ends, the relevant end here being their own maximum advantage). In coming together to form a society they must agree on principles for the distribution of benefits and burdens.

What are the principles on which such people would agree? According to Rawls, they would insist first on a form of equality. Secondly, they would require that any departure from equality should benefit everyone, and especially those who are least advantaged. When introducing the notion, Rawls says that the first principle 'requires equality in the assignment of basic rights and duties'.[4] Later he is more specific, confining the first principle to liberty, which he regards as the most basic of rights.[5] Elsewhere he describes his statement of the two principles as a special case of a general conception of justice that combines the two but in a more general way: 'All social values—liberty and opportunity, income and wealth, and the bases of self-respect—are to be distributed equally unless an unequal distribution of any, or all, of these values is to everyone's advantage.'[6]

In the later discussion the general conception is repeated with some variation: 'all social values' becomes 'all social primary goods', but the condition for unequal distribution, instead of being 'everyone's advantage' becomes 'the advantage of the least favored'.[7] In one place Rawls adds that the special conception differs from the general one because it ranks the two principles 'serially'.[8] We shall see shortly that 'serial' ranking is allotting a special kind of priority.

Each of the hypothetical contractors, Rawls believes, would think that the combination of the two principles offers the best chance of maximum advantage. Each person is ignorant of particular facts and so does not know whether he will be well or ill endowed and placed as compared with his fellows. For all he knows, he may be among the least advantaged. Therefore he will choose a scheme that aims at the greatest possible benefit for everyone and especially for the least advantaged. Such a scheme need not be, indeed is unlikely to be, completely egalitarian; for a non-egalitarian plan that gives $x+1$ units of good to the least advantaged makes them better off than does an egalitarian plan that gives x units to everyone. This is why the second principle is added to the strictly egalitarian first principle.

Rawls believes that the content of his two principles would commonly be

---

[4] *A Theory*, 14. [5] Ibid., esp. 60, 302. [6] Ibid. 62.
[7] Ibid. 303. [8] Ibid. 541.

regarded as fair. He also claims that the method of reaching them would be thought fair since it gives everyone an equal opportunity of joining in and influencing the outcome. Because the method is fair and agreed to be fair, it can and should continue to be used for the application of the two principles to rules for specific spheres of action. This later process, however, cannot be conducted under the veil of ignorance, which is accordingly lifted in stages.

As I have said, one of Rawls's aims is to provide an alternative to utilitarianism. The most popular alternative historically, he says, has been intuitionism. He uses this term to mean any theory which holds that there is a plurality of basic principles of right action. Intuitionism suffers from two defects. First, it is unable to explain why its principles should be followed: they just have to be accepted as fundamental moral 'intuitions'. Secondly, it gives no guidance for decision when two or more of its principles point to conflicting courses of action in a particular situation: here again it says simply that we must judge by moral intuition which alternative has the greater claim. These are familiar objections. Most utilitarians (but not Sidgwick nor the 'Ideal Utilitarians', Rashdall and Moore) base the principles of moral action on factors in human psychology (desires and feelings) instead of intuitions; and most of them again (with Sidgwick once more the outstanding exception) offer the principle of utility as a single fundamental principle that forms the justification for secondary principles and is therefore the criterion for resolving conflicts between secondary principles in any particular situation. But since utilitarianism has its own difficulties, is there some other way of meeting the objections that face intuitionism?

Rawls's originality lies in giving a novel answer to this question. In the preface to his book he disclaims originality, saying that his theory is 'highly Kantian in nature', but this is false modesty. He is in fact exceptionally modest and exceptionally ready to listen to his critics. All students of philosophy profess themselves ready to learn from criticism, but few of us are modest enough or pliant enough to get far with it in practice. In progressing from his early articles to *A Theory of Justice* and then to a later book, *Political Liberalism*, Rawls has modified various details of his theory in order to meet criticism. That sometimes leads to apparent uncertainty or even inconsistency, but one has to admire a philosopher who lives up to the tenets of his subject.

Rawls deals with the first defect of intuitionism by proposing a contractual hypothesis as a method of arriving at principles of justice without having to rely simply on intuition. If that could be done successfully, it would be a great gain. Not only would it explain what intuitionism leaves unexplained. It would also resolve a material disagreement, for there is no consensus on the substance of the principles of justice, as there is on most other common principles of morality. As things are, one large group of people stands pat on the intuition that justice requires distribution according to merit, while another large group insists on an alternative (or additional) principle of distribution, sometimes regarded as based on simple equality, sometimes as based on need. Rawls sides with the second group and thinks that his contractual hypothesis leads to that conclusion. The hypothesis is supposed to avoid a recourse to intuition because it depends on a judgement of prudence instead of morality.

The hypothesis does not state the meaning of justice or fairness. When the man on the Clapham omnibus says something is just or fair, he clearly does not mean that it is in accordance with principles that would be chosen by rational persons, making a social contract in order to maximize their individual interests, in circumstances in which they knew lots of general truths but were ignorant of particular facts. Rawls does not suppose this. He tells us what would be judged *prudent* in the hypothetical circumstances, and his view is that this coincides in *content* with what we normally judge to be just. He says that the kind of account he has given is an 'explication', not 'an analysis of the meaning of the term "right" as normally used in moral contexts'.[9] I think he would apply the remark to 'just' as well as to 'right', for he talks later on the same page of 'the theory of justice as fairness, or more generally of rightness as fairness'. But he goes on to declare that the explication is a 'sound analysis' or 'definition' in the sense that it provides a satisfactory substitute for a troublesome expression and thereby enables us to eliminate that expression. I take it this is consistent with what I have said above. Rawls's account does not tell us what we mean by saying that something is just, but it is an alternative method of lighting on the same idea with intellectual satisfaction if we are puzzled by the term 'justice'. We can say it is what prudence would recommend to us in the hypothetical circumstances of Rawls's contract.

Since one of the circumstances (the 'veil of ignorance' about particular facts, especially concerning oneself) makes the same choice prudent for everyone, the prudential judgement takes on a universality, an impersonality, that we do not ordinarily associate with prudence. That is why it can be a substitute for the impartial judgement of what is just, fair for all. Lots of philosophers have tried to substitute a judgement of prudence for one of morality. A simple substitution is unsatisfactory because the two things are plainly different. Hume pinpointed one of the essential differences: the notion of morals and its language differ from 'the language of self-love' in taking a universal point of view.[10] Rawls's hypothesis is a means of conferring a universal point of view on the prudential outlook.

---

[9] *A Theory*, 111.
[10] David Hume, *Enquiry concerning the Principles of Morals*, IX.i (ed. Beauchamp, pp. 74–5, §§5–6; ed. Selby-Bigge, §§221–2).

The originality of Rawls's thought is shown again, but less persuasively, in dealing with the second defect of intuitionism, its vagueness on resolving a conflict between principles. Rawls calls this the priority problem, the problem of deciding which moral principle should have priority in a situation of conflict. The weakness of intuitionism is especially striking here, for the intuition to which it appeals is different from the intuition of principles. The intuition of principles is commonly held to be a rational understanding of what is necessary and universal, comparable with the understanding of *a priori* truths; the resolution of a conflict of principles in a particular situation is held to be an intuition of preponderant 'weight' or 'stringency', comparable with a judgement about the relative weight of evidence for alternative solutions to an empirical problem. If it is unhelpful to speak of intuition, it is doubly so to use the same term for two different forms of judgement.

Utilitarianism says that the rational way of solving the priority problem is to regard the principle of utility as the court of appeal: where common rules of morality dictate conflicting courses of action in a particular situation, the right action is the one that seems likely to contribute most to the general happiness. This is the only rational method, according to utilitarianism, because the common rules of morality all depend on the more general principle of utility; for example, the rule of justice that merit should be rewarded holds good simply because actions called meritorious are actions that are generally useful and because the encouragement of such actions by the incentive of reward is useful.

The main difficulty with the utilitarian solution is that *some* moral principles, and especially some aspects of justice, do not seem to depend on utility. Where such a principle conflicts with another, an appeal to utility may seem irrelevant. Indeed, some of the most perplexing conflicts are conflicts between the principle of utility itself and an aspect of justice. This can be illustrated within the very theory of utilitarianism. The theory really consists of two principles, one prescribing the maximum increase of the total sum of happiness, the other prescribing the distribution of happiness to as many persons as possible. These two principles can conflict. In a particular situation, an individual, or, more realistically, a set of legislators, may be faced with two alternative policies. The first seems likely to increase the total national wealth more than the second, but the second seems likely to spread it more widely. Which policy is to be preferred? Utilitarianism gives us no answer.

Certain theories purport to do better than classical utilitarianism, at least verbally, by framing a single overriding principle. Thus, for example, one form of 'agathism' says that the single principle is to *realize* (not *produce*) a maximum of good; then equal or widespread distribution of happiness, no less than the production of means to happiness, can be called 'a realization of good'. In practice, of course, this does not help, for we still have to decide how to measure the 'good' of wide distribution against the 'good' of increased total happiness. We start off with the problem of deciding which is 'right', and we end up simply by being told to switch our language from 'right' to 'better'. The problem itself remains.

Rawls makes the novel proposal that we should get away from looking for a single overriding principle and should instead rank moral principles in a 'lexical' or 'serial' order. By this he means giving priority to principle A until it is *fully* satisfied (or unless it does not apply) before we are allowed to move on to implement principle B, which in turn must be fully satisfied before we may move on to implement principle C, and so on. At his first introduction of the idea Rawls admits that it does not appear promising, and he expects to use it only in a limited way. Still, it is an interesting suggestion, and one looks forward to seeing it worked out later in the book.

In the end it is not worked out at any length. Rawls's proposal is that his first principle of justice (the claim of equal liberty) should be ranked first in the serial order, his second principle of justice (which stresses the claim of need) should be ranked second, and the principle of utility should be ranked third. If we are to take him seriously, this must mean: (*a*) that, in any conflict between equal liberty and need, the claim of liberty should prevail; (*b*) in any conflict between need and utility, the claim of need should prevail; and (*c*) in any conflict between liberty and utility, the claim of liberty should prevail. The first at least of these claims is confirmed by Rawls's own statement of his first priority rule: 'The principles of justice are to be ranked in lexical order and therefore liberty can be restricted only for the sake of liberty'.[11]

Let us now consider critically the two novel features of Rawls's theory of justice. The main one is the hypothetical social contract. The conclusions of the contractors are given first in a 'general conception' of fairness and then in a 'special conception'. There are two differences between them. First, the general conception calls for equality in 'basic rights and duties' or in 'all social values' (or 'all social primary goods'), while the special conception calls for equality of maximum liberty. Secondly, the general conception allows for inequality if this gives added benefit to everyone, while the special conception adds that the increased benefit must come 'in particular for the least advantaged members of society' and that there must be equality of opportunity for reaching all positions.

The second of these differences is an insistence upon the maintenance of equality so far as possible even when an inequality is permitted for the sake of overall benefit. This is obviously true of the equal opportunity requirement. The requirement of added benefit for the least advantaged 'in particular' does not really modify the general conception's requirement of added benefit 'for

---

[11] *A Theory*, 302.

everyone'; but in some statements of the special conception Rawls writes of added benefit for the least advantaged without saying also that there must be added benefit for everyone; and perhaps this is his final view, for his priority rules imply that need has priority over general utility.

The first difference, a move from 'rights and duties' or 'all social values' to the single right (or value) of liberty, calls for explanation. Rawls does not give any explicit reason for the change, but it seems that here too the reason lies in the priority rules, for Rawls says that the essential difference between the general and the special conceptions is that the special conception places the principles of justice in serial order: liberty is given first priority and any departure from equality for the sake of greater benefit can apply only to rights or values other than liberty.

Plainly, then, we need to ask why liberty is given this special priority. Why should we suppose that the hypothetical contractors in the original position would think that liberty is the most fundamental right or value, not to be curtailed for the sake of anything else? One is inclined to say that some people, but not all, would think so, and that Rawls is unwarrantably attributing to everyone the attitude of a person brought up in the USA or in modern Western Europe, as contrasted with the probable attitude of people brought up, say, in Russia or China or the undeveloped countries of Africa. Well, can we try to abstract from the effect of upbringing? Rawls's contractors are supposed to be ignorant of the stage of civilization that their society has reached. For all they know, they might find themselves in the affluence of modern America or in the famine of Egypt at the time of Joseph. In the latter event they would put bread before freedom (cf. Gen. 47: 19). If their choice as contractors is to be prepared for all eventualities, should they not make the means of subsistence their basic good?

However, we learn from some brief passages near the end of the book that the priority assigned to liberty does not apply to all stages of society. Rawls tells us that the value of liberty, as compared with other goods, rises as civilization progresses. '*Beyond some point* it becomes and then remains irrational from the standpoint of the original position to acknowledge a lesser liberty for the sake of greater material means and amenities of office' (emphasis added).[12] How does this help to show that liberty is to be given priority in a *lexical* series as explained earlier? Lexical priority means that the claims of liberty are to be satisfied as fully as possible *before* the claims of other goods are implemented at all. What Rawls is now saying is that, *after* certain other goods have been achieved up to some point, liberty comes to be preferred to a *further* increase in those other goods. This is brought out quite clearly on the next page. 'Until the basic wants of individuals can be fulfilled, the relative urgency of their interest in liberty cannot be

---

[12] Ibid. 542.

firmly decided in advance. . . . But under favorable circumstances the fundamental interest in determining our plan of life eventually assumes a prior place.'[13] In other words, liberty is not prior to the satisfaction of 'basic wants'; liberty comes to the fore when and only when these basic wants are satisfied.

Rawls acknowledges this more openly in his later book, *Political Liberalism*: 'the first principle covering the equal basic rights and liberties may easily be preceded by a lexically prior principle requiring that citizens' basic needs be met, at least insofar as their being met is necessary for citizens to understand and to be able fruitfully to exercise those rights and liberties.'[14] The concession does not go far enough. The plain facts of life surely show that the original first principle *should*, not 'may', be preceded by a lexically prior principle of meeting basic needs. Rawls's further qualification in this quotation implies that he wants to make the new prior principle dependent upon the old: basic needs can be given priority only because they are a necessary condition of understanding and exercising basic rights and liberties. But if the contractors are to think in terms of self-interest, they will give priority to basic needs simply because that is a necessary condition of staying alive.

Even though the lexical ranking of principles has been amended to place basic needs first, we may still ask how the contractors in the original position will know that liberty should be given absolute priority once basic needs are satisfied. I think Rawls is relying on his admiration for Rousseau and Kant, whom he regards as his mentors in contractual theory. Rousseau is a social contract theorist who also makes a powerful case for treating liberty as the essence of human personality. It is not clear to me why Rawls should classify Kant as a social contract theorist, but it is true that Kant continues and elaborates Rousseau's thesis about liberty. Rawls explains in §40 of the first book why he regards his theory of justice as Kantian: he is following Kant's doctrine of autonomy, freedom of choice and action as the vital constituent of a person.

The contention of Rousseau and Kant on this matter undoubtedly has the ring of truth for most of their philosophical readers. Can we therefore suppose that Rawls's hypothetical contractors, thinking about social institutions from the standpoint of self-interest, would appreciate and give prominence to the central role of liberty for human personality? Rawls's assignment of priority to liberty is carefully examined in an article by the late Professor Herbert Hart.[15] Criticizing Rawls's view that liberty may be restricted only for the sake of liberty, Hart points to generally accepted restrictions on liberty whose purpose is to

---

[13] *A Theory*, 543.

[14] John Rawls, *Political Liberalism* (New York: Columbia University Press, 1993), 7.

[15] H. L. A. Hart, 'Rawls on Liberty and its Priority', *University of Chicago Law Review*, 40/3 (Spring 1973); repr. in Daniels (ed.), *Reading Rawls*.

prevent harm or suffering, not to enhance liberty elsewhere; examples are the restraint of libel, slander, the invasion of privacy, and the unlimited use of private property (such as dangerous speeding in motor vehicles). He also observes that Rawls has given no sound reason for thinking that the hypothetical contractors, deciding from the standpoint of self-interest, would not sacrifice some liberty for the sake of an addition to their material comfort. The priority of liberty is to come into effect when basic needs have been met, and that suggests that the standard of living would still be relatively austere. Would not self-interested contractors be likely to go for greater material comfort before insisting on the liberties that Rawls specifies, such as the right to vote and stand for political office, freedom of conscience, and the right to own property?

In *Political Liberalism* Rawls replies to the second criticism by revising a presupposition of his earlier book. He now suggests that 'the basic liberties and the grounds for their priority can be founded on the conception of citizens as free and equal persons' and so 'rest on a conception of the person that would be recognized as liberal and not, as Hart thought, on considerations of rational interests alone'.[16] That is a radical change from the approach of *A Theory of Justice*, which aimed to explain the idea of justice through a subtle use of rational self-interest. In *Political Liberalism* we are asked to think of the two principles as expressing 'an egalitarian form of liberalism'.[17] Liberalism will of course count liberty as its foremost political principle; that is what liberalism means. And an egalitarian form of liberalism will of course add equality. Tautology is a poor substitute for the earlier attempt at enlightening explanation.

I now want to ask, why should the political principle of liberty be treated as a principle of *justice*? The question is pertinent for the original view of *A Theory* as well as for the revised view of the later book. Although the account was not intended to give the meaning of 'justice', we were told that the content should accord with generally accepted views; and in *Political Liberalism* we are told that the parties to the contract 'must agree to certain principles of justice on a short list of alternatives given by the tradition of moral and political philosophy'.[18] The traditional principles of justice have concerned equality and desert, together with a less firm tendency in some quarters to add the relief of need. Rawls's statement in *Political Liberalism* allows him to be selective and he has chosen to include equality and need and to exclude desert. The traditional list does not include liberty. Liberty is certainly a prime principle—if you will, *the* prime principle—of politics, but not all such principles are accounted as elements of justice. The parties to Rawls's social contract are asked to specify principles of social order, and so it is legitimate enough for them to include liberty; but the remit is too wide if their conclusions are supposed to accord with traditional ideas of *justice*.

[16] *Political Liberalism*, 290. [17] Ibid. 6. [18] Ibid. 305.

Following on from that, we should ask why Rawls has chosen to exclude desert from his conception of justice. He discusses the matter briefly in §48 of *A Theory*. He has two arguments for the exclusion. One is that in practice rewards are allotted for reasons of utility, not for moral worth. The other is that the concept of moral worth is dependent upon the prior existence of principles of justice, and so cannot enter into the selection of those principles by the parties to the social contract. I shall deal with each of these in turn.

The argument about actual practice is familiar. Rawls thinks chiefly of economic life, where one may speak of a just or fair wage, but it is determined by utility, not moral worth. Weight is given to the recipient's contribution but the value of that contribution is assessed by supply and demand. Scarce talent is given a premium reward for the same reason, and in any event possession of the talent is a matter of good fortune, not moral merit. The one thing that can genuinely claim moral merit is effort, but even that, according to Rawls, is largely dependent upon native ability, for which one is not responsible. People who think that all this is unfair, and that justice calls for the reward of moral worth so far as that is feasible, are linking reward with punishment, distributive justice with retributive. This, Rawls contends, is a mistake; the two are quite different: retributive justice, the criminal law, is designed to 'uphold basic natural duties', while distributive justice serves social utility.

The reference to criminal law is fleeting and undeveloped. It is unfortunate that Rawls has deliberately confined his large book to social justice and has left aside the huge role of justice in the law. At the beginning of his book he distinguishes between 'strict compliance (or ideal) theory' and 'partial compliance theory'. The first is concerned with 'the principles of justice that would regulate a well-ordered society' in which 'everybody is presumed to act justly and to do his part in upholding just institutions'. The second 'studies the principles that govern how we are to deal with injustice'.[19] Rawls chooses to deal with the first alone.

I would agree with him that in practice rewards are largely (I would not say wholly) founded on utility; but I think that his neglect of the criminal law has blinded him to a cardinal feature of the concept of justice, its insisting upon ill desert as a necessary condition of penal sanctions, and thus protecting the innocent against the claim of social utility. Apart from that, Rawls is unjustified in denying the link between reward and punishment. The *concepts* of reward and punishment, like the concepts of praise and blame, are indeed linked as opposites, and this remains true despite the fact that the practical application of *each* of them has much to do with utility (as utilitarian theory attests). One does not need to say that this implies an erroneous linking of distributive with retributive

---

[19] *A Theory*, 8.

justice; the reward of good desert, as well as the punishment of ill desert, can be assigned to retributive justice. The words 'retribution' and 'retributive' carried both senses in the past, as the word 'requital' still does. A modern philosopher, E. F. Carritt, included reward with punishment under retributive justice and confined distributive justice to the concept of equality.[20] However, the most important point, and indeed the strongest objection to utilitarianism, is that justice protects the innocent individual against the claims of general interest.

Rawls's second argument, which he evidently regards as crucial, is that 'the concept of moral worth . . . cannot be introduced until after the principles of justice and of natural duty and obligation have been introduced'.[21] I suppose he means that the notion of moral worth or moral desert carries with it and presupposes the idea of a just claim to reward, and for that reason 'such a principle would not be chosen in the original position'.[22] But he seems to have forgotten that the contractors in the original position are expected to think in terms of self-interest and not in explicit terms of justice, lighting upon the content of justice by an indirect route. They can easily come to a principle of desert by that route.

Let us go back to the two principles which Rawls says they would choose. I have criticized the first, the principle of equal liberty, but have not as yet queried the second, which Rawls calls the difference principle because it gives the grounds for allowing differences, departures from equality. It emphasizes concern for the least advantaged, aiming at the maximum benefit for those who have the minimal position in society. Rawls refers to this aim as maximin. A rationally prudent contractor would reflect that he might be in the minimal position and so he should ensure the maximum benefit for it. This argument depends on the assumption that it is the part of prudence to prepare for the worst, an assumption that Rawls in fact makes. But we may also ask, why is it necessarily rational to play safe rather than gamble a little?[23] Rawls supposes that a rational man, moved by self-interest and not knowing whether he will be among the lucky ones or the unlucky, will prefer to maximize the good of the latter rather than offer glittering prizes for the former. But what about a middle course, a sort of welfare state, in which the unlucky are guaranteed a bare subsistence while the lucky can go for not so glittering but still quite attractive prizes? Is it clearly rational to put that aside? There is a chance after all that one will end up among the lucky people; and even if one does not, there is, as Adam Smith said, a vicarious satisfaction to be obtained from contemplating the

---

[20] E. F. Carritt, *Ethical and Political Thinking* (Oxford: Clarendon Press, 1947), 97–101.
[21] *A Theory*, 312. [22] Ibid. 310.
[23] Cf. Michael Lessnoff, 'John Rawls' Theory of Justice', *Political Studies*, 9 (1971), 76.

pleasures of 'the rich and the great', especially since Rawls's contractors are supposed to lack envy.

It is not only possible, but plausible, to argue that rational contractors would positively prefer such a system. A welfare-state system includes a natural incentive to aim at bettering one's position: the prizes above the guaranteed line of subsistence may depend initially on luck but they can be improved by effort, and that introduces a notion of reward for merit—not in terms of a moral principle of justice but simply as a self-interested policy that works. Like Rawls's principles, however, it coincides in content with an element of justice, in this case the concept of merit, for merit proper does not depend on the luck of the game but on a person's effort to do the best he can with the abilities and circumstances that fall to his lot. The initial contractor does not know what his individual abilities and circumstances will be, compared with those of other people. He does know (it is part of his supposed knowledge of general principles) that it is equally within everyone's power to use, or fail to use, to the full such abilities and opportunities as he will have. Since *this* depends, not on chance, but on his own choice, a rational man will plump for a system that distributes advantage according to merit.

Rawls's hypothesis does not provide a method of deciding between rival conceptions of justice. It is tailored to fit one of these, but can be stretched to cover another; and we are given no reason why it should not be differently tailored anyway. Rawls favours a conception of justice that leans towards egalitarianism and distribution according to need. He rejects the principle of distribution according to desert and supposes that his hypothesis leads to his own conception. But, as we have seen, it is perfectly possible to say that his rational contractors would choose a system that included desert. Then again, Rawls adds to his hypothesis the proviso that his initial contractors lack envy. This is to avoid their choosing a strictly egalitarian system in which the level of goods, for each as well as for all, is less than it might be. Rawls is ready to accept inequality provided that it means increased benefit for all groups including the poorest. Someone who thinks that justice (as contrasted with some other principle of morality) insists on strict equality could still use Rawls's hypothesis but without depriving the contractors of envy, in which case they could be supposed to go for a bare egalitarianism.

Nevertheless Rawls's hypothesis of a social contract does tell us something about the notion of fairness which we do not normally see. Fairness is a notion that is acquired at an early stage of life: young children are quick to complain that action which discriminates in favour of one child or one group is unfair, and they do not confine this complaint to thought of their own advantage but are ready to speak up for the claim of others. This seems a surprising expression of altruism at a stage when the child's concern is still largely centred on himself.

When Rawls explains why his hypothetical contract is a method of fairness, he brings out the connection between fairness and self-interest. This is especially clear in the early paper 'Justice as Fairness' (§4):

> Justice is the virtue of practices where there are assumed to be competing interests and conflicting claims, and where it is supposed that persons will press their rights on each other. That persons are mutually self-interested in certain situations and for certain purposes is what gives rise to the question of justice in practices covering those circumstances. Amongst an association of saints, if such a community could really exist, the disputes about justice could hardly occur; for they would all work selflessly together for one end.

The last sentence recalls Hume's perception that the need for distributive justice arises from the facts of scarcity and limited benevolence. Rawls refers to Hume when he takes up the theme in *A Theory*, where he rightly stresses the factor of scarcity.[24] Hume's account does include the role of self-interest but Rawls's contribution adds the insight that agreement to take in the self-interested aims of each person is a good part of what we mean by fairness.

Rawls's second innovation of method, lexical priority, fares less well than the hypothetical contract. How can the second principle of justice be implemented at all if the first principle has lexical priority? The first principle requires a maximum of equal liberty for all. The second says that inequalities (of liberty as of other things) are justified only if they benefit people in all positions and especially the least advantaged. Now if the first principle has lexical priority, this means that no question of inequality, even for the sake of benefiting the needy or the society as a whole, may be considered unless there is full satisfaction of the first principle, maximum equal liberty for all. A maximum of equal liberty is the same as a minimum of restraints on liberty equally for all. Restraints on a person's liberty, according to Rawls, are justified only as necessary means to the protection of a like liberty for others; so that all the restraints in a situation of maximum equal liberty are necessary for the protection of that maximum. Then if a restraint on liberty is lightened in one quarter, this must have the consequence of adding to the impediments to liberty in another quarter. In other words, any increase of liberty for one individual or group must involve a decrease of liberty for some other individual or group; it must involve a falling short of the maximum of equal liberty that existed before. So lexical priority for maximum equal liberty implies that unequal *liberty* may never be considered at all.

Furthermore, some other inequalities, such as inequality of wealth and inequality of power or authority, involve unequal liberty. Wealth increases the

---

[24] *A Theory*, 127–30.

freedom to acquire possessions that one would like to have, and to enjoy activities that one would like to pursue; power and likewise authority increase the freedom to get other people to do what one would like them to do; so that inequality of wealth or power or authority includes inequality of liberty. Lexical priority for maximum equal liberty implies that such inequalities, too, may never be considered.

Rawls states his priority rules about halfway through the book. He delays giving any argument for them until near the end, and when it does finally come it is restricted to presenting a case for the priority of liberty. The argument is that the value of liberty, as compared with other goods, rises as civilization progresses. As we have seen, this implies that in the first stages liberty is not prior to the satisfaction of 'basic wants'. The original notion of lexical priority for liberty has disappeared.

Although the argument is unsatisfactory, at least there is an argument given in the end for assigning priority to Rawls's first principle of justice. When it comes to priority among goods, he is less accommodating. He defines primary goods as 'things that every rational man is presumed to want',[25] and he distinguishes natural primary goods, such as health and intelligence, from social primary goods. The social primary goods, he says, are liberty and opportunity, income and wealth, and self-respect. It seems odd to put income and wealth in the same category as liberty, opportunity, and self-respect. In the ordinary way one thinks of income and wealth as means to basic goods rather than as goods themselves; and since there are forms of society (some of them highly rational) in which income and wealth do not exist as private possessions, one expects some argument for classing them as 'things that every rational man is presumed to want'. The argument never comes. Rawls does explain why he thinks great importance is to be attached to liberty and to self-respect, but so far as the list of social goods as a whole is concerned he simply says that he will not argue the case for it 'since their claims seem evident enough'.[26]

I conclude with some general reflections on Rawls's more fruitful innovation of a hypothetical contract. Strictly speaking, the hypothesis is not coherent. It does not really make sense to suppose that people might know the general laws of psychology and the social sciences while being unacquainted with any individual facts about their own abilities and the character of their own society. The sciences in question are empirical, not *a priori* like pure mathematics, so an understanding of them depends on acquaintance with individual facts of the kind on which the general laws are based; and if a hypothetical person were debarred from having experiential knowledge of his own abilities and his own society, he could not have experiential, or derived, knowledge of *anyone's* abilities or *any* society. Even if

---

[25] *A Theory*, 62.   [26] Ibid 434.

this objection were invalid, it would still be true that the general knowledge postulated by Rawls would be so thin as to be useless. Since the contractors are ignorant of the stage of civilization of their society, the 'laws' of psychology, economics, and politics that they know must be such as would apply equally to tribal as to industrial society. A difference in form of society often means a difference of psychology as well as of social institutions, and the sort of psychological and economic 'laws' that apply throughout the whole gamut would tell one virtually nothing about predictable behaviour.

However, an insistence on strict coherence may be misplaced. A tale of fantasy is similarly incoherent if details are pressed; yet we can understand it on the superficial level intended by the author, and can see its point. A philosophical hypothesis like that of Rawls is admittedly fantastic but can be intelligible and have point. In one place Rawls compares his hypothesis with the more realistic situation of 'delegates to a constitutional convention, and ideal legislators and voters',[27] where similar though less strict limitations apply. A legislator has to frame policies for the future, relying on knowledge of general facts and ignorant of the way in which they will work out in detail for individual cases. We may recall the classical theory of utilitarianism as expounded by Bentham. It represents the legislator as motivated by benevolence although behaviour in private life is largely motivated by self-interest. That is an idealization, like Rawls's reference to 'ideal' legislators, but it is not a fantasy, and it is a way of making the point that the standard of right action, as utilitarians understand it, coincides with the choice that legislators would make if they acted purely from benevolence. It explains the judgement of right by describing a hypothetical fact, just as Rawls tries to do.

More to the point is the question whether Rawls's hypothesis achieves his purpose of eliminating intuition. The details of the hypothesis are manipulated so as to yield a preconceived view, that is, a particular moral intuition; and even then the hypothesis does not necessarily lead to Rawls's conclusions, which are thus shown again to rest on intuition. Now Rawls knows very well that there is an alternative method of trying to dispense with intuition, the method followed by empiricist moral philosophers, including some of the leading utilitarians. It is to base moral judgement on factors of moral and social psychology, and notably on sympathy. Rawls rejects the concept of a sympathetic spectator for this purpose. He takes it to be a device of utilitarian theory for thinking of the interests of society as if they were the interests of a single person, and he says the trouble with utilitarianism is that 'it does not take seriously the distinction between persons'.[28] One can reasonably complain of utilitarianism that it does not take the distinction seriously *enough*, but not on the grounds alleged by

[27] Ibid. 449.   [28] Ibid. 27, 187.

Rawls. The concept of the sympathetic spectator, as used by classical theorists, does not blur the distinction between persons. This is true even of Hume, who did found utility on sympathy. It is more obviously true of Adam Smith, who developed the notion of the sympathetic spectator in order to *oppose* utilitarianism and to support an empiricist version of natural law theory.

I mentioned at the beginning of this discussion that it is not clear whether the contractual hypothesis is supposed to apply to moral judgement as a whole or only to judgements of distributive justice. When introducing it, Rawls says that his version of the contract theory is intended only to apply to justice,[29] and that if this were found to be reasonably successful, one might (though he will not, in this book at least) go on to consider whether the idea could be extended to the more general notion of rightness and perhaps to a still wider conception of all moral relationships. Yet later he often writes as if his theory did apply to the concept of rightness in general. Indeed, if this were not the case, Rawls would not have given us an alternative to utilitarianism. The main objection to utilitarianism is that our intuitive convictions often oppose justice to utility and at times give justice priority. A non-utilitarian view of justice can account for the opposition but not for the priority. For the latter purpose we need a theory of right. Utilitarianism says that the right action (both when it is and when it is not also a just action) is always the most useful action. If we want to deny that, if we want to say that sometimes the right action (being also a just action) is not the most useful, we need to show what is the criterion of rightness. This cannot be the same as the criterion of justice, for there are also times when we judge that the right action *is* the most useful one even though it is not also a just action and indeed may be an alternative to the just action. I gave an example in Chapter 9: in time of war the most useful method of selecting men for military service or demobilization is not the fairest method, as we ordinarily conceive of fairness; yet most people would agree that it is right in those circumstances for the national interest to prevail over fairness.

Rawls would probably say that his theory allows a decision to follow utility in such a situation, provided that the useful result will benefit people in all positions and especially the most needy. If so, he is regarding his theory as one of rightness, not of justice or fairness as commonly understood. Unfortunately it does not give us a criterion for deciding when utility should prevail over fairness and when it should not; we have to fall back on the intuitive moral judgement that he wanted to eliminate.

However, the disappointments of Rawls's contractual theory do not detract from the value of what he says about the sense of fairness. I do not think it covers

---

[29] *A Theory*, 17.

the whole picture, since a developed sense of fairness can be quite disinterested, but Rawls's account in terms of mutual self-interest is an enlightening suggestion for the origin of this state of mind. It would not have occurred to him apart from his reflections on the idea of the social contract.

Chapter 19

ROBERT NOZICK

Robert Nozick's theory of justice is to be found in his book *Anarchy, State and Utopia*,[1] the main purpose of which is to advocate a minimal state in the spirit of John Locke, that is to say, a state whose functions are confined to the protection of rights. Nozick therefore opposes the idea of a welfare state that expands its functions into redistributing income and wealth so as to provide for the needs of citizens who cannot easily provide for themselves. He devotes a large part of his book to the concept of distributive justice because that is commonly taken to be the ground for the welfare state.

His own conception of justice is one of 'entitlement'. Essentially it is what David Miller calls the rights view of justice, but Nozick's formulation has important distinctive features. The chief of these is his emphasis on the *historical* character of the rights of justice. An entitlement is a just 'holding', and a holding can come about in either of two ways: direct acquisition by the holder, or transfer from some other person or persons through voluntary exchange or gift. In either event the holder's entitlement arises from an action in the past.

Not all holdings are just entitlements: a holding can be acquired unjustly, by theft or fraud, for example, or by forcible seizure contrary to the wishes of the original holder. A person is entitled to a holding only if it has been justly acquired or justly transferred. If a holding has arisen from a past injustice, it may be just to rectify it. ('May be' rather than 'will be' because there can be countervailing reasons, such as the lapse of time, for leaving well alone.) Rectification is a third principle of justice, to be added to the two principles of just acquisition and just transfer. Like them, the justice of rectification depends on a past event, the unjust action which it aims to undo. All three principles of justice, then, have a historical character.

Nozick contrasts this feature of justice, as he understands the term, with the

---

[1] Robert Nozick, *Anarchy, State and Utopia* (New York: Basic Books; Oxford: Blackwell, 1974).

non-historical character of alternative conceptions of justice. They use 'current time-slice principles' of justice: they look at a situation as it is now, in the current slice of time, and they assess its justice or injustice by reference to some 'structural' principle or principles of just distribution. A utilitarian, for example, judges one distribution of benefits to be more just than another if it is likely to produce a greater total sum of happiness; and where there is no discernible difference between the two distributions on this score, then the one that is a more equal form of distribution is to be rated the more just. There is no need to look at the past; all that matters is the degree of general utility and, sometimes, the tendency to equality in the distribution itself. Welfare economics, says Nozick, operates on this conception.

He goes on to show that it is plainly too narrow as an account of what is normally understood to be a just distribution. Nearly everyone would agree that some reference to the past is also relevant. The justice of imprisonment under the criminal law depends on what the imprisoned person has done, in consequence of which he *deserves* to be punished, deserves to be deprived of benefits that other people enjoy. Again, many people, certainly all socialists despite their advocacy of the structural principle of equality, would say that desert for past action is the determinant of justice in an entitlement to the fruits of one's labour.

Nozick then broadens his conspectus of non-historical ideas of justice based on a structural principle of distribution. They need not be confined to a 'current time-slice' but can take in a series of time-slices. For example, someone who adopts equality as his structural principle need not necessarily say that justice requires an equal share of benefits for everyone right now; he might think that an individual who has had a lesser than average share of benefit in the past should be given a greater than average share in order to compensate for the past. The reference to the past may seem to imply that this view should not be called non-historical. But Nozick would doubtless say that its essential character is dependence on the structural principle of equal distribution, applied to a whole lifespan rather than to the one, currently existing, slice of time. To accommodate the wider conspectus, Nozick replaces the name 'current time-slice principles' by 'end-result or end-state principles'.

He next draws a different distinction within the class of historical conceptions of justice, contrasting entitlement principles with 'patterned' principles. A patterned principle calls for distribution in accordance with variations in some 'natural dimension' (or in a combination of natural dimensions), such as moral merit or usefulness to society or needs. It is not clear why these characteristics should be called natural. I suppose they are called dimensions because they admit of degrees. They are historical because the ground for differential distribution is made up of past actions (meritorious or useful deeds) or past passivities (such as deprivations leading to need). The commonly suggested principles of distributive justice are nearly all patterned: they claim that the distribution of benefits should follow a pattern, should accord with variations in a general feature of human life. Entitlement principles, on the other hand, are not patterned: they refer to particular past actions as the ground for justice in holdings.

Nozick thinks that the very idea of 'distributive' justice, of a just redistribution of goods, is misleading because it implies that an existing state of holdings is the result of a deliberate or planned distribution by state authority, whereas in fact it has come about from a haphazard collection of actions by individuals or groups of persons. If you think, as so many theorists do, that justice is a matter of filling in the blanks in the formulae, 'To each according to his . . .' and 'From each according to his . . .', you make an unreal separation between production and distribution. When a person makes something, having bought or contracted for any holdings needed for the process, he is entitled to what he has made. 'The situation is *not* one of something's getting made, and there being an open question of who is to get it. Things come into the world already attached to people having entitlements over them.' If you insist on describing justice in terms of the popular formulae, then it is choice that should fill in the blanks: 'From each according to what he chooses to do, to each according to what he makes for himself . . . and what others choose to do for him and choose to give him.'[2]

Nozick illustrates the incompatibility of choice with a patterned conception of justice through a lively hypothetical example. Suppose that there is a society in which a patterned principle of distributive justice has been put into effect. It might, for example, be a strict principle of equality, so that everyone has been given the same amount of money. One of its members is Wilt Chamberlain, the incomparable basketball player. Knowing his popularity with spectators, he signs up for a team in a contract stipulating that for each game played at the home ground he is to receive twenty-five cents from the price of every ticket sold. Lots of people are happy to go along with this in order to see Wilt Chamberlain play; they gladly place twenty-five cents of the admission fee into a special box marked with his name. At the end of the season a million tickets have been sold for home games, and Wilt Chamberlain has received $250,000, a far larger income than anyone else has earned. This grossly upsets the supposedly just distribution imposed at the beginning. Is the new distribution unjust? Everyone is happy about it; it is the result of voluntary choice; nobody has been done down. If people are not to be allowed to choose what they do with their money, what is the point of giving them any in the first place? A free choice of action is essential to justice, and such freedom will upset any patterned principle of distributive justice.

What is the example supposed to prove? Nozick introduces it with the state-

---

[2] Nozick, *Anarchy, State and Utopia*, 160.

ment: 'It is not clear how those holding alternative conceptions of distributive justice can reject the entitlement conception of justice in holdings.'[3] True; but why should they not hold both? Having given the example, Nozick says it shows that no patterned principle of justice 'can be continuously realized without continuous interference with people's lives'.[4] True again; but no one other than theorists of an extreme communism have supposed that their favoured pattern can or should be realized totally, let alone continuously. The usual aim has been to mitigate what is seen as injustice, not to get rid of it completely and for ever. Nozick advocates a minimal state and opposes a welfare state. The idea of the welfare state is as well described in Lord Beveridge's *Report on Social Insurance and Allied Services* as anywhere. It envisages state help for the needy up to a modest level of subsistence, with encouragement for people to rise above that level by their own efforts. If one is to think of it as animated by a sense of justice, then that sense includes both a communal responsibility to meet needs and an individual responsibility to better one's condition. The second of these is not the same as Nozick's freedom to act as one chooses, but it presupposes such freedom, with an implied sanction that anyone who chooses to be idle cannot expect any further help from the state.

Nozick does not say explicitly that a true concept of justice is confined to his notion of entitlement and rectification, but that seems to be his view. What reasons could he give? He might remind us of the incompatibility between the entitlement conception and any patterned conception, shown up by the tale of Wilt Chamberlain. A concept that is to guide social life, he might say, must be self-consistent. No doubt that is desirable; but a true account of a concept must accord with the relevant evidence, and the relevant evidence is the way the concept is in fact used. Justice is a complex concept and we noted earlier that the distributive principles of merit and need can conflict with each other. So it is not surprising to be told that either of them, or indeed any principle of distributive justice, can conflict with an aspect of the rights conception of justice. In fact this is implicitly recognized in my description of the rights conception as conservative justice, liable to be revised by reformative justice. The conflict does not require us to say that one or other of the conflicting conceptions is not true justice. If both are commonly described in terms of justice, we should accept that.

In the case of the conflict between the principles of merit and need, it is possible to query the inclusion of need within justice since this is a relatively late development and is not firmly established in the use of language. That does not mean querying the genuine ethical character of the claim of need: Nozick would presumably allow that the relief of need is a duty of beneficence and is an ethical claim in that sense, although he would challenge subsuming it under the rubric

---

[3] Ibid.   [4] Ibid. 163.

of justice. We are often faced with a conflict of prima facie duties and must decide which to regard as paramount. Such a conflict may be between a duty to help the needy and a duty to respect established rights (what Nozick calls entitlements). The essential features of the situation are the same irrespective of whether the duty to relieve need is attributed to beneficence or to justice, though an attribution to justice perhaps implies a stronger degree of obligation. A potential incompatibility between ethical claims is a constant feature of human life and there is no good reason to say that it cannot occur within the sphere of a single ethical concept as well as between two (or more) such concepts. There can be a conflict between two claims of beneficence or between two claims of justice. Incompatibility between the claim of entitlements and that of 'patterned' principles is no reason to deny the validity of either as a species of justice.

Nozick's primary concern is to make a case for the minimal state. He examines the concept of justice only because he thinks that 'patterned' principles of social justice are used as the ground for expanding the functions of the state. Consequently he tends to think of 'patterned' justice solely in relation to the state and seems to forget that ideas of fairness are used of relations between people in all sort of groups. Children will complain of unfair treatment if there is discrimination favouring some over others in the allotment of good things; this might occur in the family, or in the school, or in the children's own gatherings at play.

Nozick refers briefly to the family at one point. He says that radical advocates of a patterned principle of social justice have an ambivalent attitude towards the family: they think of its loving relationships as a model to be emulated in the society as a whole, but at the same time they denounce it as being too concerned with its own narrow affairs and so becoming blinded to the need for radical change in the wider society. He goes on to say that 'it is not appropriate to enforce across the wider society the relationships of love and care appropriate within a family, relationships which are voluntarily undertaken'; and he then notes that love is a historical relationship, like the entitlements of justice, and is attached to particular persons. A footnote adds that Rawls's difference principle would be inappropriate in a loving family since it would require specially favourable treatment for the least well-off and least talented child, holding back the other children.[5]

The discussion gives the impression, perhaps unintentionally, that in a loving family there is no place for 'patterned' justice. It is true that parental love may override the merit principle of distributive justice, but then it does so by regarding the equality principle as more appropriate. Indeed parental love may

---

[5] Nozick, *Anarchy, State and Utopia*, 167–8.

itself be subject to correction by the justice of equal regard. Sometimes a parent happens to love one child more than another, as Jacob loved Joseph above all his brethren; it is undoubtedly right for such a parent to reflect that justice calls for the favouritism to be subordinated to the principle of equality. As for Rawls's difference principle, that is a form of the needs conception of justice. A loving family would surely agree that the special need of the least well-off and least talented child warrants some discrimination, though I agree that it would be unjust to discriminate so far as to 'hold back' the other children or (Nozick's elaboration) to make payment for their education conditional upon their lifelong commitment to 'maximizing the position of their least fortunate sibling'. To agree that this would be unjust is to judge that the entitlement right of the other children outweighs the needs claim of the disadvantaged child if they should conflict; it does not imply that the needs claim has no validity at all.

The requirement on parents to take account of 'patterned' justice applies to anyone in a position of care or authority over a group of people. He or she is expected to allot benefits equitably: that is to say, equally where there is no relevant reason to discriminate, and, where it appears that there is reason to discriminate, to count as relevant reasons either merit or special need.

The requirement would apply to Nozick himself as a university teacher: he has a duty to deal equitably with his students, notably in the award of marks or grades for their performance in essays and examinations, a task in which he must follow the principle, 'to each according to his or her merit'. He might say that the duty arises from a tacit contract with each of his students, not from a general principle of justice; but that would not cover a similar duty in awarding marks or grades as an external examiner of students whom he has not taught and with whom he has had no contact.

In short, if we wish to understand the concept of justice, we should not restrict our attention to the role of justice in the state. Nozick has given no good reason to confine justice to entitlements and to dismiss any addition from 'patterned' principles. His discussion does, however, make a positive contribution to clarifying our thought about justice in bringing out the special features of entitlement: its historical character and its connection with free choice.

Chapter 20

BRIAN BARRY

When John Rawls's *Theory of Justice* appeared, Brian Barry was its most resolute critic. While others wrote articles or reviews concentrating on two or three main issues, Barry wrote a sizeable book, *The Liberal Theory of Justice*, that went through the whole of Rawls's work with a fine toothcomb. Yet, although his comments were largely critical, he also paid tribute to the value and importance of Rawls's novel treatment of the topic of justice. Since that time Barry has been thinking hard about the subject for himself and has been engaged in recent years upon a large-scale *Treatise on Social Justice*. In it he repeats his praise of Rawls, if anything more warmly than before, and thinks of himself as following in Rawls's footsteps[1] because he accepts the idea that the content of justice is what would receive the agreement of all participants in a hypothetical contract.

Two volumes of Barry's *Treatise* have appeared at the time when I write: Volume I, *Theories of Justice*, was published in 1989, and Volume II, *Justice as Impartiality*, in 1995. There is to be a third volume on *Principles of Justice* and a fourth collecting together a number of individual essays. Barry's own view of the essence of justice is given in Volume II, and I shall confine myself mainly to that, with some corroborative reference to Volume I. This treatment is bound to be inadequate, since the third volume will put flesh on the bare bones of the general theory set out in Volume II. The positive exposition of Barry's theory in Volume II is in fact rather limited; by far the greater part of the book is taken up with criticism of an alternative approach and of writers who, in Barry's view, have opposed the idea of justice as impartiality. But it would be wrong to omit discussion of Barry from my survey, since his interpretation of impartiality is novel and his project as a whole is a massive affair that cannot be ignored. Not that the massive size is itself a virtue; a more concise version could have been more easily understood and perhaps more persuasive.

[1] Brian Barry, *Justice as Impartiality* (Oxford: Clarendon Press, 1995), 7.

Barry's first volume, *Theories of Justice*, is not a comprehensive account of many theories. He deals with two, justice as mutual advantage and justice as impartiality, treating them as the most serious contenders for acceptance. He says that the theory of justice as mutual advantage was first put forward in Plato's *Republic* by Thrasymachus and Glaucon, was best expressed by Hobbes, and is found also in Hume and, among modern thinkers, in David Gauthier. Barry himself rejects it and goes instead for the alternative view of justice as impartiality.

It is misleading to describe the position of Thrasymachus and Glaucon in Plato's *Republic* as a theory of justice: I have explained in Chapter 4 that their argument is a wider hypothesis about law and morality in general. It is equally misleading to apply the same description to Hobbes: Hobbes does indeed revive most powerfully the position of Thrasymachus and Glaucon, but again as a general hypothesis, this time about the authority of the state. Hobbes does also have a definite view about the specific concept of justice, which I have discussed in Chapter 7; it is only marginally related to his overall political theory. Like Rawls, Barry does not always distinguish sufficiently between justice and the more-inclusive concept of what is right.

The two theories of justice that Barry discusses seem at first sight to be ill matched as alternatives. The first presents mutual advantage as the purpose of justice and hence the motive that gave rise to it; the alleged rival, impartiality, one would naturally say, is a different sort of thing, the leading principle of justice. Indeed the notion of justice as impartiality does not seem to be a theory at all, but just a phrase that labours the obvious, unless it is intended to *limit* justice to this one feature. Hardly anyone, even among supporters of the mutual advantage theory, would deny that justice requires impartiality, at least in courts of law, and perhaps most people would be ready to agree that impartiality is the cardinal concern of justice. David Gauthier, whom Barry calls 'the contemporary champion of justice as mutual advantage',[2] in fact applies his sophisticated theory of mutual advantage to morality as a whole, and he takes it for granted that the *content* of morality, and of justice in particular, is impartiality. He obviously does not regard impartiality as a rival of mutual advantage.

It turns out, however, that Barry gives the term 'impartiality' a peculiar sense when he writes of justice as impartiality: he uses it to describe any theory of justice that conforms to some version of the type of hypothetical contract or agreement introduced by Rawls. Barry's own version of the contract, derived from T. M. Scanlon, dispenses with Rawls's 'veil of ignorance' and supposes that the participants are motivated by 'the desire for reasonable agreement'.[3] Scanlon

---

[2] Ibid. 42. Gauthier presents his theory in *Morals by Agreement* (Oxford: Clarendon Press, 1986).   [3] Ibid. 67, quoting Scanlon.

uses it as a device to decide whether an act is wrong. Barry substitutes 'unjust' for 'wrong' and thinks this makes no substantial difference. He introduces his peculiar usage of the term 'impartiality' at an early stage of *Justice as Impartiality*:

A theory of justice which makes it turn on the terms of reasonable agreement I call a theory of justice as impartiality. Principles of justice that satisfy its conditions are impartial because they capture a certain kind of equality: all those affected have to be able to feel that they have done as well as they could reasonably hope to. Thus, principles of justice are inconsistent with any claims to special privilege based on grounds that cannot be made freely acceptable to others. This still leaves it open that inequalities may be legitimated; but it rules out immediate claims to advantage based on, for example, high birth, ethnicity, or race. For although you would benefit from a principle establishing your skin colour (say) as a basis for privileged treatment, you cannot reasonably expect this to be accepted by those who stand to lose from the operation of such a principle.[4]

The first sentence of this quotation gives some hint of Barry's reason for making justice as impartiality an alternative to justice as mutual advantage. Both theories offer a suggested origin and ground of a system of justice. One says that the concept and its system of rules arise from the desire of all (or nearly all) to find a *modus vivendi* that will be of mutual benefit. The other says that they arise, or at least could arise and be grounded on, the 'reasonable' agreement of all who will be affected. The second sentence of the quotation uses the term 'impartial' in its normal sense and purports to justify the name given in the first sentence to a type of agreement theory.

In his earlier Volume I, Barry is more explicit and explains the juxtaposition of the two theories in terms of *motive*. They give alternative answers to the question 'Why be just?' The one says the motive is personal advantage; the other says it is 'the desire to act in ways that can be defended to oneself and others without appealing to personal advantage' (an unhelpful, because purely negative, statement). The passage also tells us: 'Because of the practical nature of justice, a theory of the motivation for being just must at the same time be a theory of what justice is.'[5] A little later Barry offers a positive account of the second theory: since it puts aside personal advantage, it is 'an appeal to what can be approved of from an impartial standpoint'.[6] The reference to motive is echoed in *Justice as Impartiality* when Barry describes Scanlon's revision of Rawls's 'original position': the participants in the contract 'are actuated solely by a

---

[4] *Justice as Impartiality*, 7–8.
[5] *Theories of Justice* (Hemel Hempstead: Harvester-Wheatsheaf; Berkeley and Los Angeles: University of California Press, 1989), 359.
[6] Ibid. 362.

motive that has force with almost all of us to some degree, the desire to act in ways that can be defended to others'.[7]

Why should a contractual theory based on that motive be called a theory of justice as *impartiality*? I said just now that the second sentence of my long quotation uses the term 'impartial' in its normal sense and purports to justify the name given to the theory in the first sentence. Does it in fact justify the name? The first sentence says that Barry is using the name 'justice as impartiality' for 'a theory [presumably any theory] of justice which makes it turn on the terms of reasonable agreement'. Well, a theory of mutual advantage can satisfy that definition: the social contracts described by Glaucon and Hobbes receive the agreement of all participants for the sake of mutual advantage and can, precisely because of that, be called 'reasonable' agreements. I have said that the subject of Glaucon's hypothesis goes wider than justice, but it certainly includes justice. And while Hobbes's social contract is not an agreement about justice, it is taken by Barry to be the most impressive model of the mutual advantage theory. When referring thus to Hobbes in *Justice as Impartiality*, Barry quotes Hobbes himself on the reasonable character of the motivation: 'Hobbes's next move ... was to argue that by taking counsel people could hope to do better for themselves. "Reason suggesteth convenient Articles of peace, upon which men may be drawn to agreement." '[8]

Of course the remainder of my earlier long quotation from Barry shows that he requires more than that from an impartiality theory: in particular he requires 'a certain kind of equality', emphasized on the following page as 'a fundamental commitment to the equality of all human beings'. But to say that agreement can be reasonable only if it acknowledges equality is to give an idiosyncratic meaning to 'reasonable' (adding to the idiosyncrasy of Barry's use of 'impartiality'). It is certainly true that impartial treatment implies equal treatment, with exceptions on morally relevant grounds; but that is not the only kind of practice that can properly be called reasonable. Egalitarian rules of justice are commonly called reasonable and have been compared to rules of logic; but a prudent pursuit of self-interest is also commonly called reasonable.

Barry goes on, in the long quotation, to say that all those affected by the agreement 'have to be able to feel that they have done as well as they could reasonably hope to', and that 'you cannot reasonably expect [privilege] to be accepted by those who stand to lose' from it. That assumes an acknowledgement of equality. Well, the participants in Glaucon's social contract do not expect or demand equality; but the weaker brethren accept greater power for the few and 'feel that they have done as well as they could reasonably hope to' because, without the agreement, their plight would be much worse. Hobbes's

---

[7] *Justice as Impartiality*, 10. [8] Ibid. 31.

social contract acknowledges a rough factual equality—of ability—which implies that no one person can be assured of achieving domination by his own efforts, and so it is prudentially reasonable to come to an agreement authorizing a sovereign power to be supported and obeyed by all. Hobbes also writes of a normative equality of treatment, or 'equity', that is prescribed by a law of nature and imposes a 'natural' duty on the sovereign. Hobbes thinks of this as applying to judgements of law. The exercise of government in other respects is apparently unaffected, and it is, for Hobbes, a pragmatic question whether that government should be monarchy, oligarchy, or democracy; he evidently thinks that monarchy is most likely to exercise the function successfully. Monarchy and oligarchy both involve privilege, but since the overriding issue is the security afforded by successful government, we must suppose that participants in Hobbes's social contract, as in Glaucon's, would 'feel that they have done as well as they could reasonably hope to'.

A social contract, then, can be a reasonable agreement without including an acknowledgement of equality. At a later stage in his book Barry refers to the obvious fact that a theory of justice as mutual advantage can be based on a social contract, though he does not take into consideration the fact that the contract can properly be called a *reasonable* agreement. He says that both theories, justice as impartiality and justice as mutual advantage, appeal to a hypothetical agreement.

> What divides them is the basis of the agreement. For justice as mutual advantage, the terms should reflect the balance of power between the parties, providing each with a prospect of gains over what may be expected from the absence of agreement. For justice as impartiality, the terms should be worthy of free acceptance under conditions where power relations do not play a part in the negotiations.[9]

So Barry's version of a reasonable agreement, entitling a contractual theory of justice to be called an impartiality theory, has two special requirements: that the participants should have a commitment to equality and that power relations should play no part in the negotiations. These special requirements, especially the first, are what bring impartiality into the proceedings. If so, what need is there for a social contract? Since the participants must already be committed to equality, why do they need to make a contract in order to include that commitment in their conception of justice? The contractual element of Barry's theory will no doubt have a role in his subsequent elucidation of the principles of justice, but it is not needed for the bare concept of impartiality. He obscures the picture when he uses the term 'impartiality' to describe the contractual character of the theory as contrasted with its normal sense of describing a primary principle of justice.

---

[9] *Justice as Impartiality*, 210.

The obscurity is compounded when Barry distinguishes his two senses of impartiality with the names 'first-order' and 'second-order' impartiality without explaining why he uses these expressions. He introduces them thus:

> What the theory of justice as impartiality calls for are principles and rules that are capable of forming the basis of free agreement among people seeking agreement on reasonable terms. If we call impartiality in this context second-order impartiality, we can contrast it with first-order impartiality, which is a requirement of impartial behaviour incorporated into a precept. Roughly speaking, behaving impartially here means not being motivated by private considerations. This is often cashed out by claiming that to be impartial you must not do for one person what you would not do for anybody else in a similar situation—where your being a friend or relative of one but not the other is excluded from counting as a relevant difference.[10]

Barry goes on to refer to the 'two levels' (rather than two senses) of impartiality and to complain that critics often conflate them and assume that 'any principles which can be impartially justified must of necessity be principles that mandate universal impartiality'. He elaborates his criticism later in the book and connects it with William Godwin's notorious thesis that if you could rescue only one person from a burning building and you had to choose between Archbishop Fénelon and his chambermaid who happened to be your mother (or his valet who was your father or brother), justice would require you to choose Fénelon because he was more valuable to mankind. Godwin takes a utilitarian view of 'justice' (he means moral rightness), and the point is that he denies the morality of rating the special claim of kinship above the general claim of social utility. Barry says that the critics of justice as impartiality mistakenly suppose that this conception of justice resembles Godwin in decrying the special claims of kinship or friendship as against the general moral claim of impartiality. I hold no brief for any critics who suppose this (though I do not think that all of those cited by Barry are in fact criticizing an impartiality notion of *justice*); but Barry's distinction between two 'orders' or 'levels' of impartiality is not a helpful way of correcting their error.

What one would like to know is how Barry relates impartiality to relevant claims for departing from equality. The special moral claims of kinship and friendship stand outside the general claim of justice. In contrast to them, there are moral claims that fall within the ambit of justice but require a departure from equal treatment. Desert is the clear example; the claim of need would be added by some, not by others. Both can be related to equality, though in different ways, but the immediate action that they require is a departure from equality.

Let us look first at the special claims of kinship and friendship. Barry has told

[10] Ibid. 11.

us that behaving impartially means 'not being motivated by *private* considerations' (emphasis added) and that being a friend or relative is not a 'relevant difference' for departure from the general rule. This suggests that a person is required to follow the general rule of impartiality when acting in a public capacity such as the office of a judge or civil servant or teacher. Barry himself cites the role of a judge as the prime example and says that partiality 'is the introduction of private considerations into a judgement that should be made on public grounds'.[11] He is, however, aware that the matter is not clear-cut when we think of restrictive rules or practices about membership of a club: is that a public or a private concern? Barry also notes that parents are expected to show impartiality in the treatment of their children, though they are not thereby required to suppress every vestige of special affection for a particular child: is parenting a public or a private form of activity? At any rate being a parent is a relevant moral reason for departing from impartiality in one's dealings with children generally. One has a special moral obligation to one's children, and also to other close kin and to friends. These are not the only obligations of special relationship: there are the obligations of a professional person to patients or clients or pupils, obligations of gratitude for special help or benefit, obligations of loyalty to bodies with which one has been closely associated. All these have nothing to do with justice. If any of them should happen to conflict with a claim of justice, one has to reach a judgement of priority as in any conflict of moral claims.

Unlike these obligations of special relationship, the moral claim of desert, a relevant ground for unequal treatment, does not stand outside the claims of justice. Would Barry subsume it under impartiality or would he regard it as a separate principle of justice? Some people would place the claim of need in the same boat; others would not. Presumably these matters will be discussed in Barry's Volume III on the principles of justice. Still, it is surprising that a book devoted to justice as impartiality should say nothing at all about the concept of desert, even when it refers to relevant grounds for departure from equality. So far as need is concerned, Barry does in one place write briefly of Rawls's 'difference principle', with its special consideration for the 'least advantaged', and tells us that his own view, to be expounded in Volume III, will be fairly close to Rawls's principle.[12]

Barry's 'first-order' impartiality is, as he himself says, the common-sense idea of the term. His innovation is to add the 'second-order' usage. This is a quite different sense of the word and therefore confusing. It stands for a particular form of social contract, in which the participants must have a preceding commitment to equality. This commitment, I have said, implies that they already accept an

---

[11] *Justice as Impartiality*, 13.   [12] Ibid. 95 n.

obligation to practise 'first-order' impartiality, so why do they need a social contract to say so? Barry himself poses what is more or less the same objection.

It might be said that, in the way in which I use it, the Scanlonian construction is little more than a device for talking about what is fair, on a certain fundamentally egalitarian conception of fairness. I would not regard that as a devastating criticism. I make no pretence of getting something for nothing: what you get out is what you put in. There are, however, two reasons for making use of the Scanlonian construction . . . The first . . . is simply that the question 'Is it fair?' is illuminated by phrasing it as 'Could it reasonably be rejected?' The second is that the Scanlonian approach opens up the idea that I have introduced . . . of the circumstances of impartiality.[13]

The second reason concerns a topic that I shall discuss shortly, Barry's view of the relation between justice and 'the good'. What about his first reason? It is certainly helpful to be given some illumination of the notion of fairness. All of us, including children at an early age, understand the question 'Is it fair?' (and such statements as 'It's not fair', 'It's only fair'), yet we find it difficult to say precisely what the little word means. But is the question really illuminated by Barry's rephrasing? I do not find that it is. The rephrased version seems to me to cover a wider span than the original, being equivalent to 'Is it acceptable?' in the sense of 'Is it worthy of acceptance?' Fairness is one, but not the only, good reason for accepting (or declining to reject) a suggested course of action. Another good reason is beneficial consequences (either with no consequences that are adverse or as an overall balance of good over bad). The rephrased version does not catch the specific notion of fairness, which must surely have reference to the effect of the suggested action, and normally to a comparison between persons affected, rather than reference to the reaction of those persons to the suggestion. In Chapter 18 I said that Rawls illuminates the notion of fairness when he says that agreement to take in the competing self-interested aims of each person is a good part of what we mean by fairness. That insight by Rawls refers to effect and comparison, as I have specified; Barry's statement does not.

I turn now to the relation between justice and 'the good'. At the beginning of *Justice as Impartiality* Barry writes of the book's two main themes. One is the assignment of 'two distinct roles' to the concept of impartiality, and the other is the thesis that 'a crucial task of justice as impartiality is to mediate between conflicting conceptions of the good'.[14] These two themes are the distinctively original features of Barry's theory of justice. My preceding discussion has concerned the first of these themes, in which 'first-order' impartiality is an uncontentious account of 'the common-sense idea' while 'second-order' impartiality is the novel use of the term. My conclusion has been that the novel use is misleading

---

[13] Ibid. 113.   [14] Ibid. 11, 12.

and unhelpful. The second theme is described in the Preface as a 'highly controversial feature: the claim that [justice] is in some sense neutral between different conceptions of the good, and thus offers a fair basis for agreement among those who hold different conceptions of the good'.[15]

It is a little surprising to find that somewhat archaic term 'the good' in a present-day thinker who is especially well versed in down-to-earth politics. One would suppose that by a 'conception of the good' he must mean some people's view of what things are good in themselves or of what they regard as the most valuable of those good things. In one place Barry writes of regarding something as 'an important component of the good life',[16] but more commonly he substitutes 'interests and concerns' for 'the good'. He tells us that an impartial conception of the good is one 'that does not give any special weight to the interests or concerns of the agent but treats all interests or concerns in the same way', while a partial conception 'is one that attributes more weight to the interests and concerns of the agent or of those connected to him . . . than to those of others'. He adds that an 'impartialist theory' need not limit itself to the interests and concerns of human beings. It can be anthropocentric, confining itself to the good of human beings, zoocentric, covering the good of all animals, or ecocentric, attributing value to the whole of nature, inanimate as well as animate.[17]

Some conceptions of the good conflict and Barry thinks that 'the object of justice as impartiality is to find some way of adjudicating between them that can be generally accepted as fair'.[18] The solution is the simple one of being neutral between all of them and decreeing that all are permissible. Barry's argument for neutrality is as follows. Justice as impartiality rests on 'a desire to reach agreement with others on terms that nobody could reasonably reject'. There is no conception of the good that is immune from reasonable rejection because all such conceptions are inherently uncertain.[19] We must therefore leave everyone free to follow whatever conception of the good he prefers.

Barry illustrates the issue with the example of freedom of religious worship and then adds the further example of freedom for consensual sexual relations, thinking particularly of giving homosexuals equal freedom with that given to the heterosexuals. He puts the two examples together because he thinks that freedom of practice for religion (including the freedom to reject it) and for sexual relationship are both crucial in most people's conception of the good life. The religion example has been discussed in past political thought under the rubric of toleration, that is to say, of according freedom to an activity irrespective of whether it is approved or disapproved. Similar considerations do indeed arise in discussion of homosexual relations.

[15] *Justice as Impartiality*, p. ix. [16] Ibid. 82. [17] Ibid. 20–1.
[18] Ibid. 82. [19] Ibid. 168–9.

Why does Barry think that both examples are matters of *justice*? Because the favoured solution of equal freedom is *fair* to all parties. True enough, but that misses the main point. The chief concern is freedom, not fairness. Freedom to engage in activities crucial for a good life is essential for the flowering of human personality. Deprived groups know what *they* are missing and that is what stirs them. Comparison with the more fortunate does indeed add to their resentment but is not the heart of their grievance. Suppose a ruling body were to remove unfairness by banning religious practice for all; would we think that catered adequately for a crucial element in the good life? Fairness does come into Barry's examples but is not the primary consideration. To say that 'the object of justice as impartiality is to find some way of adjudicating' between conflicting conceptions of the good is to depreciate the role of justice and to discredit the theory. In any event the so-called adjudication is not hard to find. It is apparently the same simple verdict for all cases: 'No contest; all conceptions of the good are uncertain; let them all continue—and remain in conflict.' The second main theme of Barry's discussion turns out to be trivial:

> *Parturient montes, nascetur ridiculus mus.*

It seems to me that Barry's theory of justice fails to live up to expectations because he focuses his attention upon motive. He does not claim that adjudicating between conflicting conceptions of the good is the sole object of justice, though he does appear to think it is the most important. He also describes it as the origin of the idea of justice as impartiality: 'I have endeavoured to explain how the idea of justice as impartiality emerges as a solution to an otherwise intractable problem—the problem . . . created by unresolvable conflicts about the good.'[20] This recalls my comments at the start about Barry's juxtaposition of justice as impartiality with justice as mutual advantage: he regards the character of each as stemming from its origin.

Towards the end of his first volume, *Theories of Justice*, having effectively criticized the theory of justice as mutual advantage, Barry asks what is the alternative to regarding self-interest as the only good reason for acting justly. His answer begins: 'That something is just, as justice is understood by the second [the disinterested] approach, can be in itself a good reason for doing it. The motive is the desire to act justly . . .'. That is unexceptionable but also unenlightening, and Barry commendably tries to make the motive more explicit.

The motive is the desire to act justly: the wish to conduct oneself in ways that are capable of being defended impartially. . . . What I am saying is that the desire to be able to justify our conduct in an impartial way is an original principle in human nature and one that develops under the normal conditions of human life.[21]

---

[20] Ibid. 111.   [21] *Theories of Justice*, 363–4.

This is still unexceptionable, but Barry understandably wishes to be more perspicuous in the face of the widespread view that the motive must at bottom be self-interested, and a few pages later he comes up with a further idea: 'to postulate that they [the parties to the contract] are, under ideal hypothetical conditions, seeking to reach agreement on principles that nobody could reasonably reject.'[22] This is the idea that the carries over to *Justice as Impartiality*; if I am not mistaken, the initial bare statement that 'the motive is the desire to act justly' is not repeated, though no doubt it is to be understood. An alternative formulation, given at the beginning of the book and quoted early in this chapter, is that the relevant motive is 'the desire to act in ways that can be defended to others', a motive that is said to have 'force with almost all of us to some degree'.[23]

It seems to me that the elaborated view must be mistaken. A motive is a desire or thought that prompts a person to do an action. If you were to ask someone exercising authority over others (or in some analogous position) why he or she aims at being impartial, the answer might well be, as in Barry's initial statement, 'Because it is just'. Now suppose you pressed on with the further question: 'Is your motive, then, the desire to act on agreed principles that nobody could reasonably reject?' (or 'Is your motive, then, the desire to act in ways that can be defended to others?') That question would surely be met with astonished protest such as, 'What has that to do with it? The idea has never crossed my mind.' If the idea has never crossed his or her mind, it cannot be the motive—unless Barry were to foist upon us the Freudian notion of an unconscious motive; but then that would make nonsense of his hypothetical agreement and it would also undermine his own criticism of the rival theory that the motive is always self-interest.

I am not seeking to deny that impartial action may in fact conform to Barry's formulae. My argument is that those formulae do not represent the agent's motive. The trouble with Barry's account of impartiality is that it is framed in terms of the agent's motive instead of the intended result for the people affected by the agent's decisions. I think this has come about because Barry, impressed by Rawls's social contract but critical of its specific form, has substituted an alternative form while retaining the general idea of a contract or agreement. He therefore makes universal agreement the essence of his novel (so-called 'second-order') impartiality, instead of attending simply to the common-sense idea of ('first-order') impartiality, concerned with the *treatment* meted out by impartial action.

[22] *Theories of Justice*, 370.   [23] Cf. n. 7 above.

Part III

Historical Fruits

Chapter 21

FAIRNESS

What can be learned from my historical survey? It is of course a limited survey and calls for some caution. I said at the start that it would be selective and that the selection depended to some extent on what had happened to interest me. It has also been confined to the tradition of Western civilization with its roots in Judaeo-Christian religion and Graeco-Roman culture. Attention to other traditions might disclose major differences in concepts of justice or of something analogous to justice. Like many other people I have some sketchy acquaintance with Islamic tradition on penal process, and I have in the past read a few relevant anthropological books on tribal societies. Both in Islamic and in tribal thought one sees a resemblance to the idea of justice as it has appeared in the Western tradition, so that the omission of them from my survey may not be a great loss for the purpose of understanding justice. I cannot, however, entertain a similar consoling supposition about Buddhism or the other indigenous religions of Asia, since I know nothing of what they have to say on this topic. Still, it is pertinent to note that the main features of the Western tradition have acquired a near-universal acceptance in international law; and if we hope to discern a future trend from past history, the history of the Western tradition is the place to look for it.

A further caveat arises from the predilections of particular thinkers. Apart from Chapters 1–3 and 6, this book has been concerned with the writings of individual philosophers. Some of them have sincerely tried to report prevalent ideas of justice before going on to give their own conclusions, while others have simply advocated their personal convictions. We cannot assume that a marked change in systematic theory reflects a change in popular understanding; but if it is a change that has influenced several theorists, it is likely to exert a wider influence in due course.

Justice as a specific notion, distinguished from morality in general, clearly began as the guiding principle of law. Hence its connection with stable order in early Greek thought. It seems to have been especially associated with punishment for breaches of the law, that is to say, for disturbance of public order. The psychological origin of punishment obviously lies in the resentment and impulse to retaliate that arise naturally when a person is deliberately harmed by another. But that does not in the least warrant the charge often made that a call for penal justice is simply an expression of the desire for revenge. On the contrary, the institution of penal justice replaces personal revenge with an impersonal, cool infliction of painful experience intended to put a stop to disorder.

The idea of punishment is matched with that of reward, though reward rarely appears (as it can) among the activities of law courts. Reward has a psychological origin matching that of punishment: gratitude for having been benefited is a natural analogue of resentment for having been harmed. The impulse to retaliate that accompanies resentment is not clearly matched by an immediate desire to reciprocate a benefit; rather, the feeling of gratitude engenders a sense of obligation to reciprocate if and when occasion arises in the future. Still, reward and punishment are similar enough to warrant their being classed together in moral thought under the rubric of desert, and this is a leading principle of the idea of justice or fairness. It may perhaps have been the first principle historically, but the principle of impartiality comes close behind—or even neck and neck, for the substitution of legal process for personal revenge implies replacing a partisan by an impartial outlook. The early biblical command to pursue justice prohibits the showing of favour.

Impartiality, however, is not immediately identical with a regard for equality. To avoid showing favour is to ignore 'irrelevant' inequalities, that is to say, inequalities other than inequality of desert: one must not favour the rich and the great out of esteem for their wealth and power, and one must not favour the poor and the weak out of pity for their need and vulnerability; esteem and pity have a place as approved motives of action, but not when impartiality is called for. Impartiality, then, discounts inequalities (apart from desert) and so gives equal treatment to equals and unequals alike; but that is not, on the surface at least, to think of them as having equal worth in some general sense.

Emphasis on equality in connection with justice seems to have begun with Aristotle. I have not found in my references to the Bible any association of the concept of justice with equality. In Aeschylus' *Oresteia* there is a hint of associating justice with democratic voting and so perhaps with universality, but not explicitly with equality. In Aristotle the connection between justice and equality is firm and prominent. He is building on the fact that the Greeks used their word for 'equal' to express the idea of 'fair', showing that they saw an association between justice and equality. Aristotle exaggerated the association in fastening upon an alleged equality in corrective justice between a wrongdoer's gain and his victim's loss, and again in his account of distributive justice, where he extended the idea of equality to cover an *unequal* distribution in accordance with differences of worth, calling it 'proportionate equality' because the differences of benefit were 'in proportion' to the differences of worth. He does, however, show insight in observing that the democratic idea of justice, unlike the aristocratic and the oligarchic, associates it with a genuine equality (what he calls 'arithmetical proportion'). This observation, incidentally, confirms that a concept of justice or fairness does not necessarily imply a belief in the equal worth of all the people affected. We may recall that our own idea of judgement by one's peers, retained in the jury system, once meant different procedures for lords ('peers' of each other) and for commoners. As Perelman put it, the equal treatment required by justice is for all members of one 'essential category'.

It is, of course, possible to think of humanity as one category, and in the course of time this one category came to be linked to the idea of the rights of man or, as they were called later, human rights. The change of name was due to Eleanor Roosevelt when acting as Chairman of a United Nations Commission charged with reviving the rights of man and making them effective. A delegate from one benighted country said he trusted that the expression 'the rights of man' meant what it said, the rights of man, not of woman; and Mrs Roosevelt promptly knocked that idea on the head. Human rights have now come to be treated as a key concept of international law and as a ground for imposing requirements on states. Rights to liberty and equality are, of course, prominent among human rights, as they were in the eighteenth-century concept of the rights of man; and since international law is a vehicle for publicizing more than for enforcing international justice, we can certainly say that the concept of justice now implies a regard for human equality.

One of Aristotle's observations about equality is relevant here. It is a further example of his insight into the democratic cast of mind despite his predisposition to favour aristocracy; but it is perceptive also in associating equality with friendship as much as with justice. He says that justice and friendship rest on a sense of equality between the parties and that the extreme inequality of master and slave does not rule out such relationships since there is an equality of men simply as men, so that a master may be a friend of his slave *qua* man though not *qua* slave. He then adds that 'there is most room for friendship and justice in democracies, where the citizens, being equal, have many things in common'.[1]

Initially the idea of justice consisted of two elements, the requital of desert and the practice of impartiality. After a considerable time a third element, the relief of need, was added by some thinkers but questioned by others and is still not universally accepted. Everyone of course agrees, and always has agreed, that the relief of need is a strong moral obligation; the difference of opinion concerns only the classifying of this obligation under the rubric of justice. Those

---

[1] Cf. Ch. 5 above.

who do so have no hesitation in thinking that a 'fair' distribution of resources includes special help for the needy, but some of them mark the exceptional character of this aspect of fairness or justice by ascribing it to 'social justice', using that term not only to distinguish moral from legal justice but also to acknowledge that the traditional notion of moral justice did not include the relief of need: it was classified rather as an obligation of charity or benevolence.

The nineteenth-century development of social justice, 'To each according to his needs', was not altogether new: it was a revival of the doctrine of Philo, Augustine, Peter Lombard, and Aquinas, that helping the poor and needy was a requirement of justice, a doctrine perhaps based on isolated statements of Isaiah and Jeremiah, though in general the biblical prophets did not speak of justice when stressing the obligation to help the needy. The revival did not in fact have to wait until the nineteenth century. Reid propounded it in the eighteenth, basing his argument on theology. He draws an analogy between a family and mankind as the family of God, and says that since justice requires a family to meet the necessities of those members who cannot fend for themselves, 'justice as well as charity' makes the same requirement for 'the great family of God'.[2] The use of the word 'justice' is questionable in this argument: one would not naturally say that family obligations to helpless members are a matter of justice; they are obligations of special relationship, and precisely for that reason they cannot be equated with a general obligation to mankind, since that would remove their status of being special. Reid's point is really that help for the needy is a duty of strict obligation, not one of discretion. We should recall that Kropotkin took the same view and thought that the claim of need arose from common humanity rather than justice. Those who speak of justice in this connection no doubt intend, like Reid, to indicate a strict obligation as contrasted with the discretion associated with charity. I think that the adjective 'social' is added for a similar reason: help that is left to the discretion of individuals is inadequate to meet the need, and so the obligation must be firmly assigned to society as a whole. That is what Kropotkin had in mind with his communistic outlook.

It is not essential to turn to the concept of justice in order to declare that the relief of need is a strict obligation. Unlike Reid, most people do not speak of justice when they acknowledge the strict obligations of special relationship, such as obligations to family, friends, and close associates, or the obligations of keeping faith, in promises, contracts, and shunning deceit. We do not say that these things are just or fair, and obligatory for that reason; they convey the sense of obligation from their own specific nature. Why should we not think the same of the obligation to help the needy? What is the point of calling it just or fair?

---

[2] *Active Powers*, v.5 (Thomas Reid, *Essays on the Human Mind* (Edinburgh, 1808), iii. 432).

Is it possible to pinpoint the meaning of fairness so as to understand why it has come to be applied to the relief of need? If one is asked what is meant by 'fair', it is easy enough to give the denotation of the word, to say what things one would describe as fair: the requital of desert; impartiality, including equal treatment in the absence of relevant reasons for discrimination; and perhaps, but questionably, special help for the needy. That is what I have been describing up to now in this chapter. But what about the *connotation* of the word, its meaning as a concept, enabling us to say that it is appropriately applied to the things listed above? It is not at all easy to deal with that question.

Although I have frequently written of justice 'or' fairness as if the two terms had the same meaning, they are not quite synonymous. In the law the concept of justice is distinguished from equity, which *is* pretty well synonymous with fairness. Quite apart from the use of 'justice' to refer to the legal system as such, law has a pretty clear concept of justice as its main purpose. Justice sets out rigid rules and can be qualified by equity. Equity is not rigid: it is, as Aristotle said, malleable like lead and can be adjusted to special circumstances. The relationship between justice and fairness in moral discourse is not so clear-cut, but there is a hint of the notion that justice is bound by a regard for firm rules while fairness has more of a free rein. That makes fairness, and equity in the law, seem more attractive; yet the firmness of justice can give it the edge over fairness in serious matters: a 'miscarriage of justice' would seem less heinous if we were to describe it as a breach of fairness or equity. We speak of a just war, meaning a war that meets certain lawlike criteria; the expression is a translation of Aquinas's Latin rather than a native growth, but it would sound odd and almost flippant to substitute 'a fair war'. We do have the proverb 'All's fair in love and war', apparently rejecting the concept of a just war limited by prohibitory rules, and we speak of one person beating another in 'fair fight', meaning that the success was achieved purely by the exercise of fighting abilities and without gaining advantage from extraneous means.

'Fair fight' is similar to 'fair play'. We speak, too, of fair competition and a fair field. A substitution of 'just' in such expressions would fail to catch the nuance of 'fair'. This arises, I think, from the presence of comparison: the fairness is a matter of making or allowing the same provision for each or all of the persons concerned. That does not always apply to situations described as just: a just punishment is one that fits the crime. You could say that it is compared with the crime and contrasted with heavier or lighter punishments for other crimes; but it is not necessarily compared with other instances of punishment for the same crime. If such a comparison is made and a difference of treatment is found, we say the difference is 'unfair'—and we could reasonably add or substitute 'unjust'. But such comparison is not needed in order to describe the punishment as just in the first place.

The difference in meaning between justice and fairness shows itself not only in a difference of linguistic usage but also in the feelings that we experience when applying the terms. The judgement that a situation is fair or unfair is, of course, an expression of approval or disapproval, states of mind that include both thought and feeling. It seems to me that with fair and unfair the feeling has a specific nuance, that it is not quite the same as the feeling that comes with a judgement of justice or injustice. It also seems to me that this particular feeling is experienced both when one judges that the requital of desert is fair and that equal treatment is fair in the absence of relevant grounds for discrimination. (I speak of judgements that are made with honest independence and not just as a matter of convention.) Why, I wonder, do we have the same reaction to two categories of situation that are not obviously similar? One can, of course, ask the same question about the (contested) fairness of helping the needy. I take it that people who differ about classifying the relief of need as fair really do experience different feelings; at any rate this is suggested by the warmth that they often show in expressing their judgements.

It is not difficult to say why the idea of fairness, with its specific feeling, should be applied to the relief of need. The needy are especially disadvantaged, prominently below a level of well-being experienced by the general mass of people in the society concerned. Since equality has come to be thought an element of fairness, gross inequality seems unfair, and action that reduces it can be seen as aiming at fairness. The difference between those who do and those who do not regard the relief of need as an obligation of justice is a difference of opinion about the proper primary motive for helping the needy: you can say that it is to reduce the gross inequality under which the needy labour, or you can say that it is to reduce their suffering. Those who concentrate on the inequality should in consistency, and usually do, also think that reducing inequality at the other end, by imposing higher taxes than normal on the rich, is likewise a requirement of fairness or social justice.

So one can understand how the relief of need comes to be classified as fair: it is assimilated to the equality element of fairness. Is it possible to explain why the old element of requiting desert is put together with equal treatment? One can understand why each of these two elements came to be a moral requirement, but why are they classed together under the one concept? Why do we experience the same specific feeling of fairness in regard to two quite different things (or two things that appear to be quite different)?

It cannot be because they both answer to the traditional legal definition of justice as rendering to each person what is his due (one reasonable understanding of 'his own'); for this definition does not distinguish the sense of fairness and unfairness, with its specific feelings (of satisfied approval and dissatisfied protest?), from the sense of justice in general. Even if my notion of a separate nuance for fairness is dubious, the definition is too wide when transferred from law to ethics, for 'rendering what is a person's due' can apply to various moral obligations outside the sphere of justice, such as honouring parents or keeping promises.

Nor can it be, as a utilitarian might say, because the two things, requiting desert and equal treatment, are similar in having acquired approval from general utility; for that, on the utilitarian thesis, is true of all principles of right conduct—*except* the principle of equality. A good case can be made for attributing to utility much, though not the whole, of the approval of requiting desert, but that does not explain why it is classed together with equal treatment under a particular concept confined to these two things and the relief of need.

J. S. Mill did not take that particular utilitarian line. As we saw in Chapter 12, he was troubled by the relation between desert and impartiality or equality, and one of his suggestions was to assimilate impartiality to desert as a special case of requital, equal treatment for equal desert: the idea being that, if we have no knowledge of differences in desert, we should assume that there are none. I criticized this on the ground that it is factually unrealistic and that, while we would certainly think it unfair to discriminate in the absence of relevant knowledge, the unfairness cannot rest on a pretence which we know to be false.[3]

Adam Smith's view of 'fair play' affords a much more interesting suggestion. As in the whole of his ethical theory, he relies on the reaction of spectators, known to agents through the imagination. He says that, if a competitor seeks to gain an advantage by means other than ability in the relevant activity—for example, jostling a rival in a race instead of relying simply on running ability—spectators will have no sympathy for the selfish motive that drives him.

This man is to them, in every respect, as good as he: they do not enter into that self-love by which he prefers himself so much to this other, and cannot go along with the motive from which he hurt him. They readily, therefore, sympathize with the natural resentment of the injured, and the offender becomes the object of their hatred and indignation.[4]

Smith's suggestion is that the judgement of unfairness in such a situation is one of ill desert and is founded upon a presumption of equality. It will not apply to all examples of ill desert, since not all examples are breaches of fair play. Where it does apply, however, it is a persuasive explanation of the conjunction of desert and equality. It has the further advantage of showing that a judgement of fairness is not always concerned to accommodate self-interest. In Chapter 18 I commended Rawls's insight that agreement to take in the self-interested aims of

---

[3] Cf. Ch. 12 above.
[4] Adam Smith, TMS II. ii. 2.1; p. 83. Cf. Ch. 11 above.

each person is a good part of what we mean by fairness, but it is salutary to be reminded that this is not the whole of the story: as I said at the time, even young children soon come to think of fair treatment as due to others as well as themselves.

Adam Smith then offers a similar explanation for another connection between desert and equality: the sense of fairness requires that the punishment should match the crime because the spectators' sympathy matches the victim's resentment. He brings in the matching of feelings in spectator and victim because he treats all moral judgement as a reflection of sympathetic feeling in spectators. But this does not really explain the specific moral judgement of fairness: it gives us a reason why a punishment satisfying the victim's resentment is judged morally right, but it does not explain why the punishment should be fair in the sense of matching, being equal in amount, to the crime. After all, natural resentment often prompts an injured person to strike back harder. The idea of just or fair punishment is one of *talio*, like for like, as distinguished from the stronger reaction that resentment might prompt and from the more lenient penalty that mercy might advise.

That particular equality may be the connecting link between the requital of desert and impartiality so as to bring both within the concept of fairness. The fair requital of desert is an equal reciprocation of the good or evil that a person has done, like for like. In practice, a benefactor is, more often than not, left unrewarded and simply given praise instead, while a malefactor may have his punishment reduced or waived when justice is tempered with mercy, or, on the other hand, he may have the punishment increased so as to be 'exemplary' in the interests of utility; but the basically fair requital for both types of action is that the agent should receive good or ill equal to that which he has done. The suggestion that this explains the fairness is Aristotelian in spirit. In his discussions of justice Aristotle does not in fact say anything about the requital of desert,[5] but if he had turned his attention to it he would probably have brought in an application of equality, as in his account of other aspects of justice.

These thoughts about the element common to all three species of fairness suggest that it is always a concern with equality of some sort. That may explain why the ancient Greeks used the word for 'equal' to express the idea of fairness, and why the Romans followed suit with *aequitas* (from which 'equity' is derived). Linguistic usage illustrates the difficulty of hitting upon the distinctive connotation of fairness. We saw from Aristotle's discussion that he uses the word for equal or fair to distinguish moral justice from legal justice, and that the moderating principle of equity in the law was described in ancient Greek by a different word which otherwise has the very general meaning of the fitting or

---

[5] Cf. Ch. 5 above.

suitable. Biblical Hebrew does not seem to have any word for fairness alongside that of justice, which itself (like the Greek *dikaiosyne*) is less firmly distinguished from the wider notion of moral rightness than in modern languages. Later Hebrew coined a word for fairness by altering the vowel pointing in the word for justice. Among other modern languages, French, German, and Italian all make the word for 'just' do duty for 'fair' also; French offers the alternative of *équitable*, but *juste* is used far more commonly. The English word 'fair' is different. According to the *Oxford English Dictionary*, the earliest recorded instances of the word have the sense of beautiful (still in use, of course). Other meanings were developed from that: delightful or desirable in general; bright or light in colour; free from blemish, and so free from moral blemish; then, more specifically, free from bias or taking undue advantage, that is to say, impartial.

The equality involved in a 'fair' requital of desert does not have a close similarity to the equality of treating people in the same way. Is there any practical advantage in classifying the two under the one concept of fairness? Does it, for example, help to decide the relative strength of conflicting obligations? The claim of need can conflict with the claim of desert, and if the relief of need is taken to be required by benevolence while the requital of desert is taken to be required by fairness, we have no common quality by which to compare the moral strength of the two requirements. Can we say that we do have a common quality, and so a measure for comparison, if they are both classified as fair? That would be true if the common element, equality, were the same sort of thing in both, but in fact it is not; you cannot measure the equality of reciprocated good or ill against the ideal equality of basic well-being that is the goal of relieving need. I cannot see any practical advantage in classifying together as fair the two categories of action, equal treatment and the requital of desert. I can only suppose that the juxtaposition is the result of history. Both have an intelligible place in legal process, where the idea of justice first made itself felt; and when the notion of moral justice emerged as a concept on its own, it retained, as associated together, the elements that formed the content of legal justice.

Chapter 22

THE DEVELOPING ROLE OF JUSTICE

The history of concepts of justice helps us to see how the role of justice has developed. I have said that justice has both a conservative and a reforming role. Sidgwick described the latter as giving effect to an ideal conception of justice. The historical survey shows that the ideal conception is not static: it engenders some addition in the light of experience, perhaps as part of a more general development of ethical thought. The conservative role, too, develops, not merely in accepting changes from reformative justice but also in clarifying its original task. Let me begin with that.

In Aeschylus' *Oresteia* we twice hear the maxim 'What you do shall be done to you'. First the Chorus in the *Agamemnon* report it as 'enduring so long as Zeus reigns', and then the Chorus in the *Choephoroe* say it is told as 'an old, old tale'. Is it to be taken as a statement of fact or as a norm? Are we to understand that being treated as we have acted is what happens as the way of the world, or that it is what ought to happen as a moral imperative? The first report, referring to the reign of Zeus, suggests that it is a norm, a divine commandment, though this can be a way of expressing what we now mean by a (scientific) 'law of nature'. The second report of an old, old tale is more readily understood as a statement of fact drawn from experience. Probably we should not distinguish sharply between the two interpretations: on both occasions the Chorus are describing what happens in the world and are assuming that what happens regularly in the world is due to the will of the gods. Elsewhere in the trilogy both Orestes and the Furies take it for granted that they are under an *obligation* to avenge the murder of kin.

The impulse to take revenge arises naturally as an element of human psychology. If it is generally acted upon, it becomes 'the norm' in the sense of custom, what usually happens; and since custom is the main origin of early law, the norm in the sense of custom comes to be a norm in the sense of moral requirement. Justice, the concept that gives expression to moral requirements that affect the stability of society, takes this one under its wing. So early justice proclaims that what you do shall be done to you: you *ought* to receive what you have inflicted; that is what you deserve.

A number of philosophers nowadays are too ready to say Hume showed that an 'ought' cannot be derived from an 'is'. While Hume's discussion is part of a section entitled 'Moral Distinctions not deriv'd from Reason', the passage in which he writes of 'is' and 'ought' uses the word 'deduction',[1] I think deliberately. Hume is there criticizing Samuel Clarke (and possibly other thinkers) who explicitly tried to give a deductive proof of basic moral obligations from factual truths about 'the nature of things'.[2] Hume's criticism refers to the undoubted fallacy of importing into the conclusion of a deductive inference a term that is not included in the premisses. But that does not impugn the reliability of 'deriving' a norm from a fact in the sense of suggesting a causal explanation. Hume's own theory that moral distinctions are 'deriv'd' from sentiment is an example of such a causal explanation, and so is the more detailed theory of his friend Adam Smith.

My suggestion about the early role of justice is concerned only with *harmful* action and primarily with murder. The maxim 'What you do shall be done to you' should apply to beneficial action too; but since that does not generally need to come under the aegis of the law, it is not included in the primitive notion of justice and is certainly not in the mind of the Chorus in the two Aeschylean plays. It does, however, recall the Golden Rule, 'Do as you would be done by', often said to be a summary of moral conduct as a whole. Leibniz held that the Golden Rule is the basic principle of justice. He was mistaken but one can see why he should have thought so, especially when we compare the Golden Rule with the 'old, old tale' of the *Oresteia*. When the Choruses speak of the old tale, they are thinking of the retaliation of harmful action. Harmful action is a more basic concern for justice and morality in general than is beneficial action; that is why a primordial code like the Ten Commandments gives prominence to prohibitions and why the Golden Rule first appears in its negative form. 'Do not unto others what you would not wish to be done unto you'.

The verbal affinity of the positive Golden Rule to the 'old tale' does not, of course, give them the same meaning. One might say that the truth of the old tale evokes the negative Golden Rule: to avoid retaliation of harm, refrain from harming. But that is to give to the Golden Rule a self-interested interpretation that minimizes its significance. Even in its negative form, the Golden Rule is a properly ethical principle, requiring that we think of other people's wishes as we

---

[1] David Hume, *Treatise of Human Nature*, III.i.1, last para.
[2] Cf. Ch. 9 above.

think of our own, that (to quote Kant on the fundamental principle of morality) we 'make their ends our own'. It shares with justice the mandate of treating all human beings as equal, though it is not the same as justice.

Some of the theorists in my historical survey believed that there is an essential connection between justice and rights. Reid and Mill said so explicitly; Hume, followed by Kames, implied it by defining justice in terms of property rights. Like Leibniz, they were understandably mistaken: mistaken because there can be justice in the absence of rights and rights in the absence of justice, as I observed in Chapter 10; yet understandably mistaken because there is often a link between rights and justice.

There are two main senses of a right, commonly described by theorists nowadays as liberty-rights and claim-rights. I have in the past called them rights of action and rights of recipience. Rights are more closely connected with obligations than with justice and each of the two senses can be defined in terms of obligation. A liberty-right is a right to do something (hence my name of right of action); it is a freedom from obligation to refrain from the proposed action. We speak of a right to act if there has been some challenge or query about the action concerned. We can express the same thought by saying that one 'may' do the action or that there is nothing wrong in doing it. A claim-right is a right to receive something (hence my name of right of recipience) as one's due; it is a right against some other person or persons obliged to provide that thing; it may be defined as the correlative, the other end, of a strict obligation owed by some other person or persons to the person said to have the right. I speak of a 'strict' obligation because not all obligations entail correlative rights: some obligations, such as those of charity or courtesy, are discretionary or of moderate stringency, and so are not deemed to be joined to rights.

The association of justice with rights chiefly concerns claim-rights. We would not normally speak of a right to act as being a matter of justice. When Hume and Kames assign to justice the function of protecting property rights, they no doubt intend to cover both claim-rights and liberty-rights, for the ownership of property includes both: it carries an exclusive liberty-right for the owner to use or dispose of the property as he wishes, and it also carries a claim-right against other people that they do not try to make use of the property or to interfere with what the owner does. Property rights are legal rights, and both Hume and Kames are thinking of the law when they speak of justice as the guardian of property rights. But when we are considering justice as a moral concept and rights in the sense of moral rights, we would not be likely to cite these rights of ownership as relevant examples. We might say justice requires that everyone should have a fair chance (an equal opportunity) of acquiring property with its legal rights; and if we were to call the fair chance a right of justice, it would be a claim-right, a right to receive equality of opportunity. I think the same thing is true of all liberty-rights. They do not depend on any thought of justice for their validity: the mere fact that a person wants to do something is sufficient warrant for doing it unless it would breach some moral consideration. Justice or fairness comes into the matter only if a question arises about unequal opportunities for different persons to do this sort of action if they want to, and then the reference to justice concerns the claim-right of equal opportunity.

We should, then, confine ourselves to claim-rights. Equality is the aspect of justice that is most obviously linked to the notion of rights. The obligation of impartiality in exercising a public office is correlated with a right of those affected to receive impartial treatment. Bentham's maxim that everyone should count for one and nobody for more than one is a claim-right as well as an obligation. If we turn to desert and need, the other main aspects of justice, we do not find such a clear link with rights. As I have said before, many of those who regard the relief of need as an obligation of justice would hesitate to say that the people in need have a right to the help, at least when it is discretionary help from individuals or private charitable institutions; if the help is part of a statutory scheme as in a welfare state, then it is certainly a right, legal as well as moral. As for desert, when a good deed merits reward, it lays a measure of obligation on the beneficiary and may give rise to some expectation in the benefactor, but neither the benefactor nor people at large would say he has a *right* to reward or reciprocal benefit. With ill desert, few of us will follow Hegel in thinking that a criminal has a right to the punishment he undoubtedly deserves, though many will say that justice gives victims of the crime a right to see it punished.

An explicitly distinct notion of rights seems to have arisen later than that of justice. Any society that recognizes the concept of private property must include in it the idea that ownership implies an exclusive relationship of the owner to the thing owned, a relationship that ought to be respected by other people. But that does not necessarily evoke immediately a special verbal expression for the relationship. No word for a right is to be found in biblical Hebrew (though there is one in the later legal disquisitions of the Talmud). There is likewise no specific word for a right in ancient Greek. Instead the adjective 'just' was pressed into service for both liberty-rights and claim-rights: 'I have a right to do X' was expressed by 'I am just [*dikaios*, no doubt meaning justified] to do X', and 'to obtain one's rights' was expressed by 'to obtain the just things [*ta dikaia*]'. A right in Latin is *ius*, a word having the initial meaning of a bond and so coming to mean law (in the sense of a system of law), and also giving rise to *iustus* and *iustitia*; so when it was used with the additional meaning of a right, it associated that concept with both law and justice. The notion of rights was, in addition, signified, as in Greek, by 'just things' (*iusta*). This does not show that Latin resembles Greek in focusing on justice first but it confirms the readiness of justice to take in additional elements.

The most striking additional element is, of course, the relief of need, discussed in the preceding chapter. Although the attribution of this obligation to justice remains controversial, I think we have to concede that it is now true of public action in the welfare state: state benefit for the needy is thought to be required by fairness as well as humanity. The relief of need is, however, not the only important addition to the concept of justice in the course of time. Another is concern for the individual.

In my historical survey this feature of justice appears first in Adam Smith and is then found in Mill, Sidgwick, and Rashdall. I do not know whether Smith was in fact its originator; it may be connected with emphasis on the individual in other spheres of thought, and that began before the eighteenth century, appearing in the epistemology of Descartes and the moral philosophy of Hobbes.

Adam Smith does not treat concern for the individual as a major feature of justice. It comes up in his criticism of a utilitarian view of punishment and is merely one of several arguments. Smith is thinking of the individual who suffers injury from a criminal action; he argues that thought about the justice of punishing the action is the thought of what is owed to the individual victim of the crime, not a concern for the interests of society. I commented that Smith's argument was defective because the law punishes crime as an offence against the state and leaves the injured individual to seek redress for himself under the procedure of a civil action.

It might be said, in response to my criticism, that the practice of the criminal law fails to meet the sense of justice and would do better if it looked to redress for the victims of crime. Many early systems of law had alternative penalties for serious crime (not only murder), namely capital punishment and the payment of blood money, and some of those systems left the choice to the victim or to the kin of a deceased victim. The practice, for murder at any rate, still exists in some systems of Islamic law and is no doubt felt to satisfy the sense of justice. It can, however, be abused so as to seem vindictive rather than just. Not long ago a court in Saudi Arabia convicted two British nurses of murdering an Australian colleague and, in accordance with custom, left it to the victim's next of kin to say whether the death penalty should be commuted to the payment of blood money. As it happens, the verdict of guilt was controversial, because there was dispute about the validity of an incriminating statement, later retracted, by one of the accused. However, the Australian brother of the victim at first insisted that the death penalty should be carried out, and then, when persuaded to choose instead the option of blood money, he set the amount at an extraordinarily high level quite out of line with the usual practice in Saudi Arabia. Transferring responsibility for punishment from the victim (or the victim's kin) to the state is a measure of liberalization: the anger of the vendetta is replaced by the cool judgement of a public authority. In this regard the change is a move away from the individual to the social body.

Mill gives a more prominent place to the concern of justice for individuals, but his account resembles that of Smith in referring to the victims of harm and in connecting that with thought about punishment. It is possible that Mill derived the idea from Smith, for his reliance upon sympathy in chapter 3 of *Utilitarianism* suggests that he was familiar with the ethical theories of both Hume and Smith. He does, however, give a wider application than Smith to the idea of concern for individuals, treating it as a constant essential feature of justice. He lists six ethical categories that come under the aegis of justice: legal rights, moral rights, requital of desert, keeping faith, impartiality, and equality. He then looks for a common element in all six categories and suggests that there are two: a breach of justice involves harm to one or more definite (or 'assignable') individuals and makes us wish to see it punished. Since Mill also thinks that the second of the two ingredients, the desirablility of punishment, applies to all breaches of moral duty, it is the first ingredient, the relation to assignable individuals, that is specifically distinctive of justice. Mill associates this with the notion that the individuals concerned have a personal right, and in the end he concentrates on the rights aspect and seems to forget about the 'assignable individuals' themselves. Still, the emphasis was there and gave the theory of justice a novel perspective.

Sidgwick's reference to individuals is of less consequence. Writing of a wider and a narrower meaning of term 'justice' in the law, he says that justice in the narrower sense deals with the distribution of benefits and burdens to individuals. He could have said individuals and groups: his point was simply to distinguish justice as a particular feature from justice as a name for the whole system of law. Later he contrasts two versions of ideal justice, calling one of them individualistic and the other socialistic. The former is 'the free-market interpretation', which accepts market value as the just or fair rate of remuneration, while the socialistic ideal relies on the estimate of 'enlightened judges'. The term 'individualistic' is used simply because decisions in the market are made by individuals with their own interests in mind, as contrasted with the hypothetical enlightened judges who think of the interests of society at large. The reference to individuals in the free-market interpretation of a just wage has no special significance for a change in the role of justice.

Rashdall's discussion is altogether more serious, though his reference to individuals is only a small part of his struggle with the problem presented to utilitarianism by the concept of justice. His main concern is to reconcile the promotion of good with the claims of equality and merit. He does not think that these claims of justice are entirely centred on individuals: he writes also, with obvious deep feeling, of the 'sacrifice of unfortunate minorities—the weak in mind or body, the sick, the halt, the maimed—such as common humanity would condemn', and he says 'it is a matter of life and death to our position' to find a common measure for justice and benevolence.[3] But he does recognize that often the claim of justice is a matter of 'sympathy and mercy to individuals' or 'solicitude for individual interests': the sense of justice evinces a concern for individuals as contrasted with care for the general interest. 'Benevolence assets the value of good. Justice asserts the value of persons.' They can be reconciled, 'for good is ultimately the good of definite individuals'. Yet 'Too great a sacrifice of the individuals does present itself to us as unjust even when it might be prescribed by the principle of maximum good.' In commenting on this I said that Rashdall's solution to his problem is inadequate, but I also paid tribute to his perception that the concern of justice for individuals pinpoints the difficulty for utilitarianism.

My own perception of this concern arose from reflection on the retributive theory of punishment. At first sight the retributive theory seems to express only a stern, backward-looking demand for requital; and so a utilitarian theory, in terms of prevention, deterrence, and reform, appears more acceptable ethically. But then one sees that a purely utilitarian theory would justify punishing an innocent person in some circumstances, and then the notion of justice cries out against it, insisting that punishment is permissible only if there is guilt: once guilt has been established, punishment *may* be imposed, which is not to say that it *should* be. My view is that, once punishment is permissible, utilitarian considerations should determine whether to impose it. The wrongdoer deserves to be punished but that does not necessarily imply that the relevant authority is obliged to give him what he deserves. I think that a defensible retributive theory of punishment would be better called the desert theory: it holds that desert is a necessary though not a sufficient condition of punishment. I elaborated my view in a paper, 'Justice and Liberty', published in 1951[4] and wrote that, while moral thought now recoils from justifying punishment by mere retaliation, justice has acquired the role of protecting innocence, 'the raising of a moral *obstat* to the infliction of pain on an innocent individual'. The protection is, of course,

---

[3] Cf. Ch. 14 above.
[4] *Proceedings of the Aristotelian Society* NS 51 (1950–1); repr. in D. D. Raphael, *Justice and Liberty* (London: Athlone Press, 1980), essay 3. The discussion of punishment is in §iii and the passage quoted is on p. 41 of the book.

not confined to individuals; it applies just as much to innocent groups who come to be accused of wrongdoing; but the process of bringing charges under criminal law is normally used against 'assignable' individuals (to recall Mill's term), though occasionally against corporate bodies treated as legal 'persons'. It is, therefore, reasonable to think of the protecting role of justice as defending the innocent individual.

The age-old principle of justice which says that those who do wrong deserve to suffer what they do, of course implies that only wrongdoers deserve that: those who are innocent of wrongdoing were always exempt from the rule, so that punishing them, as if they were guilty of wrongdoing, was always contrary to the requirement of justice. Yet one does not find in early expressions of the concept of justice, so it seems to me, any explicit perception of justice as the protector and champion of innocence. I think this is because the establishment of a system of criminal justice was more concerned with the stability of the general social order. Later on it developed a particular concern to avoid oppression of the accused: this is illustrated in the procedure of trial by jury and in the dictum of Blackstone, 'It is better that ten guilty persons escape than one innocent suffer.'

All but one (Sidgwick) of the writers listed here as having attributed to justice a concern with the individual have been thinking of a difficulty for utilitarian theories of ethics. Utilitarianism is intended to be a progressive doctrine and on the whole it succeeds in that aim. In seeking the criterion of right action it urges us to look to the future instead of the past, to judge by the standard of improvement, good consequences, and to make the task intelligible with a single explanation for the several principles to which appeal is made in everyday life. This is a laudable programme and it has served to show up unconscious prejudice in some traditional attitudes. Utilitarianism has also been remarkably successful in fitting ethics, law, and politics into one coherent system. But in sticking to simplicity at all costs it becomes too big for its boots and cannot accommodate all the evidence. As Mill and Rashdall realized, the most serious difficulty comes from the concept of justice. Whether utilitarianism takes as its simple criterion the maximum total of happiness or the maximum total of intrinsic good or the maximum total of preferences, it looks to a *general* goal and fails to take adequate account of the *persons* whose desires, choices, and experiences make up the approved general product. Rashdall puts the point succinctly, though too crudely, when he says 'Benevolence asserts the value of good. Justice asserts the value of persons.' The aphorism is too crude because, as Rashdall himself says later, 'good is ultimately the good of individuals'. Still, the criterion used by utilitarianism is not focused upon that 'ultimate' fact and can allow the individual person to be sacrificed to realizing a greater amount of total good. Utilitarianism, as I have said, is a progressive doctrine, but it resembles the earlier concept of justice in concentrating on the good of society as a whole. Its successfully progressive and comprehensive character leads its advocates to think it can account for everything in ethics, politics, and law. That has provoked a keener perception of the implications of justice and a widening of its role. A concept that began as a shield of the social order has come to be the shield of the individual against encroachment by social authority.

Index

Abraham 12, 16–17
Adam, James 41–2
Adeimantus 34, 36, 52
Aegisthus 22–5
Aeschylus 7, 19–29, 32, 234, 242–3
Agamemnon 22–5, 28
Ambrose, St 57, 60
Amos 17
Anouilh, Jean 20
Antigone 20
Apollo 24–9
Aquinas, St Thomas 6, 19, 57, 59, 236, 237
Aristotle 6, 19, 31, 36, 40, 140, 176
    on equality 234–5
    on equity 54–5, 237, 240
    on justice 43–55, 57–9
    in Hobbes 76–7, 79
    in Leibniz 86
    in Rashdall 153
    in Sidgwick 145
    in Smith 115
Artemis 22
artificial:
    bonds or obligations 66, 72–3, 95
    virtue 66, 90–1, 93–5, 96–9, 104, 107–8
Athena 25–7, 29
Atreus 22–3
Augustine, St 19, 57, 59–60, 86, 236

Barry, Brian 186–8, 220–30
Beckett, Samuel 20
Benn, S. I. 188
Bentham, Jeremy 126–7, 135–6, 148, 153, 211, 245
Beveridge, Lord 217
Bible 7, 11–18, 33, 130
Blackstone, Sir William 122, 249

Blanc, Louis 7, 160
Bradley, F. H. 157–8
Broad, C. D. 140
Butler, Joseph 140
Butler, Samuel 89

Campbell, A. H. 58
Carmichael, Gerschom 94
Carritt, E. F. 207
Cassandra 23
categorical imperative 7, 162–3, 178
Cephalus 31–3, 36
Chamberlain, Wilt 216–17
charity and justice 59–62, 236
    in Jewish doctrine 60
    in Kropotkin 163
    in Leibniz 82–3, 85–6
    in Locke 61
    in Reid 107–8
    in Smith 114
Charmides 42
Cicero 56
Clarke, Samuel 93, 243
Clytemnestra 22–6
communism 160, 163–6
Corneille, Pierre 20
Cornford, F. M. 41
covenant, *see* promise
Critias 42

Del Vecchio, Giorgio 57–8
Denning, Lord 3
Descartes, René 66, 80, 246
desert 5, 33, 134–5, 144–6, 158, 234
    communist principle of 160
    and fairness 238–41
    in Hume 88–90
    in Mill 134–5
    in Miller 185, 192–3

Index

desert (cont.):
  and punishment 248
  in Rashdall 158
  in Rawls 206–8
  in Sidgwick 144–6
  socialist principle of 166
discrimination 5, 12, 141–2
Dreyfus, Alfred 137

Electra 24–5
Emslie, Lord 3
Engels, Friedrich 190
entitlements 4, 171, 173, 174–5, 214–19
equality 128, 134–6, 149, 151, 195
  in Aristotle 234–5
  in Barry 222–4
  a claim of fairness 103, 198
  of consideration 151–3, 156
  of human beings 53, 152–3, 235–6
  in Kropotkin 161–3
  and need 5–6, 178–9, 185, 189–90, 208, 235, 237
  in Nozick 215–16
  in power 79, 103
  in Rawls 198, 202, 208
  and rights 245
equity 2, 118, 219, 237
  in Aristotle 54–5
  in Hobbes 76–8
  in Kropotkin 161, 163
  in Sidgwick 148–9
  in Smith 113–14
  see also fairness
ethics:
  political 1–2, 6
  social 1–2, 4, 6
expediency 5, 127, 133, 137; see also utility

fairness 1, 4, 237–41
  in Barry 227, 229
  opposes utility 102–3, 136
  in Rawls 197, 208–9
  and rights 107–8

fair play 119
Fénelon, Archbishop 225
freedom, see liberty, rights
Freud, Sigmund 230
Furies 24–9

Gauthier, David 221
Glaucon 34–5, 37, 40–2, 81, 221, 223–4
God 12–13, 16–17, 80–2
Godwin, William 163, 225
Golden Rule 83–5, 161–3, 243
Gratian (Gratianus Franciscus) 60
Grotius, Hugo 58, 124

Hammurabi, Code of 14
Hardie, W. F. R. 50
Hart, H. L. A. 204–5
Hegel, G. W. F. 19, 245
Helen (of Troy) 22
Herodotus 22
Hesiod 51
Hitler, Adolf 98
Hobbes, Thomas 18, 19, 34, 65–79, 92, 246
  in Barry 221, 223–4
  in Hume 92, 95
  in Leibniz 81
  on promising 65–75, 128
  on punishment 78–9, 147
Homer 20, 31
Hont, Istvan 114
Horace 126
Horne Tooke, John 129
Hume, David 19, 66, 87–103, 243, 244
  in Kames 104–6, 110–11
  in Mill 247
  in Miller 184, 190
  in Rawls 200, 209, 212
  in Reid 106–11
  in Smith 117
Hutcheson, Francis 91–5, 97, 117

Ibsen, Henrik 20
Ignatieff, Michael 114

Index

impartiality 12, 128, 134–5, 221–30, 234
individual 121–3, 133, 137–8, 141, 146, 157, 246–50
individualism 163–6, 192–3
intuition 199–201, 211–12
Iphigeneia 22–3
Isaiah 15–16, 17, 59, 236

Jacob 219
Jeanne d'Arc 137
Jefferson, Thomas 144
Jeremiah 15, 236
Jesus 14, 16, 33
Joannes Teutonicus 60
Job 13, 16–18
John Chrysostom, St 57
Joseph 219
justice:
    commutative 37, 52–3, 57–8, 70, 86, 115
    conservative 2, 4, 142–3, 174–5, 184–5, 242
    corrective (in Aristotle) 49–50, 57–8; (in Nozick) 214
    definition of (in Hobbes) 65–8; (in Kames) 105; (in Leibniz) 82–3; (in Mill) 129; (in Miller) 184; (in Nozick) 214; (in Plato) 30–3, 37, 40–2; (in Rawls) 200; (in Reid) 107; (in Roman law) 1, 56–9; (in Smith) 115
    distributive 5–6, 46–9, 58, 70, 115, 206–7, 216
    ethical notion of 2, 12
    formal and concrete 169–74, 180–1
    of God 13, 16–17
    ideal 142–6, 184, 242
    in law 1–2, 11–15, 141
    natural 2–3, 53–4
    reformative (or prosthetic) 2, 4, 175, 184–5
    retributive 22, 26, 118, 206; see also punishment
    social 15, 18, 59–62, 86, 184, 190, 236, 238
Justinian 56

Kames, Henry Home, Lord 104–6, 109–10, 111, 117, 128, 244
Kant, Immanuel 6–7, 19, 69
    and categorical imperative 163, 178–9, 181, 244
    in Rawls 199, 204
    on retributive punishment 158
Kelly, P. J. 127
Kemp Smith, Norman 91–2
Kierkegaard, Søren 19
Kronos 29
Kropotkin, Peter 7, 160–7, 184, 187, 190, 236

Lactantius 57
Laird, John 68
liberty:
    in Barry 228–9
    in Rawls 198, 202–5, 209–10
    in Sidgwick 143–5
Lane, Lord 4
law:
    canon 60
    civil 1–2, 121–2
    code 35
    common 35
    criminal 1–2, 121–2
    of England 3–4
    following precedent 180–1
    international 233, 235
    Islamic 246–7
    military 123–4
    natural 72–3, 79
    Roman 1, 14, 33, 35, 56–9, 86
    of Scotland 3
    statute and case 2–3
    of USA 3
Leibniz, G. W. 57, 80–6, 243–4
lex talionis 13–14, 16, 24–5, 28, 50, 118, 240

liberty 1
  in Barry 228–9
  in Rawls 198, 202–5, 209–10
  in Sidgwick 143–5
Lloyd George, David 46
Lloyd-Jones, Sir Hugh 28
Locke, John 6–7, 92
  in Kames 105
  in Nozick 214
  on property 96, 98, 104
  in Reid 108
  on rights and justice 60–2
  in Sidgwick 144
Lot 12, 16
Lucas, D. W. 28

Mandeville, Bernard 92
Marcel, Gabriel 20
Marx, Karl 6–7, 34, 159–60, 178, 190
Menelaus 22
merit 4–6, 33, 38, 48, 88–90
  in Perelman 171–2, 176–7
  in Rashdall 153–6, 158
  in Rawls 206, 208
  in Smith 116–17
  see also desert
Mill, J. S. 19, 126–38, 141, 244, 249
  on impartiality 134, 239
  on individuals 246–7
  on promises 66
Miller, Arthur 20
Miller, David 162, 183–95, 214
Mollat, Georg 80
Moore, G. E. 150, 199
moral philosophy 19
moral theology 16–18, 20, 108–11, 148, 236
motive 222–3, 229–30

need 4–5, 235
  as claim of beneficence 217–18
  and equality 178–9
  and fairness 237–8, 246
  in Kropotkin 160–1, 163–7

in Miller 185–90, 194–5
in Rawls 202–5
in Smith 114
and utility 177–8
see also equality
Nietzsche, Friedrich 19
Nowell-Smith, P. H. 89
Nozick, Robert 214–19

obligations:
  of special relationship 225–6, 236
  strict 244
Oedipus 20
O'Neill, Eugene 20
Orestes 24–9, 242
Ouranos 29

Paris (of Troy) 22
Pelops 22
Perelman, Chaïm 168–82, 183, 235
Peter Lombard 59–60, 236
Peters, R. S. 188
Philo 60, 86, 236
Phrynichus 22
Plato 6, 19, 20, 21, 30–42, 58–9, 150
  in Barry 221
  contrasted with Aristotle 43–4, 45–6, 51–2
  in Leibniz 221
Polemarchus 32–4, 58
Priam 23
promise:
  in Hobbes 65–75
  in Hume 66, 87, 95, 102
  in Kames 106, 109–11
  in Mill 66, 128
  in Reid 110–11
property 87, 96, 100–1, 104–6, 108–9, 244
Proudhon, P. J. 163
Pufendorf, Samuel 58, 61, 86, 94
punishment:
  and fairness 240
  and guilt 5, 249

INDEX

in Hobbes 78–9
in Mill 133
origin 234
in Rashdall 157–8
in Rawls 206–7
retributive 147, 158, 248
in Smith 119–24
Pylades 25
Pythagoreans 50–2

Racine, Jean 20–1
Raphael, D. D. 184–5
Rashdall, Hastings 150–9, 199, 246–9
Rawls, John 6, 7, 183, 195, 196–213, 218–19, 239
   in Barry 220–2, 226–7, 230
recompense 114, 151
Reid, Thomas 104, 106–12, 128, 236, 244
requital 118, 144–6, 207, 240
retribution 22, 25–6, 78–9, 118–19, 147, 157, 207
reward 5
   correlated with punishment 158, 206–7, 234
   origin 234
   of public service 154–5
   as recompense 151
   and retributive justice 118, 207
   utility of 176, 206
   of virtue 155
Rhadamanthus 51
rights 2, 94, 107–8, 184–5, 191–2, 244–6
   acquired 108–9
   to freedom 143–4, 198
   human 235
   legal and moral 127–8, 133
   liberty- and claim- 73, 244–5
   natural 61–2, 73, 82, 90, 104, 108–9, 143–4
   notion of 245
   perfect and imperfect 58, 61
   see also entitlements

Riley, Patrick 80
Roosevelt, Eleanor 235
Ross, Sir David 46, 50
Rousseau, Jean-Jacques 19, 204
Russell, Paul 95

Saint-Simon, C. H., Comte de 160
Sartre, Jean-Paul 20
Scanlon, T. M. 221–2, 227
Schulz, Fritz 58
self-contradiction of promise breaking 70–2
Shakespeare, William 20–1
Sidgwick, Henry 139–49, 150, 184, 199, 242, 246–7, 249
Simonides 33, 59
Smith, Adam 104, 107, 113–25, 147, 207, 243
   on fairness 239–40
   on four stages theory 105–6
   on individuals 121–2, 137, 246
   on imperfect rights 61
   in Kropotkin 166
   in Mill 247
   in Rawls 212
social contract:
   in Barry 221–4, 230
   in Hobbes 68, 74–5
   in Plato 34, 196
   in Rawls 196–9, 202, 212–13
socialist 146, 149, 151, 154, 159, 160
sociology 180–2, 183, 190–5
Socrates:
   the historical character 21, 30–4, 38, 136, 137
   the mouthpiece of Plato 30, 40–2, 59
Sodom and Gomorrah 12, 16–17
sophists 35, 69, 95
Spencer, Herbert 135–6, 184, 190
Spinoza, Benedict 18, 19
Stoics 20

talent 5, 145, 176–7
Taylor, A. E. 69

Theognis 31
Thrasymachus 30, 33–5, 45, 81, 221
Thucydides 21
Thyestes 22–3
tragic drama 19–21

Ulpian 56, 58–9
utilitarian:
    aspects of punishment 147, 148
    conflict with equality 151
    explanation of praise and blame 89
    ideal 150
    in Mill 131–2, 134–8
    in Nozick 215
    in Rawls 197, 199, 201, 211–12
    reason for following precedent 180–1
    in Smith 120–5
    success and failure 249–50
    unconscious 141, 148
    view of justice in Bentham 126–7
    view of merit 158
    view of rights 94–5
utility:
    in Bentham 126–7
    and fairness 102–3
    in Hume 90–1, 99, 101–2
    in Mill 127, 135, 137
    and need 177–8
    and principles of worth 176–7, 201
    of reward 206
    in Sidgwick 141, 146–9
    in Smith 120–2

vendetta 22, 28, 51
Voltaire (F. M. Arouet) 16

welfare state 15, 46, 188, 207–8, 214, 217, 245–6
Wollaston, William 93
Wordsworth, William 22
worth 38, 48, 88, 176–7

Zeus 24, 27–9, 242